Women Fight, Women Write

Women Fight, Women Write

TEXTS ON THE ALGERIAN WAR

MILDRED MORTIMER

University of Virginia Press | *Charlottesville and London*

University of Virginia Press
© 2018 by the Rector and Visitors of the University of Virginia
All rights reserved
Printed in the United States of America on acid-free paper

ISBN 978-0-8139-4204-9 (cloth)
ISBN 978-0-8139-4205-6 (paper)
ISBN 978-0-8139-4206-3 (e-book)

First published 2018

9 8 7 6 5 4 3 2 1

Library of Congress Cataloging-in-Publication Data
is available for this title.

Cover art: Celebrating Algerian independence, July 1962. (© Marc Riboud/Magnum Photos)

In memory of three extraordinary women:

Yamina Echaïb Oudaï, called Zoulikha
Assia Djebar
Djamila Amrane

CONTENTS

Acknowledgments — ix

Introduction: Women Write, Women Fight — 1

1 Writing Women into History: Danièle Djamila Amrane-Minne's *La guerre d'Algérie (1954–1962): Femmes au combat* — 21

2 Herstory Is the War Story: From Assia Djebar's Early Fiction to *L'amour, la fantasia* — 49

3 Mapping the Traumascape: Yamina Mechraka's *La grotte éclatée* — 77

4 Wounded Memories: Maïssa Bey's *Entendez-vous dans les montagnes . . .* — 103

5 Collective Trauma, Collective Memory: Leïla Sebbar's *La Seine était rouge* and *Une enfance dans la guerre: Algérie, 1954–1962* — 131

6 Testimonial Literature: Self-Reflection in the Works of Zohra Drif, Louisette Ighilahriz, and Eveline Safir Lavalette — 158

7 Remembering Zoulikha in Assia Djebar's Film and Fiction — 188

Conclusion: The Silence Has Been Broken . . . — 213

Notes — 225
Bibliography — 239
Index — 255

ACKNOWLEDGMENTS

I am very grateful to the writers, critics, friends, colleagues, and students who, over the years, have inspired me and encouraged me to complete this book. The book project originated as a paper presented at an African Studies Association panel in 2008 organized and chaired by Maureen Eke. It then evolved into an article for a collection of essays that Eke, Marie Kruger, and I edited for *Research in African Literatures* entitled "Memory/History, Violence, and Reconciliation," published in the spring of 2012, and finally, this book.

Special thanks to those who read and commented on parts of the manuscript: Patricia Brand, Catharine Harris, Darcie Fontaine, Natalya Vince, Valérie Orlando, Pamela Pears, Allison Rice, and my husband, Rob Mortimer, who read the work in its entirety. I also thank many others for sharing their thoughts and opinions, personal memories, contacts, as well as somewhat obscure publications and unpublished works: Skyler Artes, Khedidja Akacem, Maïssa Bey, Odile Cazenave, Amel Chaouti, Anne Donadey, Amina Amrane Far, Nicole Grimaud, Feriel Lalami Fatès, Nassima Guessoum, Nicholas Harrison, Susan Ireland, Arun Kapil, Dalila Mechakra Martini, members of the Oudaï family (Mohammed, Abdelhamid, Khadidja, Rafik), Leïla Sebbar, and Phyllis Taoua. Sadly, three whom I cannot thank enough are no longer with us: Djamila Amrane, Assia Djebar, and Clarisse Zimra. At the University of Virginia Press, I thank my editor, Eric Brandt, as well as my anonymous readers and my meticulous copyeditor, Joanne Allen.

The author and publisher are grateful for permission to reproduce the following copyrighted material: selections of my study "Tortured Bodies, Resilient Souls: Algeria's Women Combatants Depicted by Danièle Djamila Amrane-Minne, Louisette Ighilahriz, and Assia Djebar," published in *Re-*

search in African Literatures 43, no. 1 (Spring 2012): 101–17; an earlier version of my article "Probing the Past: Leïla Sebbar, *La Seine était rouge/The Seine was Red*," published in the *French Review* 83, no. 6 (May 2010): 1246–56; and a revised version of my article "Zoulikha the Martyr of Cherchell in Film and Fiction," published in *PMLA* 131, no. 1 (2016): 134–39.

Women Fight, Women Write

INTRODUCTION

Women Fight, Women Write

As the first successful anticolonial war in Africa, the Algerian War continues to capture the attention of historians, writers, students, and the general public in Algeria and beyond its borders. Initiated by a group of militants committed to armed conflict in order to free Algeria from the yoke of French colonialism, the war that ensued did not seem to foreshadow victory for the colonized and the eventual defeat of the colonizer. Yet, after eight years of violent struggle the revolutionary movement achieved its objective, independence. The liberation struggle had begun on November 1, 1954, when guerrillas of the Front de libération nationale (FLN; National Liberation Front) attacked military installations, police posts, communications facilities, and public utilities in various parts of the country. The war that followed was fought in the cities and in the countryside by revolutionaries actively engaged in the armed struggle and by their supporters, who carried out acts of resistance by sheltering rebels and distributing arms, tracts, and supplies. Led by the FLN and its military arm, the Armée de libération nationale (ALN), Algeria gained its independence on July 5, 1962. After 132 years of political domination, French colonialism came to an end and the new era of Algerian independence dawned.

Independence had not been gained easily, however, and the transition to a new social order was difficult as well. By the time the conflict ended, a million Algerian lives had been lost, more than three million rural Algerians had been displaced from their homes, hundreds of villages had been razed, and fields, pastures, and forests destroyed (Ruedy, *Modern Algeria*, 190). Among those who had resisted independence, most *pieds-noirs* (French Algerians) fled the country, many fearing reprisals at the hands of the Algerians. And many *harkis* (Algerians who had collaborated with the French colonials) were killed in retribution by Algerians, with others relocated to camps in France. Moreover, as a newly independent nation, Algeria was faced with millions of impoverished, uprooted peasants poorly equipped to enter a new phase of their political existence. Thus, the summer of 1962, while exhilarating for those who had won the war, proved difficult not just for those who had lost but for the entire nation. Exile and dislocation were experiences common to both the former colonizer and the ex-colonized.

This book focuses on the struggle of Algerian women to appropriate the Algerian War story as participants, taking their place in the history of their nation's liberation movement, and chroniclers, writing their story in autobiographical narrative and fiction. Although Algerian women were actively engaged in the anticolonial struggle, their contributions to the war effort have never been fully acknowledged.[1] As the Algerian historian Danièle Djamila Amrane-Minne states, "Qu'il s'agisse d'œuvres de fiction, de témoignages ou de recherches universitaires, les écrits sur la guerre d'Algérie sont de plus en plus nombreux et divers mais tous ont en commun d'ignorer le militantisme des femmes" (*La guerre d'Algérie,* 13; Whether in works of fiction, memoirs, or university research, writings on the Algerian war have grown in volume and diversity, yet they all ignore women's militancy).[2] Her historical work, published three decades after the war ended, corrects this omission, provides clues to women's silence, and encourages further exploration.

Drawing upon the three sources Amrane-Minne cites—fiction, memoirs, and historical texts—I propose to extend her analyses, exploring the role of women's individual and collective memory in evoking and recording events of the violent anticolonial conflict, and examining the ways in which their war experiences transformed and affirmed their sense of self. I do so with the perspective of two additional decades, including Algeria's traumatic *décennie noire,* the "dark decade" of the 1990s, which saw a violent struggle between the Algerian army and Islamist fundamentalists. Those turbulent times caused a significant number of women writers to find parallels between their role as dissident voices in contemporary Algeria and that of women militants during the liberation struggle; these writers were looking to the women who had preceded them for inspiration and courage.[3]

I first encountered the Algerian War in 1961, when, as an American student of French literature, I spent the academic year in France, a country deeply involved in an anticolonial war; the French government was still committed to keeping Algeria French. As a result of political tensions in France at the time, I immersed myself in the history of French colonialism in Africa, with special attention to Algeria, and discovered Algerian fiction written in French, the language of the colonizer. The Algerian War ceased to be an abstraction for me when I arrived in Algeria in 1964, two years after the war ended, to pursue graduate studies at the University of Algiers. Traces of violent confrontations were still evident: gutted structures that had once been homes to families in the Casbah of Algiers and villages in the countryside scarred by napalm. Individual and collective memories of the war were fresh; the young and old spoke of their war experiences, although some chose to remain silent.

Looking back on that period more than a half century later, I—and fellow scholars—now have additional perspectives acquired from fifty years of political and historical analyses, interviews, memoirs, novels, short stories, poetry, essays, and films. It is with these new perspectives that we now approach Algerian women's relationship to the Algerian War and the literary works, both fiction and nonfiction, that their war experiences inspired. Probing the ways in which women are part of the war story and have authority over the narrative, this study poses two additional, interrelated questions: To what extent does the search for the "truth" about the past reveal hidden and forgotten histories? How do the dynamics of gender intersect with efforts at social restoration? These queries come together in a specific way in Algeria, where the dynamics of gender tend to keep women from speaking publicly about private matters, including personal loss and trauma, forcing them to be silent about their war experiences. Silence, sometimes a form of protection, at other times a form of resistance, and far too often a result of intimidation, contributes, of course, to obscuring history. Yet, when Algerian women break their silence, they not only revise perspectives on their nation's history but also destroy the stereotype of the mute and passive "Oriental woman." They do so with testimony that speaks of women's courage, fortitude, and resiliency.

Men on the Battlefield, Women at Home

As I undertook this project, I realized that to grasp the complexities of Algerian women's relationship to the independence struggle, I would have to reexamine my notions of women's role in armed warfare. These concepts originated for me, I believe, with one of the earliest works of fiction I clearly recall, Louisa May Alcott's *Little Women*, a classic of American children's literature. Having read the work at the age of nine or ten, I still have vivid memories of the fictional lives of the March sisters—Meg, Jo, Beth, and Amy—four captivating New England girls whose devoted mother, Marmee, kept the home fires burning as well as she could while their father, Mr. March, served as a chaplain to the Union soldiers in America's tumultuous Civil War. As Alcott's nineteenth-century novel introduced generations of American girls to feisty Jo, the rebellious daughter whose dreams surpassed the limitations placed upon women of her time, it also clearly delineated female space as private, not public, the hearth, not the battlefield. In this regard, Jo March tells her sisters: "'We haven't got father, and shall not have him for a long time.' She didn't say 'perhaps never,' but each silently added it, thinking of father far away, where the fighting was" (3). Jo's words confirm the division in physical space and emotional experience between the male warriors and the women who waited patiently for them to return.

Only years later did I learn that Alcott, unlike her fictional female characters, did not spend those war years on the sidelines. She joined the war effort as a volunteer nurse for the Union army in Georgetown, Virginia, tended to wounded and dying soldiers, and subsequently wrote about the experience in *Hospital Sketches*, a series of vignettes based on letters sent to her family. Unlike *Little Women*, the latter text has been largely forgotten.[4] As a nurse, however, Alcott shares the experience of a significant number of Algerian women who served in the same way, tending to the wounded and the dying during the Algerian War.

A children's classic neither shapes nor defines a tradition that places men on the battlefield, women safe at home. It does, however, represent culturally constituted myths, memories, and values. The political theorist Jean Bethke Elshtain explains in her study *Women and War* that we in the West are indeed the heirs of a tradition that assumes that in time of war men occupy one space, the dangerous battlefield, women another, the safe and secure home. Rare were the legendary women warriors she terms the "ferocious few" (173). Elshtain notes that as we embrace the assumption that men are the "life takers" and women are the "life givers" (195), we also place women in the position of designated weepers over war's inevitable tragedies and losses (4). Weepers, however, play only a limited role in war and do not write its history.

Elshtain uses the terms *Just Warrior* and *Beautiful Soul* to designate men's and women's roles in time of war, borrowing these terms from the German philosopher Georg Wilhelm Friedrich Hegel. She writes that Hegel, in *Phenomenology of the Spirit*, defines the Beautiful Soul as a mode of consciousness that allows the individual to conserve "the appearance of purity by cultivating innocence about the historical course of the world" (4). Although Hegel makes no gender distinctions—both men and women can be Beautiful Souls—Elshtain maintains that the Western world has cast women as a collective Beautiful Soul, writing: "Embodying ethical aspirations but denying women a place in the corridors of power; recapitulating aesthetic visions of the 'lady' unbesmirched by the sordid wheelings and dealings of commercial society, but insulating her from the nameless perils of uncharted social waters, by lodging women solidly in the domain of *Privatrecht* or 'private right,' a sphere that persists in tension with the *Kriegstaat* or 'war state'—the Beautiful Soul constellation of enshrined ideas dooms women to lose certain battles over and over again" (141). Thus, she finds that one battle women lost concerned authority over the war story. In other words, the gender division permeating the story of war has led to the assumption that only those who have experienced combat have the authority to speak and write about it. Because women, as she notes, are exterior to war to the extent that they do not engage in combat on the battlefield, men have been granted legitimacy in the role of "the great war-story tellers" (212). Yet, this legitimacy remains ambiguous. Stephen Crane's classic of the American Civil War, *Red Badge of Courage*, appeared in 1895, three decades after the war ended. Crane was a talented male novelist who had never taken part in his nation's civil war.[5]

The binary construct of men on the battlefield, women at home, has remained the dominant paradigm for centuries. We know of no women soldiers at Waterloo, Gettysburg, Verdun, or Omaha Beach.[6] However, as historians of the Algerian War clearly show and anyone who has seen Gillo Pontecorvo's film *Battle of Algiers* will confirm, the battle zone was not clearly demarcated in the Algerian War; battles spilled into the streets and into the homes.

Interrogating Western history to explore women's relationship to war, Elshtain does not delve into the political struggles of non-Western colonized women. It would have been interesting if she had done so. As the historian Judith Tucker notes, various nationalist movements of the region—Turkey's War of Independence (1919–23), the Iranian Constitutional Revolution (1906–11), and the Egyptian Revolution of 1919, all of which preceded the Algerian War of Independence and the ongoing Palestinian conflict—involved women as demonstrators, organizers, and even fighters (110).

In terms of Algerian women's participation in the anticolonial struggle, Frantz Fanon's writings are particularly pertinent. A practicing psychiatrist in Blida, Algeria, as well as a member of the FLN during the Algerian War, the Martinican-born theorist of anticolonial revolutions was in a unique position to analyze Algeria's liberation struggle. In "L'Algérie se dévoile" ("Algeria Unveiled"), a chapter in *Sociologie d'une révolution*, published in English as *A Dying Colonialism*, Fanon not only posits the Algerian woman combatant as a key element of the revolution, but celebrates her liberation and empowerment through her participation in the war. In his text, published in 1959, while the war was being waged, Fanon affirms his conviction that women combatants had gained respect and social equality among their Algerian compatriots and that their gains during this period of social upheaval would continue in independent Algeria.

Drawing attention to the difference between conventional wars, fought by armies on the battlefield, and revolutions, fought by rebel armies, he states that the latter are total wars, in which the woman is not on the sidelines. Fanon situates her in the combat zone as a nurse, liaison agent, and fighter, adding: "La femme algérienne est au cœur du combat. Arrêtée, violée, abattue, elle atteste de la violence de l'occupant et de son inhumanité" (48; The Algerian woman is at the heart of the combat. Arrested, tortured, raped, shot down, she testifies to the violence of the occupier and to his inhumanity [66]).

An important aspect of the woman's participation, he explains, involves the veil. Beginning with the concept that the veil ensured Algerian women's identity and was a form of national resistance against the colonial occupier, he charts the progressive transformation of the veil during the liberation struggle: "Voile enlevé puis remis, voile instrumentalisé, transformé en technique de camouflage, en moyen de lutte" (42; Removed and reassumed again and again, the veil has been manipulated, transformed into a technique of camouflage, into a means of struggle [61]). Calling attention to the "dynamisme historique du voile" (45; historic dynamism of the veil [63]), he explains that just as the veiled woman was able to carry hidden tracts, weapons, and bombs under her traditional haïk, the unveiled woman, moving "comme un poisson dans l'eau occidentale" (39–40; like a fish in Western waters [58]), could do so as well. In other words, veiled and unveiled, old and young, Algerian women were less suspect and potentially more mobile in war torn Algeria than their male counterparts, a political reality that signaled potential empowerment.

Unfortunately, Fanon, the Marxist intellectual writing from his unique position as an insider (FLN militant) and as an outsider (non-Muslim, non-Algerian), underestimated the power and resilience of indigenous patriarchy, as well as the force of Islamic values and traditions. And sadly, he died of leukemia shortly before the end of the war. Thus, he never lived to see Algeria's independence come to fruition and did not know that Algerian women did not gain the power he had envisioned for them. Yet, rather than fault Fanon for events he could not foresee, we must place his essay within its historical context. In this vein, Winifred Woodhull writes: "'Algeria Unveiled' tries to *enable* the liberation of Algerian women in a form that complements nationalism and simultaneously challenges Western ideologies, including feminist ideologies, that ignore the specificity of the Algerian situation" (*Transfigurations of the Maghreb*, 22). Placed in perspective, Fanon's reflections can guide us toward later analyses.[7]

Miriam Cooke's *Women and the War Story* is one such analytical work. Published three decades after Fanon's essay, it also focuses on the experiences of women who do not figure in Elshtain's study, specifically women of North Africa and the Middle East. Cooke does not contradict Elshtain's findings concerning gender division in war—throughout the ages, men fought and women were fought for (80)—but adds a crucial element missing from Elshtain's analysis and from Fanon's as well. Women's heightened consciousness, the knowledge that male appropriation of *qissat al-harb* (the war story) makes them appear marginal and apolitical, has become a catalyst for transformation. Political awareness grants women the incentive to "re-member their pasts and then to write them," writes Cooke (5). Yet, as she notes with some irony, women must always struggle to "retain the authority to write about an experience that they are supposed not to have had" (5).

Whereas Cooke's *Women and the War Story* devotes one chapter to the Algerian war, Marnia Lazreg's *The Eloquence of Silence* is a book-length study of the colonization and decolonization of Algeria and the effect of these two historical processes on Algerian women. Significantly, both Cooke, with the choice of the chapter title "Silence Is the Real Crime," and Lazreg, entitling her study *The Eloquence of Silence*, draw attention to Algerian women's silence during the colonial period and the subsequent postcolonial era.

Cooke writes:

> The story of the Algerian war of independence from the French is a story about silencing. Throughout the 124 years of French rule, the Algerian people—both men and women—resisted but did not speak out. Finally in 1954 they mobilized in the cities and mountains and—after over seven years of fighting—they won. They were free to create the government and the society of which they had dreamed. But dreams turned reactionary: revolutionary leaders became conservative rulers. National liberation did not bring social emancipation, particularly not for women. For women, the silencing persisted. (119)

In this passage, Cooke makes the crucial distinction between two very different forms of silence: resistance to the French colonizer and submission to the Algerian patriarchal ruler. Examining the work of Algerian feminists, Cooke is highly critical of texts that, in her view, do not pay enough attention to Algerian women's war experiences or to the transformation that occurs when that experience is recorded in writing, and they do not probe the reasons for women's silencing (142).[8] In her analysis of the Algerian War's impact upon women, she expresses disappointment at what she finds to be meager results of a potentially transformative experience for self and society, stating with cynicism: "The war was not so much a consciousness-raising event as an exciting interlude in the gray monotony of an unchanging routine" (161).

Lazreg, in contrast, is more measured in her evaluation of women's gains and losses as a result of the war. She views the independence struggle as a successful anticolonial war that accomplished its objective, which was to break France's colonial grip on the country (140), and believes that women militants gained the respect of the nation for their courage and bravery, including their willingness to sacrifice their lives for their convictions (138). She discerns three reasons why women participated voluntarily in the war: some militants sought to redress the perceived wrongs of colonialism; others pursued a family tradition of resistance; still others wished to serve society by joining an organization that required them to rise above self-centered objectives (123).

In Lazreg's view, the Algerian War's impact upon women participants was positive and multifaceted and transformed their sense of self. Women who were jailed and tortured forged deep bonds in prison that cut across class, ethnicity and geographical region. Urban women, who took on educational, paramedical, and other tasks in rural areas, found a new sense of purpose. Women entrusted with dangerous missions gained confidence in their ability to assume enormous risks. Widows and women whose husbands had been arrested were called upon to run farms and businesses. Women who had rarely left home traveled to distant jails and detention centers in search of missing family members. Women who joined the revolutionaries in the maquis broke traditional social barriers by living closely with men who were not family members, often protecting them when they were wounded. Last but not least, women's participation was voluntary; the act of entering the war was an expression of will (138).

Despite these gains, Lazreg's optimism is guarded. Like Cooke, she sees the gains made at independence rapidly disappearing and writes with a heavy heart: "Women's rise to the word in post-colonial Algeria is threatened by violent silencing" (226). The phrase *violent silencing* refers to the violence perpetrated by Islamist fundamentalists against women they believed had betrayed their very strict and rigid religious beliefs.

The Dark Decade of the 1990s

Both Cooke and Lazreg published their texts during the dark decade of the 1990s. Major political strife had occurred in Algeria in 1991, when the FLN—the political party in power since independence—faced with major economic problems that included weakening oil prices and high unemployment, found itself challenge at the polls by the FIS (Front islamique du salut, the Islamic Salvation Front), an Islamist fundamentalist party. Rather than lose the second round of local elections to the opposition Islamist party, the military, in a coup d'état, canceled the elections, dissolved the FIS, and arrested its leaders. These actions sparked a civil war between the Algerian military and jihadists of the FIS and its military component, the Groupe Islamique Armée (GIA; Armed Islamic Group), a conflict that lasted throughout the decade.

In this conflict, Islamists targeted all Algerians, both men and women, who embraced a secular multicultural vision of Algerian society. Thus, this *décennie noire* was a particularly dangerous period for the nation's intellectuals—writers, journalists, scientists, physicians—forcing many French-educated professionals into exile. Although a dark period in Algeria's recent history, it was one of heightened activity for dissident women writers. Assia Djebar, Maïssa Bey, Malika Mokeddem, Leïla Marouane, Hafsa Zinaï Koudil, and others refused to remain silent, using writing as a form of resistance against oppression.

Writing to defend cultural pluralism and women's rights, they were overtly critical of what postindependence had brought to the Algerian population as a whole, to women in particular.[9] These writers criticized the government's failure to promote a modern democracy that guaranteed women's rights, and they strongly opposed Islamic fundamentalists intent upon transforming Algeria into an Islamic state that would deny women their civil rights. Finally, by choosing to write in French, they challenged their government's active educational policy of Arabization, which not only replaces French with Arabic, the national language, in Algerian schools but considers French a foreign language in Algeria.

Djebar, whose writing career began in the late 1950s, has called the younger writers the "nouvelles femmes d'Alger" (new women of Algiers), drawing attention to a new generation of politically engaged women writers as she alludes to Eugène Delacroix's painting *Femmes d'Alger dans leur appartement* as well as her own earlier collection of short stories that bears the same name (*Oran, langue morte,* 367). In contrast to Delacroix's nineteenth-century Orientalist work, which depicts Algerian women as silent, luxuriously adorned objects of a patriarch's harem in Algiers, Djebar and her fellow writers voice their protest, using their texts to combat oppression in all its forms. We find Maïssa Bey responding to the political crisis by publishing her first novel, *Au commencement était la mer* (In the beginning was the sea), in which she describes the undeclared civil war as "cette guerre qui ne dit pas son nom, plus terrible encore que l'autre, la vraie, celle où l'ennemi se découvre, s'affronte à visage découvert" (13; this unnamed war, more terrible than the other kind, the real war in which the enemy shows his face, fights in the open). Reacting to the fear and insecurity among Algerian citizens in the face of numerous political assassinations perpetrated by Islamists, Bey not only began to write but urged other women to do so as well. To this end, she founded Paroles et Écriture, an association in her hometown of Sidi bel Abbes that brings women together in writing workshops where they may hone their writing skills and are taught to use writing as an implement for empowerment and social justice.

As I have already noted, a significant number of women writers drew parallels between their role in the turbulent 1990s and the role played by militants in the liberation struggle. Amrane-Minne makes the same comparison between the women of the two periods in her introduction to *Des femmes dans la guerre d'Algérie* (Women in the Algerian War), a selection of interviews she had previously conducted with women militants for her historical account of Algerian women's participation in the liberation struggle. Giving voice to the women who fought for independence, Amrane-Minne reminds her readers that the same courage and determination motivated Algerian women at two different times in Algeria's history. She writes:

> En fait, la continuité est manifeste entre les combattantes de la lutte armée pour l'indépendance et les femmes qui, aujourd'hui, dans une société anesthésiée par l'ampleur et l'apparente irrationalité d'une violence odieuse, manifestent dans les rues, voilées ou dévoilées, mais à visage découvert, leur refus du terrorisme et leur désir de vivre en paix dans la diversité des modes de vie qui est la marque d'une Algérie en pleine évolution. (12)

> (In fact, continuity can be seen between the women fighters in the armed struggle for independence and those who today, in a society anaesthetized by the extent and apparent irrationality of hateful violence, openly show in the street—whether they are veiled or unveiled—their refusal of terrorism and their desire to live in peace among the diverse ways of life that characterize a changing Algeria.)

Clearly, the *décennie noire* served as an important catalyst for women's literary production in the 1990s and brought earlier events of the liberation struggle back into focus.

During this period, as fiction writers wrote of war, so did memoirists. Louisette Ighilahriz's memoir, *Algérienne* (Algerian Woman), published in 2001, reintroduced the accusation that Algerian women were tortured and raped by the French military during the Algerian War. Torture had first become a public issue in France during the early years of the war, when, in 1957, Georges Arnaud and Jacques Vergès published *Pour Djamila Bouhired*, a text that drew public attention to a young Algerian woman accused of participating in guerrilla warfare, tortured in prison, and condemned to death. This text was followed the next year by *La question*, Henri Alleg's account of being tortured by the French military in Algeria. In 1962, Simone de Beauvoir and Gisèle Halimi's collaborative work *Djamila Boupacha* appeared. Written by Boupacha's lawyer, Halimi, with a preface by de Beauvoir, the text traces the legal defense of the young Algerian militant Djamila Boupacha, who had confessed to terrorism under torture. Louisette Ighilahriz, however, was the first Algerian woman to bring the issue of torture before the French and Algerian public in personal testimony, describing in her own words the traumatic experience of torture and rape at the hands of the French military in Algeria.

In her text, Ighilahriz addresses the significant gap in time between the events of 1957 and her disclosure in 2001, stating that it took her four decades to find the courage describe the abuse she had suffered at the time and the moral strength to counter the wishes of her family, former comrades, and government officials, all of whom embraced the code of silence (111). Hence, not only is her testimony an important reminder of women's participation in the anticolonial war, attesting to women's sacrifice, courage, and willingness to fight for justice, but it reveals both the necessity and the difficulty of bearing witness, of articulating the trauma, and speaking of it publicly.

Trauma as a Wound

Depicting a world shattered by violent political upheaval, first the liberation struggle and later the undeclared civil war, Algerian women writers of fiction and memoirs are forced to come to terms with personal and collective trauma. Hence, their texts connect with a body of contemporary works that includes literature of the Holocaust, the Rwandan genocide, and the anticolonial wars of Vietnam and Algeria. For all, bearing witness is, as trauma specialists insist, crucial to the individual and collective healing process. Dori Laub, a survivor of the Holocaust and a psychotherapist, warns that the survivors of traumatic events who do not tell their stories become victims of a distorted memory. Silence, in his view, brings no peace of mind, but allows traumatic events to "invade and contaminate the survivor's daily life" ("Truth and Testimony," 64). Similarly, the psychologist Kai Erikson emphasizes the importance of sharing traumatic experiences, asserting that both the individual and the community benefit when trauma is shared. It can than serve "as a source of communality in the same way that common languages and common backgrounds can" ("Notes on Trauma and Community," 186). Yet, individuals who have shared trauma may be either unwilling or unable to speak of it. Focusing on the locations where trauma occurs, the sociologist Maria Tumarkin applies the term *traumascape* to places scarred by violence, war, and terror, and explains that people who experience a traumatic event are often so overwhelmed that "the ways in which they usually experience the world and make sense of their own place in it are effectively shattered" (*Traumascapes*, 11).

The sense of an irreparably altered world is reflected in Cathy Caruth's examination of trauma as a wound. Working with Freudian concepts, she explains that trauma appears to be more than the simple illness of a wounded psyche: "it is always the story of a wound that cries out, that addresses us in the attempt to tell us of a reality or truth that is not otherwise available" (*Unclaimed Experience*, 4). Drawing attention to its delayed appearance (which Freud calls "latency") and its recurrence, Caruth identifies trauma as "unclaimed experience" that "possesses" the traumatized. In other words, because of its unassimilated nature, it continues to haunt the survivor. We can understand it, I believe, by seeing it in terms of a scratched vinyl record that sticks each time the needle touches the marred groove, repeating the passage and unable to move beyond it.

Further, by noting the difficulty involved in establishing the truth surrounding a traumatic event, Caruth reveals a paradox: "that in trauma the greatest confrontation with reality may also occur in an absolute numbing to it, that immediacy, paradoxically enough, may take the form of belatedness." (*Unclaimed Experience*, 6). The phenomenon of belatedness helps explain the time lapse between the trauma suffered by Ighilahriz as a young militant, a trauma that continued to haunt her, and the public disclosure of the events many years later. Yet, the ability to recover the past is paradoxically linked to the inability to have full access to it. In Mechakra's text *La grotte éclatée* (The shattered cave), for example, we meet a traumatized protagonist struggling with her inability to reach the truth and questioning her own reliability as a narrator. Throughout her narrative, the protagonist wonders—as do her readers—where the truth of her experience lies. It is in this same vein that Leïla Sebbar's fictional informant Noria, having witnessed the violent events in Paris on October 17, 1961, admits to a faulty memory when trying to recall them. Speaking to her interlocutor, Louis, she states: "J'ai oublié de te dire . . . Louis, quand on raconte, on oublie, tout vient dans le désordre" (*La Seine était rouge*, 113; I forgot to tell you . . . Louis, when you tell a story, you forget, everything comes back pell-mell" [*The Seine was Red*, 89]).

As writers bring into play the relationship between history and memory, they introduce a theme that has become increasingly important to philosophers, historians, and literary critics in the last few decades. In *La mémoire, l'histoire, l'oubli* (*Memory, History, Forgetting*), the philosopher Paul Ricoeur narrows the gap between history and memory by emphasizing the importance of testimony, the narrative dimension of historical discourse: "Nous n'avons pas mieux que le témoignage et la critique du témoignage pour accréditer la représentation historienne du passé" (364; We have nothing better than testimony and the criticism of testimony to accredit the historian's representation of the past [278]). Yet, the historian Pierre Nora draws attention to the difference between history and memory:

> La mémoire est un phénomène toujours actuel, un lien vécu au présent éternel; l'histoire, une représentation du passé. Parce qu'elle est affective et magique, la mémoire ne s'accommode que des détails qui la confortent; elle se nourrit de souvenirs flous, téléscopants, globaux ou flottants, particuliers ou symboliques, sensible à tous les transferts, écrans, censure ou projections. L'histoire, parce que opération intellectuelle et laïcisante, appelle analyse et discours critique. ("Entre mémoire et histoire," xix)

(Memory is a perpetually actual phenomenon, a bond tying us to the eternal present; history is a representation of the past. Memory, insofar as it is effective and magical, only accommodates those facts that suit it; it nourishes recollections that may be out of focus or telescopic, global or detached, particular or symbolic—responsive to each avenue of conveyance or phenomenal screen, to every censorship or projection. History, because it is an intellectual and secular production, calls for analysis and criticism. ["Between Memory and History," 8–9])

Nora's reflections on the difference between history and memory grant objectivity to history and subjectivity to memory. Admitting that history is always problematic and incomplete, Nora nevertheless links it to the world of rationality, objective reality, and intellectual analysis, in contrast to memory, which he finds vulnerable to accommodating "those facts that suit it." In other words, memory is highly subjective.

Mohammed Harbi and Benjamin Stora similarly point to the subjective dimension of memory. In their preface to *La guerre d'Algérie, 1954–2004: La fin de l'amnésie* (2004) they write:

Les mémoires ont toujours une dimension subjective. Elles fonctionnent comme un discours de légitimation, de sorte qu'elles sont à la fois rappel d'événements et miroir déformant. L'historien ne peut ni les dédaigner ni s'y soumettre. Le propre des souvenirs c'est d'être une évocation d'un vécu passé, mais aussi un discours sur le contemporain. [. . .] Le rôle de la critique historique c'est de les entendre tous et d'analyser les conditions réelles qui furent celle d'une guerre d'indépendance avec des excès partagés, mais sans que soient escamotées la légitimité d'une révolution et l'injustice du statu quo colonial. (10)

(Memories always have a subjective dimension. They function as a discourse of legitimatization and serve as a reminder of past events and a distorting mirror. The historian can neither disparage them nor submit to them. The role of memory is to evoke a lived past but also to be a commentary on the present. [. . .] The role of historical critique is to hear them all and analyze the real conditions of a war for independence with its shared excesses but without covering up the legitimacy of a revolution and the injustice of the colonial status quo.)

Recognizing that the role of the historian includes listening attentively and then analyzing the material gleaned as well as the conditions surrounding the particular events, Harbi and Stora concede the importance of memory in the historical process but privilege the historian's objective analysis over the memoirist's subjective reality. In this vein, we find the historians of Algeria Danièle Djamila Amrane-Minne, Natalya Vince, and Joshua Cole making extensive use of personal testimony while acknowledging its limitations. Amrane-Minne, for example, considers her informants' recollections as interpretations of a historical moment and not as authentic pieces of history (*La guerre d'Algérie*, 278).

By engaging the theme of memory, historians and writers have been able to disclose hidden histories of the colonial period and the Algerian War that are both personal and collective. For example, when Djebar delved into French colonial history pertaining to the conquest of Algeria, she uncovered hidden, forgotten, or little-known incidents, including reports of *enfumade,* the French military tactic of setting caves on fire that resulted in the death by asphyxiation of the Algerian tribes taking refuge in them, as well as evidence of Algerian women on the battlefield of Staoueli. Carrying out her historical search, she came to view herself as a spelunker, an underground explorer engaged in "une spéléologie bien particulière" (91; a very special kind of speleology [77]). Djebar's exploration of the history of the French conquest of Algeria then led her to the events of the Algerian War, and the speleological endeavor resulted in her unearthing the life story of Yamina Echaïb Oudaï, called Zoulikha, a resistance leader who lived and died in Djebar's native region of Cherchell. Until Djebar embarked upon her quest, Zoulikha's political activities had been relatively unknown beyond Cherchell. Hence, Zoulikha enters history through Djebar's efforts to preserve her memory via her film *La nouba des femmes du Mont Chenoua* and the historical novel *La femme sans sépulture*.

Women Fight, Women Write

As my title, *Women Fight, Women Write,* acknowledges the courage and commitment of all Algerian women who joined the independence struggle and the importance of validating their experiences in writing, the text evolved from my personal interest in the life story of Zoulikha, militant of Cherchell, arrested and assassinated by the French military during the early years of the Algerian War. During my visit to Cherchell in 2009, Zoulikha's sons, Mohammed and Abdelhamid, accompanied me to the place where, in October 1957, French soldiers had captured their mother. Standing in the bright, peaceful clearing with two middle-aged brothers orphaned since childhood, I found myself unable to fully grasp Zoulikha's decision to commit to militant action at the risk of losing her life and thereby giving up a future with her children. In my quest to comprehend the psychology of the "ferocious few"—to borrow Elshtain's term—I embarked upon this research project, which began as a personal reflection on the concept of self-sacrifice and has become a book about Algerian women's narratives of war, personal transformation, and empowerment.

Bringing together works of fiction, memoirs, and historical studies, this volume tests the hypothesis that works of both fiction and nonfiction are necessary to our understanding of the complexity of the Algerian War. In addition, a study of works that cover a fifty-year period—from Djebar's *Les enfants du nouveau monde* (*Children of the New World*), published in 1962, to Sebbar's *Une enfance dans la guerre* (A childhood in war), published in 2016—while not strictly chronological in its presentation of the texts, allows us to discern transformations in both style and content, changes I explore in the chapters that follow.

The study is organized into seven chapters, all but one devoted to a single author. Chapter 1, "Writing Women into History," presents an analysis of Amrane-Minne's historical study of women participants in the Algerian War (1993) and of her collection of interviews, published in 1994. In addition, the chapter charts her life as a militant and examines poetry inspired by her prison experience, mostly unpublished work. Thus, we see her through a triple lens, as militant, poet, and historian. Chapter 2, "Herstory Is the War Story," offers close readings of Djebar's early war novels, *Les enfants du nouveau monde* (1962) and *Les alouettes naïves* (1967), followed by her best-known work of fiction, *L'amour, la fantasia* (1985), tracing the evolution of the writer's sociopolitical objectives and narrative techniques and revealing that the texts offer a nuanced analysis of women's transformation through the war experience. Chapter 3, "Mapping the Traumascape," examines Yamina

Mechakra's *La grotte éclatée* (1979), a novel that depicts a nurse's experience in the maquis during the Algerian War, taking the reader into the heart of the violence. Combining realism, symbolism, and surrealistic elements, the text expresses the trauma of war. Chapter 4, "Wounded Memories," probes the Algerian War's traumatic effects upon individuals who experienced the war as children. Maïssa Bey's novel *Entendez-vous dans les montagnes . . .* (2002) revisits the war from the perspective of Algeria's undeclared civil war of the 1990s, introducing a fictional voyage—a train trip across France—as a trope to explore Algerian history, a journey to self-understanding, and a search for answers to the broad philosophical issues of morality, justice, and freedom. Chapter 5, "Collective Trauma, Collective Memory," proposes a close reading of Leïla Sebbar's novel *La Seine était rouge* (1999), a work of historical fiction that reminds us that the independence struggle was carried out in France as well as in Algeria, and *Une enfance dans la guerre: Algérie, 1954–1962*, a collection of autobiographical sketches by writers who recall their childhood and adolescence in war-torn Algeria during the anticolonial struggle. With these texts, Sebbar explores the interrelated themes of collective trauma and occulted history as she brings oral and written testimony into the process of anamnesis, the recovery of historical memory. Chapter 6, "Testimonial Literature," examines testimonial writings of FLN militants: Zohra Drif, Louisette Ighilahriz, and Eveline Safir Lavalette. Drif's *Mémoires d'une combattante de l'ALN: Zone autonome d'Alger* (2014) offers an eyewitness account of a critical chapter in the history of the Algerian War, the Battle of Algiers. Ighilahriz's *Algérienne* (2001) reopens the controversy in France and Algeria concerning torture by making public her personal experience. Lavalette's *Juste Algérienne: Comme une tissure* (2013) chronicles a life shaped by political engagement. Chapter 7, "Remembering Zoulikha in Assia Djebar's Film and Fiction," explores Djebar's representation of Zoulikha Oudaï in film and text. The film *La nouba des femmes de Mont Chenoua* (1977) pays homage to the resistance leader of Cherchell but focuses primarily on a fictional protagonist haunted by memories of traumatic events of the Algerian War. The text *La femme sans sépulture* (2002) is a fictionalized biography of Zoulikha that blurs the boundaries between fact and fiction, transforming the militant into a legendary figure of the anticolonial struggle. Finally, in the conclusion, "The Silence Has Been Broken . . . ," I offer some reflections on the corpus of texts and then trace a path to new directions, including the emergence of creative work in documentary film that takes us beyond the realm of the Francophone written text.

In presenting analyses of representative works, I have chosen writers who were born and raised in Algeria and have written one or more works—fiction, memoir, or, in Amrane-Minne's case, a historical study—that describe the war from a woman's perspective. These writers are exclusively Francophone, as Algerian women of their generation, women who were young adults or children during the war, were educated in the language of the colonizer and therefore write in French. Future generations will surely produce a flourishing literature in Arabic, and one hopes that Berber-language literature will secure its place as well. In this regard, Ahlam Mosteghanemi is one Arabophone woman writer paving the way.[10]

A book that focuses on the struggle of Algerian women to appropriate the Algerian War story, both as participants and as chroniclers, is first and foremost about the appropriation of voice. The text herein present two forms of the authoritative voice: first- and third-person narratives. The subjects are women who speak, women who are spoken for, and women who collaborate in their narrative with a journalist or historian. All three avenues of expression allow women to assume their rightful place in the war story. In the words of the critic Irène Assiba d'Almeida, they serve to "destroy the emptiness of silence" (*Francophone African Women Writers*, 11). The concluding paragraph of d'Almeida's critical analysis serves as the entry point to this study: "Women as producers of texts offer a social vision that African society will find nowhere else. That vision promises a social understanding that is an invaluable resource for nations and, equally important, for individuals. It is true for communities as well as for individuals that if the story is told, the silence, and its emptiness, may be destroyed" (177). With these thoughts in mind, I propose to chart Algerian women's struggle to destroy the silence surrounding their participation in the war. While affirming the "eloquence of silence"—to borrow Lazreg's term—thereby acknowledging silence in various forms, as a form of resistance to injustice and imposed cultural values, as a crucial element of reflection, as a powerful component of the creative process, and as a recognized path to spirituality, the writers in this study distinguish between silence that is chosen and silence that is imposed through coercion, manipulation, and violence.

The "fight to write," the struggle to become the legitimate chronicler of one's own story, is being waged and won by women writers committed to replacing amnesia with anamnesis, forgetting with remembering, as they destroy the silence that had been imposed upon them. As their contributions to the war for independence enter Algeria's collective conscience, Algerian women move closer to securing their rightful place in their nation's history.

1 WRITING WOMEN INTO HISTORY

Danièle Djamila Amrane-Minne's *La guerre d'Algérie (1954–1962): Femmes au combat*

An FLN militant during the nationalist struggle, a historian in the postcolonial era, Danièle Djamila Amrane-Minne brings a unique perspective of personal experience and objective analysis to the study of the Algerian War. Highly critical of the fact that women's contributions to Algeria's war for independence were increasingly overlooked, she set out in the late 1970s to obtain her *doctorat d'état* with a dissertation that would repair this omission and correct other misconceptions. Working over a ten-year period, she combed archives and conducted interviews to trace Algerian women's participation in the nationalist cause. The results of her research appear in two publications: a historical text—originally her doctoral thesis—*La guerre d'Algérie (1954–1962): Femmes au combat* (The Algerian War [1954–1962]: Women in combat), published in 1993; and *Des femmes dans la guerre d'Algérie* (Women in the Algerian War), published in 1994, a collection of thirty interviews chosen from the eighty-eight she used for her doctoral research.[1]

Commending Amrane-Minne's efforts to restore Algerian women to their proper place in their nation's history, her fellow historian Benjamin Stora writes: "It is that silence that she decided to break in a thick book where scientific intention is allied with the intimate knowledge that comes from the experience of the militant women committed to independence" ("Women's Writing between Two Algerian Wars," 88). The "thick book" not only draws upon archival facts and figures to correct inaccuracies and uncover hidden history; it represents an innovative approach to history by incorporating women's voices, including those of women who had not usually been included in historical analyses—poor, illiterate, and often anonymous women—into the text. In this regard, she writes: "Seule la parole donnée à ces femmes peut révéler la profondeur de leur engagement et l'ampleur des sacrifices consentis" (*La guerre d'Algérie*, 215; Only these women's voices can reveal the depth of their involvement and the extent of their sacrifices willingly borne). Thus, Amrane-Minne contributes to securing Algerian women their rightful place in history with a text that articulates the commitment, determination, and collective nature of women's political engagement.

From Danièle Minne, Militant, to Djamila Amrane, Historian

Born in Neuilly-sur-Seine, France, in 1939, Danièle Minne left France as a child with her parents, Pierre and Jacqueline Netter Minne, who accepted teaching positions in Algeria in 1948. Following the couple's divorce several years later, her mother married Djilali Guerroudj, a militant in the Algerian Communist Party. Political activists committed to Algerian independence, they joined the liberation movement when the war began. They were arrested in 1957 as accomplices of Fernand Iveton, a French Communist convicted and guillotined for placing a bomb in Algiers to destroy the city's gasworks. Although sentenced to death, they were not executed and spent the remaining war years in prison.[2]

Danièle, still a teenager, followed her family's path of anticolonial resistance and joined the FLN. She became one of the bomb carriers in Yacef Saadi's group during the Battle of Algiers.[3] The historian Alistair Horne describes the mission she carried out on January 26, 1957: "The targets were the Otomatic, a favourite students' bar on the Rue Michelet; the Cafeteria opposite (second time over) and the Coq-Hardi, a popular brasserie. [. . .] Placed in the ladies' lavatory, Danièle Minne's bomb in the Otomatic seriously injured a young girl and several others" (*Savage War of Peace*, 192). The young militant was arrested and tried, and like her mother and stepfather, she spent the rest of the war in prison, first in Algeria, then in Pau, France.[4] While in prison, Djamila (the Arabic name she assumed during the war) prepared her baccalaureate. At independence, she began her university studies in Algiers. She completed a doctorate in history in 1988 at the University of Reims with a dissertation awarded the highest honors and subsequently published in both Algeria and France. After teaching for many years at the University of Algiers, she moved to France during the tumultuous and violent 1990s, Algeria's *décennie noire*, to teach history and women's studies at the University of Toulouse–Le Mirail. Upon retiring from university teaching, she returned to Algiers, where she lived with her husband, the physician Rabah Amrane, until her death on February 11, 2017.

If Amrane-Minne's path to an academic career was unusual, her unique position as a participant in and analyst of this significant chapter in Algerian history raises the question of whether a former militant can assume an objective approach and apply a critical lens to a collective history in which she was personally implicated. Her response is a carefully documented and detailed historical work that traces women's trajectory from bystander to supporter to activist-insurgent in the Algerian War. In a text that explores why women get politically involved in a nationalist movement, what their roles and missions are, and whether gender limits their actions, Amrane-Minne probes the ways women acquire agency within a patriarchal system during a turbulent period of political transformation. Thus, she grapples with the issue at the heart of this study, namely, the extent to which the experience of political engagement empowers women individually and collectively.

In her pursuit of historical accuracy Amrane-Minne used multiple sources: the Algerian ministry's files on the combatants, the Algerian press of the period, her collection of eighty-eight interviews with Algerian women combatants, women's personal written records in the form of diaries and poetry, and photographs of the period. These sources complement one another. Statistics gleaned from the archives provided the hard data concerning women combatants; the rest put a human face on events. Thus, as Amrane-Minne collected and interpreted both objective data and subjective narratives, she laid the groundwork for our study of historically based novels and memoirs. Archival sources allowed her to trace the militants' political trajectory; oral testimony shed light on their psychological transformation. And in a text that emphasizes the collective nature of Algerian women's political engagement, the collective voice that emerges not only articulates the struggle against French colonialism but challenges indigenous patriarchal structures as women express their vision of a new political and social order and show their willingness to fight for it.

Women at War: A Chronological Progression

Amrane-Minne begins her study by examining the position of women in Algeria before the revolution, then charts the emergence of women in the liberation struggle, and concludes with the reinsertion of the former women combatants into Algerian society following independence. This chronological progression allows her to trace Algerian women's absence from political life in the postindependence era back to its origins, indigenous patriarchy and French colonial policy, both of which impeded their access to public space.

Faulting French colonial educational policy in part for Algerian women's absence from public space, Amrane-Minne uses statistics to make important points. She notes that in 1954 in Algeria there were only six Algerian women doctors, twenty-five women secondary-school teachers, and no women in higher education. At the University of Algiers that year, approximately fifty Algerian female students were enrolled. These statistics are not surprising given that at the beginning of the liberation struggle nearly all Algerians were illiterate, with only 4.5 percent of women able to read and write. As a largely uneducated sector of the population, Algerian women were easily excluded from political life (*La guerre d'Algérie*, 27–29). Although they were granted the right to vote in colonial Algeria in 1947, the policy was not implemented until 1958, and only then in the vain attempt by the French colonial administration to turn Algerian women against the nationalist tide. Yet, to place the blame solely on colonial policy is, in Amrane-Minne's view, too simplistic a response; she faults Algerian political parties as well.

Examining the policies of the Parti du peuple algérien–Mouvement pour le triomphe des libertés démocratiques (PPA-MTLD; Algerian People's Party–Movement for the Triumph of Democratic Liberty) and the Parti communiste algérien (PCA; Algerian Communist Party) toward Algerian women, Amrane-Minne finds that while both parties glorified women in their traditional roles as mothers and educators, they neglected to bring them into positions of power (33). Because of women's insignificant presence in male-dominated political parties, they were obliged to work within the framework of women's organizations such as the Association des femmes musulmanes algériennes (AFMA; Association of Algerian Muslim Women) and the Union des femmes d'Algérie (UFA; Union of Algerian Women), a communist organization, in which they had a voice. Often collaborating, the two associations affiliated with the Fédération démocratique internationale des femmes (FDI; International Democratic Federation of Women) in 1952, and throughout the war they sent an Algerian delegation to the FDI conference (38). Although Amrane-Minne's research confirms that Algerian women joined the struggle once the war began, it suggests that if the nationalist parties had prepared women better for the armed struggle, and not marginalized them politically, many more would have participated actively in the revolution.

Examining the Archives and the Local Press

As Amrane-Minne charts the emergence of women in the liberation struggle, delving into multiple sources, Algerian archives reveal important data. The files of the Ministère des anciens combattants (Ministry of Former Combatants) provided her with more than ten thousand dossiers on militants that contain sociological data as well details concerning militants' military actions. With the help of this ministry, she was able to establish the number of women combatants, their roles, and their responsibilities. The ministry files revealed that among the 336,748 militants in its files, 10,949, 3.1 percent of all those taking part in active combat, were women. Of this group, 948 lost their lives (219).[5] Although the percentage of active combatants might seem relatively small, it approximates the number of European women who actively took part in World War II ("Women and Politics in Algeria," 62).

Affirming that women joined the war from its inception, Amrane-Minne parts ways with the anticolonial theorist and FLN representative Frantz Fanon, who in "L'Algérie se dévoile" ("Algeria Unveiled") writes that only after a final series of meetings among leaders was a decision made to concretely involve women in the nationalist struggle. In Fanon's view, women were brought in progressively as "l'urgence d'une guerre totale se fait sentir" (28; the urgency of a total war made itself felt [48]), and the male leaders arrived at that decision following much hesitation. He concludes: "Il faut donc exiger de la femme une élévation morale et une force psychologique exceptionnelles" (28; A moral elevation and a strength of character that were altogether exceptional would therefore be required of women [48]). Feminists today can read Fanon's words as naïve at best, condescending at worst. Amrane-Minne refutes the political philosopher's interpretation with her research and data. Examining the archives thoroughly, she finds no trace of discussions concerning women's inclusion either in official FLN texts or in the writings of the FLN leaders (247).

Delving further into the question of women's political engagement, she discerns the following motivations for their decision: the trauma of the massacre of Algerians in Sétif and Guelma in 1945; the popularity of the political leader Messali Hadj; ideas of nationalism circulated by the political parties and the *medersas* (religious schools); a family tradition of resistance; experience of poverty and hardship; revolt against injustice; and the shock of the Algerian War as it progressed (49). Two of these factors, the injustices of colonialism that she perceived, as well as a family tradition of resistance, were important motivations for Amrane-Minne herself. She concludes that women joined the war immediately, as their male counterparts did, sharing their primary motivation, the struggle for a better life, one not dominated by a colonial power (247). Significantly, their decisions seem to have been made on the basis of personal reflection, not external pressure.

If archives were one crucial source of information, French and Algerian newspapers of the period were another. *El Moudjahid,* the official journal of the FLN, confirms women's importance to the struggle but gives scant information about their actual missions. Similarly, the French newspaper *Le Monde* traces the evolution of French opinion concerning the war, but like *El Moudjahid,* it pays little attention to daily events in Algeria. It was the local press in Algiers, read faithfully by the pieds-noirs (the French settler population), that provided Amrane-Minne with the daily record of events missing from the other two. If women militants missing from the pages of history were to be found in the newspapers of the day, their representation was often inaccurate and misleading. For this reason, she dismisses *L'Echo d'Alger* as too extremist and *Le Journal d'Alger* as too focused on political opinion for her study and chooses *La Dépêche quotidienne d'Alger,* reading it attentively for its reports of women combatants' arrests, trials, and deaths.

Reading *La Dépêche quotidienne d'Alger,* Amrane-Minne finds omissions and factual errors. Reports of bombs and targeted assassinations that made the front page of the paper did not always specify the FLN militant's name. For example, on October 17, 1958, the newspaper notes: "À Oued Fodda, une bombe cachée dans une valise explose près de la gendarmerie. L'auteur de l'attentat, une femme musulmane, est déchiquétée. Un gendarme est blessé" (96n1; At Oued Fodda, a bomb hidden in a suitcase exploded near the police station. The person who placed the bomb, a Muslim woman, was torn to shreds. A police officer was wounded). Probing the incident, Amrane-Minne traces the bomb to Yasmina Belkacem, an FLN activist who survived the explosion but was seriously injured. Here, through archival research, Amrane-Minne not only puts a name and a face to an incident that had remained anonymous but also corrects the journal's account. The young militant, although severely wounded, did not die and years later gave the historian a full account of the incident.[6]

As she reads the journal, Amrane-Minne also finds a propensity for sensationalism. A case in point is the news report of August 14, 1957, an account clearly written to assure the European population that the French military was dismantling the FLN: "Grâce à une enquête particulièrement rapide menée par les paras du colonel Bigeard, onze fabricants et poseurs appréhendés. Trois femmes participaient au transport des engins qui explosèrent les 18 et 27 juillet à Alger" (107n3; A particularly rapid inquiry undertaken by Colonel Bigeard's paratroopers led to the arrest of eleven individuals, those who had made the bombs and those who had placed them. Three women participated in transporting the devices that exploded on July 18 and 27 in Algiers). Although the headline mentions a group of eleven FLN operatives, the journal draws attention to the three young women—Malika Ighilahriz, Malika Koriche, and Fatima Slimani—displaying their photos on the front page.[7]

Photos of captured young female combatants featured prominently in newspapers and magazines, along with articles that in Amrane-Minne's view were often written in the style of detective novels, served to distort reality (224). In addition to heightening the biases of their largely colonialist readership, they fostered the mystique of the woman militant as either a young urban or rural guerrilla. Indeed, in both the cities and the countryside, women participants were often quite young, and their physical attractiveness, their seemingly audacious lifestyle—they lived side by side with male soldiers in the maquis or in secret hideouts in the Casbah—and their dangerous missions caught the attention of journalists and photographers, who promoted this image.

Yet, Amrane-Minne's data gleaned from the ministry's files proved that media coverage created a misconception. Although newspaper articles and photos of the combatants fostered the belief that women participants were young girls, archival records reveal that 59 percent, a significant majority, were over the age of thirty (227). This statistic counters the notion that most women activists were zealous youth imbued with idealism; a less romantic statistic shows that mature Algerian women, with family obligations far greater than those of teenagers, formed the larger ranks of militants. Indeed, archival records show that only 2 percent were *fidayate*, urban guerrillas, and 16 percent were nurses and other aides in the maquis. The majority of them, 88 percent, were *moussebilate*, civil militants engaged in noncombatant activities, providing vital support in the form of supplies and/or refuge for the combatants (225–27). The young, however, took the greatest risks and paid the highest price. In both the countryside and the cities, female combatants risked capture, incarceration, torture, and death. Archival data acknowledge 948 deaths among the 10,949 women taking part in active combat, yet these statistics are not conclusive. Despite the exhaustive research carried out by Amrane-Minne and other historians, historical records are incomplete; lacunae remain.

Life in the Maquis

If in the Algerian public's mind the maquis, the guerrilla camp in the countryside, appeared to be a site of fearless combat against the enemy that sometimes, but not always, ended in victory, it was far less romantic for the militants who experienced it. For the combatants, it was first and foremost a series of interminable marches; the only way to escape French military surveillance was to constantly move through the countryside. Rebel combatants usually traveled as a group at night, often on precarious mountain trails. If the physical effort was intense for the peasants accustomed to the region, it was even more difficult and involved greater adaptation for those who had come to the maquis from the cities. As the maquisards encountered the challenges of building physical stamina in rugged terrain as rapidly as possible, they also confronted extreme rural poverty, a formative experience, particularly for urban women who had grown up in bourgeois homes.[8]

Amrane-Minne introduces the world of the maquis by way of the journal of a young *moudjahida*, Amina, who shared her daily log with her. Recorded in a small notebook, Amina's entries cover a twenty-seven-day period, March 18–April 14, and contain the day and month, the time, and a brief one- or two-line summary of the day's events. She writes, for example:

> 20 mars: traversée de la montagne de 9 heures (du soir) à 2 heures (du matin).
>
> 21 mars: séjour dans la forêt. Nuit: marche de 1 heure à 7 heures. Je suis tombée de cheval. Nuit désagréable: perte de Rachid. (65)
>
> (March 20: we cross the mountain from 9:00 p.m. to 2:00 a.m.
>
> March 21: we camp in the forest. Night: march from 1:00 a.m. to 7:00 a.m. I fell from my horse. A bad night: we lost Rachid.)

The entries all follow this brief format, revealing that within the twenty-seven-day period the combatants traveled for approximately one hundred hours, sometimes trekking for as long as nine or ten hours a night, usually averaging six kilometers an hour on difficult terrain. Hence, physical endurance was constantly tested. Amina notes in this regard: "30 mars: arrivée dans une khaïma. Nuit paisible. *Les frères sont abrutis par la fatigue*" (66, italics mine; March 30: arrival at a tent. Peaceful night. Our brothers are completely exhausted).

During her time in the maquis Amina receives the news from a fellow combatant that her sister has been killed in combat.[9] She writes: "À 4 heures on a su la mort de ma très chère soeur, Ghanoudja, après avoir tué deux soldats, elle est morte pour sa patrie" (73; At four o'clock we learned that my dear sister Ghanoudja died fighting for her country, after killing two soldiers). It may surprise readers that she comments no further on this very personal loss. Whatever the day's events, dramatic or banal, the tone of each day's record remains neutral, and the entry is brief. In point of fact, Amina's journal resembles a ship captain's log, recording a daily routine with great brevity. Indeed, readers will find the young girl's stoicism reminiscent of chapters in Djebar's *L'amour, la fantasia,* in which former women combatants recount their war experiences in an equally terse, laconic manner, describing emotionally charged incidents in a tone that is surprisingly devoid of emotion.

Neither elaborating on an event nor expressing personal emotion, Amina nonetheless remains an extremely conscientious diarist. With little time for elaboration or digression and her scriptural space limited to a small notepad carried with essentials in a knapsack, she never skips a day's entry. Her consistency and attentiveness to the project suggest that she was aware of the historical importance of the liberation struggle, her own place in it, and the need to document the experience. Identified in the text's annex as a young high-school student at the time she volunteered to join the nursing staff in the maquis, Amina clearly understood the importance of bearing witness and in her way contributed to the historical process that Amrane-Minne would carry further in subsequent years.[10]

Although Amina's logbook contains no intimate reflections, the oral interviews do. We may attribute the difference not only to the difficulty of keeping a journal in a combat zone but also to the close bonds between Amrane-Minne and the women she interviewed, ties that would encourage the women to speak openly of their war experiences, evoking the physical and psychological stress they had endured years before. We should note, however, that with the passage of time the former militants were able to bring greater understanding to their earlier experiences and, in the comfort of their home, were willing to discuss them with a former *moudjahida*. For example, Malika Zerrouki, a former nurse in the maquis, recalls her profound sense of helplessness when tending to the wounded and the dying, stating with great emotion:

> Il m'est arrivée très souvent de passer la nuit avec des djounoud, le lendemain il y a un ratissage et le soir je ne les retrouve pas. Alors ça, j'en suis marquée jusqu'à présent . . . (elle pleure) quand je revois les parents . . . quand j'en parle . . . Les blessés aussi j'en ai vu beaucoup, des blessés graves. Il est en vie et le lendemain je le vois étalé, mort. Il y en a qui sont encore en vie, mais très diminués, cela aussi c'est marquant, très marquant. (*Des femmes*, 90)

> (I would often spend the night with the *djounoud*, soldiers, and the next day they would be captured and I wouldn't be able to find them. That experience still haunts me [she cries] whenever I see their families, whenever I talk about it. I also saw a lot of the wounded, gravely wounded. I would see

a man alive, and the next morning he would be dead. There are some who survived in very bad shape, and that stays with you, it truly does.)

Mimi Ben Mohamed, also a nurse, not only expresses her personal anxieties but describes in detail her efforts to provide for wounded soldiers in the face of inadequate medical facilities and scarce supplies:

Je n'avais pas d'hôpital. [. . .] J'emmenais avec moi mes blesses, à pied pour ceux qui pouvaient marcher, à dos de mulets quand c'était possible. Les blessés avec des fractures j'étais obligée de les mettre dans des abris. C'étaient des petits abris creusés dans le sol avec un trou pour l'aération, je couchais le blessé, puis on refermait l'abri avec de petites planches de bois recouvertes de touffes d'herbe. (*Des femmes*, 45)

(I had no hospital. [. . .] I took my wounded with me. Those who could walk went on foot; others were carried by mules, if possible. I put the wounded with fractures in shelters; these little shelters dug in the ground had air holes. I would lay down the wounded, then close their hideout with planks that I camouflaged with foliage.)

Like other medical personnel in the maquis, Zerrouki and Ben Mohamed lived in constant fear of capture by the French military, which was seeking to round up nurses in an attempt to keep medical aid from the rebels. Zerrouki escaped arrest by crossing the frontier into Tunisia; Ben Mohamed, less fortunate, was captured and spent the last years of the war in prison.

Comparing the interviews with Amina's journal, we find that although the oral testimony offers a far more detailed view of life in the rural underground than the notebook, whose entries remain sketchy and incomplete, the journal and the interviews complement each other. The journal, initiated by the diarist, records events almost at the moment they occur; the interviews, solicited by the historian years later, recall events filtered through the pane of memory. Both forms of historical documentation, when combined with the historian's own interspersed commentary, project the same reality: life in the maquis is physically demanding and psychologically trying, particularly since the monotonous rhythm of endless treks, inclement weather, constant hunger, and fatigue is only interrupted by sudden clashes with the enemy, fierce battles that end with wounded, dying, and dead combatants on both sides.[11]

Urban Warfare: The Battle of Algiers

If in the rural areas *moudjahidate* (female FLN militants) tended to the wounded, fed the troops, and instructed the rural population in health, sanitation, and politics, urban militants performed various duties as well. In the cities, *moussebilate*, or noncombatants, gave refuge to rebels, collected money and medicine, transported messages, and took food to prisoners. At first, *fidayate*, female urban guerrillas, worked primarily as liaisons, transporting weapons and bombs. However, during the Battle of Algiers (January–September 1957), as the French paratroopers carried out repressive measures in the capital, blocking the indigenous parts of the city with checkpoints, Algerian women, particularly attractive young girls, became crucial FLN operatives; passing as Europeans, they were able to move far more easily through the city than Algerian men. Malika Ighilahriz recalls carrying false identity papers and driving a fancy American car—both provided by the FLN—to maneuver between the European sections of the city and the Casbah, passing easily as a European:

> J'avais les cheveux au vent, je passais tous les barrages avec de grands sourires. Pour rentrer à la Casbah, je stationnais boulevard de la Victoire, juste à côté de Barberousse, près de la Gendarmerie. On me voyait descendre de la voiture, à la française, j'entrais dans un immeuble où je mettais mon voile et ma voilette. Je ressortais voilée et descendais à la Casbah. Je déposais ce que je devais remettre et reprenais ce qu'il fallait sortir de la Casbah, des messages, des armes. Et je refaisais le même manège. Dans le couloir d'un immeuble, j'enlevais le voile, je remettais mon rouge à lèvres, mes lunettes, je sortais et je remontais dans ma belle voiture. (*Des femmes*, 149)

> (With my wind-blown hair and big smile, I passed through all the checkpoints. To enter the Casbah, I parked on Boulevard de la Victoire, next to the Barberousse prison, near the Gendarmerie. There I could be seen getting out of my car, acting like a young French girl. I entered a building to put

on my veil, emerged veiled, and went into the Casbah. There I dropped off whatever I was supposed to leave and took whatever messages and weapons were given to me in return. And then I repeated the earlier maneuver. In the hallway of a building, I removed my veil, put on my lipstick, my glasses, walked out, and went back to my beautiful car.)

The incident Ighilahriz describes illustrates Fanon's assertion that the female courier, unveiled, could move through the city undetected—like a fish in Western waters—and foreshadows the dramatic sequence in Gillo Pontecorvo's film *The Battle of Algiers,* in which three *fidayate* carefully disguise themselves as Frenchwomen in preparation for their mission: to plant their bombs in sites frequented by the European population.[12] The film clearly reveals that as the Battle of Algiers intensifies, some women militants abandon their supporting roles as messengers and liaisons to participate directly in political violence. To borrow the political theorist Jean Elshtain's terms, as the "ferocious few" they assume the male role of "Just Warrior," for whom "life-taking" for the national cause is considered a justifiable act.

In this tense climate of executions and bombings, as well as the occupation of the Casbah by French paratroopers, the indigenous population's anger evolves into violent acts of retribution committed by the FLN, including those carried out by women FLN activists who had not anticipated carrying out acts of terrorism. Significantly, the *fidayate* whom Amrane-Minne interviewed usually did not wish to speak about attacks that had resulted in civilian deaths: "Oh! Je n'aime pas parler de ça" (*La guerre d'Algérie,* 98; Oh! I don't like to speak about that), Baya H. exclaims. Yet, Djamila B., who chooses to do so, acknowledges her struggle of conscience:

J'avais donné à F. la bombe qui a explosé dans un trolley. *J'ai été bouleversée. Pour moi, il devait y avoir des objectifs plus valables* ... Pourtant j'ai accepté, c'était la guerre, nous n'avions pas toujours les moyens de choisir nos cibles. Mais au fond de moi-même ... Lorsque c'étaient des endroits où il y avait le simple petit pied-noir—j'avais eu des amis parmi eux—*j'avais un problème de conscience.* (98, italics mine)

(I gave F. the bomb that exploded in a tram. *I was very upset.* As I saw it, there were more important targets. ... But, I had made a commitment; we were at war and didn't always have the means to choose our targets. But, in my heart . . . When they were places with simple little pieds-noirs—I had friends among them—*I had a problem of conscience.*)

Although admitting to a crisis of conscience, Djamila justifies her actions by citing examples of colonial violence and injustice directed against the Algerian population: the executions of FLN militants; the bombings that killed innocent women and children. In contrast, the former *fidaïa* Zohra Drif, when reflecting upon her participation in violent actions—setting bombs in public places—adopts a different position, stating in her recent memoir, *Mémoires d'une combattante de l'ALN:* "Du plus profond de moi-même, je refusais de me laisser culpabiliser" (199; From my very depths, I refused to let myself feel guilty [126]). We should perhaps weigh her words in light of Fanon's statement in "L'Algérie se dévoile" that "personne n'arrête sans drame de conscience la pose d'une bombe dans un lieu public" (36; No one takes the step of placing a bomb in a public place without a battle of conscience [55]).

Significantly, Algerian militants who engage in violent actions adopt the term *terrorist*, applied to them by the colonial authorities. Borrowing the term from modern European history, they equate their resistance to colonial occupation with that of the French resistance to Nazi occupation during World War II. Amrame-Minne writes that the term *terrorist* was applied by colonial authorities to the *fidayine*, urban guerrillas, both male and female, just as the Germans applied it to members of the French Resistance; it was commonly used by the Algerian militants themselves during the war (*La guerre d'Algérie,* 91). Adding that the Arabic term *fidayate* (feminine plural of *fidaï*), a term applied to women urban guerrillas, designates women who carry out armed action, she explains that the noun *fidaï* literally means "he who has decided to give his life" and is commonly attributed to a poorly armed, inexperienced civilian who joins the struggle against a powerful army of occupation (91). Although Amrane-Minne, like Baya H., does not express her personal feelings concerning remorse or culpability and, as interviewer, always uses discretion when eliciting personal testimony, she carefully delineates the sequence of events, the retribution that resulted in escalating political violence—*la loi du talion,* an eye for an eye.

The Weight of Testimony

In her attempt to correct inaccuracies and uncover occulted history, Amrane-Minne makes frequent use of oral testimony. On the one hand, interviews allow former combatants to bring information to light in their own words. On the other hand, their large number, eighty-eight in all, projects the collective voice Amrane-Minne seeks to emphasize. It is important to note that this collective voice includes Frenchwomen who chose to join the anticolonial struggle, militants such as Jacqueline Guerroudj, who had come to Algeria from Metropolitan France, and Elyette Loup and Annie Steiner, who were of pied-noir origin.[13]

With her use of oral testimony, however, Amrane-Minne joins other historians of the Algerian War such as Yves Courrière, Mohamed Teguia, and William B. Quandt, who also use interviews in historical research.[14] Yet, given the nature of her project, to bring women into the pages of history, she places greater emphasis upon oral testimony than they do. Since women had served largely as an anonymous support group of nurses, messengers, and cooks, and not as political leaders and military chiefs, their narratives tended to focus on daily life, a subject easily discussed in an interview. Their testimony, as Amrane-Minne notes, provides a "multitude de petites touches" (*La guerre d'Algérie,* 282), numerous details, rather than information about historic battles or major political decisions.

A conversation with an admittedly political bent, the interview is a genre that favors communication. Amrane-Minne would often interview women in their own homes, where she believed they would feel most at ease. Each session was taped (unless the participant objected), then transcribed, translated (if the interview had been in Arabic), and carefully interpreted by Amrane-Minne. Following each session, she would verify the facts: names, places, dates, and the chronological order of events. Then, assuming the role of editor, she transformed the oral narrative, usually filled with repetitions, pauses, hesitations, and errors of style and syntax, into a "readable" text. Her editorial work also involved choosing excerpts for *La guerre d'Algérie* and more complete selections for *Des femmes dans la guerre d'Algérie.* Hence, she became the architect of a historical project that from conception to execution had a significant collective component. This collective spirit is most evident when the women interviewed speak of their common struggle rather than describing any individual heroic feat. In the same spirit of solidarity, they rarely asked if their names would appear in print (279).

While acknowledging the importance of the interview, Amrane-Minne admits its limitations. She does not consider it an authentic piece of history, but rather an interpretation of a historical moment. This interpretation, as she explains, would necessarily be shaped by the individual's having matured over time—more than twenty years had passed—and by the fact that changes in society had occurred as well (278). Thus, she joins other historians—Nora, Harbi, and Stora—in recognizing that the role of the historian includes listening attentively and then analyzing the material gleaned as well as the conditions surrounding the particular events. As these historians acknowledge the importance of memory in the historical process, they privilege the historian's objective analysis over the memoirist's subjective reality. In the final analysis, Amrane-Minne does too. Nonetheless, as interviewer, she is struck by the women's willingness to speak freely and spontaneously and by their desire to bring their stories to light, to place their memories at the service of their nation's history. They tell her: "Oui, il faut parler des femmes!" (279; Yes, we must speak of the women!).

Despite using oral testimony as an element of objective analysis, Amrane-Minne's interview process allows subjectivity to slip in. As a former combatant and prisoner, she shares the experiences of the women she interviews; their stories are hers. She writes:

> Les entretiens se déroulaient dans une atmosphère d'heureuses retrouvailles et de connivence favorisant le souvenir de ces années qui, pour toutes, ont été un moment exceptionnel de leur vie. Conscientes de la nécessité de ce travail et m'investissant de la lourde tâche de transmettre leur témoignage, elles se sont livrées avec une spontanéité et une franchise qui m'ont émerveillée. Certaine de les connaître grâce à nos quatre années de vie commune, voilà que plus de vingt ans après je les redécouvrais avec une émotion et une admiration renouvelées. (276)

> (These interviews took place in an atmosphere of blissful reconnection and complicity encouraging the memory of these years that for all of us had been an exceptional part of our lives. Aware of the necessity of this

work, and granting me the weighty task of transmitting their testimony, they spoke to me with a spontaneity and frankness that amazed me. Sure that I would know them given our four years of communal life, now, more than twenty years later, I rediscovered them with newfound emotion and admiration.)

Hence, the objectivity that marks other aspects of her research, supported by her meticulous examination of archives and newspapers, is complemented here by the subjective and the personal as the interviewer renews ties with women with whom she had spent four long years in prison, from 1957 to 1961. This same subjectivity is reflected in the fact that although she chooses not to bring herself directly into her text, nor does she hide her status as former combatant: "Ayant personnellement pris part à la guerre de libération nationale, j'ai gardé en mémoire l'image de toutes ces militantes que j'ai connues pendant la 'bataille d'Alger,' au maquis et dans les prisons" (13–14; Having personally taken part in the national liberation war, I have kept in my memory images of all the women militants I knew during the "Battle of Algiers," in the underground, and in the prisons).

The Prisoner Remembers . . .

Having shared the prison experience with other women combatants, Amrane-Minne is able to clearly discern the psychological effects of incarceration. For example, she notes that the prisoner is caught between a system bent upon obliterating the individual's personality and her own desire to keep her sense of self-worth and dignity (164). To maintain the latter, each prisoner follows specific principles of solidarity and activity and keeps contact with the outside world via mail, care packages, and, in some cases, correspondence courses. Nevertheless, after years of incarceration, some prisoners grow weary, their nerves increasingly frayed. In this regard, Safia, a prisoner in Pau, France, recalls:

> Pau n'était pas désagréable comme prison. C'était la meilleure du point de vue de l'ambiance, du climat et tout. Mais ce fut pour moi la période la plus éprouvante du point de vue nerveux. J'ai l'impression que c'était parce que nous étions ensemble depuis trop longtemps, c'était quand même la qua-

trième année... Je ne supportais plus la détention... au bout d'un certain temps, tu ne peux plus t'imposer une discipline permanente. (198)

(Pau was not a bad prison. It was the best in terms of ambiance, climate and everything. But for me it was the most difficult for my nerves. I believe it was because we had been together too long, it was after all the fourth year.... I could no longer tolerate detention... after a certain point, you can no longer hold to permanent discipline.)

While she acknowledges the physical and psychological hardships, Amrane-Minne's view of the prison experience emphasizes the sense of community and solidarity she observed among the women prisoners. Despite the numerous restrictions, forms of deprivation and degradation, and depersonalizing elements—the imposition of prison garb, the removal of personal items—the prison experience came to mean living in a close community with people united in a common cause.

Moreover, once the war ended, the women she interviewed felt that their participation in the liberation struggle had granted them a new sense of self-worth and wider horizons. In this vein, Fatima Benosmane states: "Mes années de prison sont des moments que je me rappelle avec une intense émotion. Nous avons eu des contacts avec des gens tellement différents, même des droits communs, c'est enrichissant de connaître des personnes aussi profondément, cela n'est pas possible dans la vie normale" (*Des femmes*, 23–24; I recall my prison years with great emotion. We had contact with such different people, even common criminals; it is enriching to get to know people so well, this is not possible in normal times).

Thus, to Benjamin Stora's rather pessimistic reflection on women in war—"The subject is somber, cruel, difficult. Images of abduction, rapes, and imprisonments immediately come to mind" ("Women Writing," 78)—Amrane-Minne offers a more nuanced perspective. Attentive to the voices of the women whose narratives she has recorded and to the vivid memories of her own war experience, she does not minimize any of the hardships, but joins Benosmane in recognizing the bonds of solidarity among the women combatants, as well as their pride in having fought for Algerian independence (*La guerre d'Algérie*, 179–80).

Speaking subjectively, Amrane-Minne explains that her own sense of regret lies not in the years of incarceration but rather in the fact that Algerian society proved unable to integrate women into political life after the war, leaving women militants with their memories of heroic exploits but nothing more. In this same vein, she regrets that women in prison were not being trained for later political activity in postcolonial Algeria; she believes that they and their nation missed an opportunity (272). Hence, when she speaks of the reinsertion of the former women combatants into Algerian society following independence, she voices disappointment.[15]

Writing both objectively and subjectively about the war as she affirms her intimate connection to it, Amrane-Minne introduces her personal voice in a rather unique way, via poems composed in prison, acknowledging her authorship in a footnote.[16] An excerpt drawn from the first poem conveys the prisoner's feeling of estrangement from normal life:

Je vois des toits
Une multitude de toits
Qui là-bas au loin
Rejoignent le ciel
Tous près des balcons
Et sur des balcons des gens libres (197)

(I see rooftops
A multitude of rooftops
Which in the distance
Reach the sky
Close by are balconies
And on these balconies people are free)

This lament is rendered all the more poignant when the reader realizes that in 1962, when the prisoner wrote these words, she was barely twenty years old and had already spent three years behind bars.

An excerpt from the second poem expresses her struggle to maintain the discipline that prison life requires and to stifle the rage she experiences but cannot express:

Les vrais murs de la prison
Ne se laissent pas oublier
Ils sont là partout
Dans tout
Le sourire qu'il faut faire
Le rire qu'il faut taire
Le mot à dire
Le mot à ne pas dire
. . . .
Et tous mes mots
Voudraient hurler
Les mots
Que j'ai dû taire (201)

(The true walls of the prison
Don't let us forget them
They are everywhere
In everything
The smile we must wear
The laughter we must stifle
The word to speak
The word not to say
. . . .
And all my words
Would like to scream
The words
I had to stifle)

With the precision of a skilled minimalist, the poet uses limited vocabulary and syntax—few nouns and verbs, neither adjectives nor adverbs, but significant and strategic repetition—to convey the constrained world she, as a prisoner, is forced to inhabit. Moreover, by adopting the first-person singular, she encourages intimacy with the reader, thereby facilitating her reader's entry into this solitary space. Finally, by bringing both previously unpublished poems to light more than two decades after they were written, she captures the spirit of her former self, the young poet who expressed so poignantly—and truthfully—her defiance and vulnerability in these difficult times.

In the third poem, "Boqala," the poet, having emerged from prison and living in an independent Algeria, now reflects upon the effects upon her psyche of the war that has just ended. Although the Francophone reader will find the title and the structure enigmatic, the Arabophone reader will understand the double meaning of the term. *Boqala* is the term for both a poetic improvisational guessing game commonly held at women's gatherings and an earthenware jug. Traditionally, when women came together for poetic recitations, they would slip pieces of paper containing short poems, usually in quatrains, into an earthenware pot. These poems, which they composed, expressed various themes: love, nostalgia, exile, hope for a better life. Hence, this poem also differs from the first two by delving into Algeria's oral tradition.

In this regard, the critic Christiane Achour draws attention to the fact that *boqala* carries two meanings, one physical, the other metaphorical. On the one hand, the term signifies an earthenware vessel used by women in their daily tasks; on the other hand, it denotes a receptacle for memories. In the critic's view, this double meaning reflects the poet's attempt at symbiosis between the traditional poetry that gives structure to the poem and the memories that are evoked (Achour, *Abécédaires en devenir,* 490–91). The excerpt reads:

> J'ai ramené la boqala du puits
> Chaque goutte qui en tombait
> Portait le nom d'un frère tué
> Et chacune de ces gouttes
> M'a brûlée pour toujours (260)[17]

> (I brought the water jug back from the well
> Every drop that fell from it
> Carried with it the name of a fallen brother
> And every drop
> Burned me forever)

By choosing as the title of the poem a word that designates a form of Arabic poetry, using a metaphor anchored in Algeria's landscape, the water well, and naming the implement, *boqala*, the earthenware water jug, the poet makes various allusions to Algeria, thereby reaffirming her commitment to her nation following independence. At the same time, she admits that though now physically free, she is still constrained by troubling memories of a past that will haunt her forever.

We find, then, that Amrane-Minne's poems, offering distinct views of the militant's experience—estrangement from normalcy, the strain of conforming to prison discipline, and finally grief over the loss of fallen comrades—all share common ground as somber personal reflections on isolation and loss. Introducing these poems ever so discreetly, she conveys, in very personal terms, the pain experienced during the war and its traces long after it has ended.

Trauma Shared, Silence Respected

Although Amrane-Minne provides readers with important testimony concerning life in prison, she withholds information in another area of inquiry. As the narrative unfolds, it becomes clear that torture is an uneasy subject of discussion for Amrane-Minne as well as her subjects. It enters *La guerre d'Algérie* as one interviewee, Fatma, recalls the arrival of abused prisoners:

> Elles arrivaient directement des lieux d'interrogatoire des tortures. Leurs vêtements étaient déchirés, certaines avaient la tête rasée. À leur arrivée, on demandait de grandes cuves pleines d'eau chaude à la cuisine et on les aidait à se laver, on leur préparait du linge. Après on lavait et on reprisait leurs vêtements. Si tu savais ce qu'elles avaient passé . . . pour chaque femme tu pourrais faire un livre. (192)

> (They arrived directly from being interrogated and tortured. Their clothing was ripped; some had shaved heads. Upon their arrival, we asked for large basins of warm water from the kitchen and we helped them wash up; we prepared clean linen for them. Then we washed and repaired their clothes. If you only knew what they had been through . . . for each woman you could write a book.)

Amrane-Minne cites testimony that makes it clear that the women had been tortured, including the visual evidence that supports the claim, but like her informant, she leaves much unsaid. Given the trauma inflicted upon torture victims, she did not feel that she could interview her subjects about their ordeal. In her view, their silence proved their wish to forget a traumatic episode in order to preserve their mental health; she, an Algerian woman with her personal sense of integrity, chose to respect their privacy (281).[18]

By acknowledging torture, Amrane-Minne opens the door to additional inquiry. Yet, by choosing not to delve further into the subject, thereby limiting her role as a historian, she contributes to stifling discussion and indeed to facilitating censorship in that realm.[19] It is clear as well that she did not want to probe the issue of sexual abuse and rape, which women captured by the French army often experienced.[20] Throughout the text, as we have seen, the author appears obliquely. In the process of unearthing hidden history, she remains a somewhat hidden informant who conceals as she reveals. She breaks the silence surrounding women's participation in the war but contributes to the silence concerning torture and its psychological consequences. With respect to the violence that touched the civilian population, she presents various points of view of the *poseuses de bombes*—Baya H., Djamila B., and Zohra Drif—but not her own. In this same vein, she neither mentions her own arrest following the Otomatic bombing nor includes any photo of herself among those of former activists that appear at the end of the text.[21]

As she withholds information to respect privacy—including hers—Amrane-Minne reveals the difficulty shared by all Algerian women combatants of coming to terms with the trauma they suffered. Although trauma specialists, such as the psychologist Kai Erikson, tell us that when trauma is shared it can serve as a source of strength for both the individual and the community ("Notes on Trauma and Community," 186), individuals who have lived through a traumatic experience often choose to remain silent. In chapter 6, devoted to three memoirists, we will find the former prisoners Zohra Drif, Louisette Ighilahriz, and Eveline Safir Lavalette expressing the reasons why they kept their silence for many years and then decided to break it. Clearly, the choice to divulge personal trauma may come after many years of reflection.

Sharing her informants' concern for privacy, Amrane-Minne uses interviews as an important tool in her research but applies discretionary guidelines for their implementation. Interviews are, in her view, conversations, not interrogations; the interviewee's privacy must always be respected. Moreover, as she decides what to reveal and what to conceal from the conversations she has had, she is fully aware that the interviewee, despite her spontaneity, may be withholding information consciously or indeed unconsciously, by experiencing memory lapses.

Challenging the Male Gaze

Given Amrane-Minne's dual focus on writing Algerian women back into their nation's history and providing an accurate account of the war, it is not surprising to find her commenting on Gillo Pontecorvo's documentary-style film *The Battle of Algiers* (1966). The film, which allows viewers to witness the techniques used by the French army during the Battle of Algiers—including torture—to put down an urban guerrilla movement, charts the daily struggle of the inhabitants of the Casbah of Algiers against extremely repressive measures and shows women participating in various realms, as *poseuses de bombes* as well as in supporting roles: hiding combatants, transporting weapons.[22]

In an article published a decade after her historical text and her collection of interviews, "Women at War: The Representation of Women in *The Battle of Algiers*," Amrane-Minne applauds the film for paying tribute to women activists but points out that women appear in only 15 of the film's 121 minutes and are almost totally silent throughout the film. Hence, she finds their representation sorely lacking. Focusing on the bombing sequence in which three *fidayate* prepare for and then carry out their respective missions, a sequence that lasts 9 minutes, including the 1 minute and 27 seconds devoted to the women's disguising themselves as Europeans, she notes that it is filmed in silence; the women never speak. Viewers may argue that silence heightens the dramatic quality of this sequence. Amrane-Minne, however, interprets Pontecorvo's aesthetic choice differently. In her view, the "complete absence of speaking roles for women activists" betrays the fact that women were never silent; the atmosphere within resistance groups was "characterized by a close camaraderie between men and women, sustained by lively debates" (347). Thus, she applauds the filmmaker for depicting the *fidayate* but faults him for denying them their voice, their mastery of the word.

The question of women's representation in film can be extended to historical accounts, particularly since the three young women who set off their bombs in downtown Algiers on September 30, 1956, were not characters drawn from fiction. Zohra Drif,[23] Samia Lakhdari, and Djamila Bouhired were FLN militants in the ZAA (Zone Autonome d'Alger, Algiers Autonomous Sector), led by Yacef Saadi.[24] Brought to the screen, these women, although never specifically named in the film, appear in numerous historical works, including Alistair Horne's *A Savage War of Peace*. Published in 1977, Horne's text appeared almost a decade after the film.

Horne's work, as I noted in the beginning of this chapter, includes a passage referring to Amrane-Minne—then known as Danièle Minne—as an FLN operative who was arrested, tried, and convicted of placing a bomb in a student bar in downtown Algiers on January 26, 1957. In the same chapter, he recounts in detail the mission of Drif, Lakhdari, and Bouhired. Here, Horne's historical text becomes problematic, and perhaps more so than Pontecorvo's film. If, as Amrane-Minne contends, Pontecorvo silences women combatants in his film, Horne reduces them to objects of the masculine gaze in his text.

In an essay entitled "Yacef Girls," the literary critic Danielle Marx-Scouras begins her dispute with Horne by calling attention to the chapter division in his text entitled "Yacef Girls: The First Bombs" (*Savage War of Peace*, 185). The heading is inaccurate, she explains, on several counts. First, the first bomb was set by the French on the Rue de Thèbes in the Casbah, not by FLN operatives. Second, the phrase *Yacef girls* is highly problematic. Suggesting that the young women were acting under their leader's influence, not necessarily following their own convictions, it robs them of autonomous thought and indeed makes them appear as their leader's possessions. Unfortunately, as Marx-Scouras notes, the phrase also conveys misplaced familiarity, if not promiscuity ("Yacef Girls," 259).

In this vein, Marx-Scouras asks of Horne and other historians she sees continuing the colonial paradigm: "Just how different are their representations of Algerian women from those of the erotic picture postcards sent by the French in Algeria during the first quarter of this century?" (259–60), alluding to Malek Alloula's *Le harem colonial* (*The Colonial Harem*), a sociohistorical study of the erotic postcards Europeans commonly circulated in colonial Algeria during the first thirty years of the twentieth century.

Dismayed by Horne's terms, which she finds imbued with sexual innuendos, Marx-Scouras cites the following passage from *A Savage War of Peace*: "Djamila Bouhired, who appears to have been personally devoted to Yacef, acted as his chief *procureuse* of suitable girls" (185, Horne's italics). Clearly, "personally devoted" and *procureuse*, terms that transform a committed political activist into a seductive, dependent, and manipulative object, are poor choices for an objective historian, male or female.

Following Marx-Scouras's lead, I have found that Horne, in his preface to his text, published in 1977, describes his relationship to French history in similar terms, stating: "Writing about the history of France has the elements of a love affair with an irresistible woman; inspiring in her beauty; often agonizing and maddening, but always exciting, and from whom one escapes only to return again" (11). One can only wonder whether a historian accustomed to using metaphors that define Western women in terms of erotic temptation and seduction can deal objectively with women representing a colonized Arab and Berber Muslim culture. Hence the importance of multiple voices, multiple narratives.

It may surprise readers, however, that Amrane-Minne, who cites Horne's text briefly, in its French translation, *Histoire de la guerre d'Algérie*,[25] fails to seize upon Horne's seemingly derogatory manner in depicting the militants he calls "Yacef girls." The explanation for this apparent oversight most probably lies in the fact that Amrane-Minne carefully examined primary sources—archives and oral testimony—in order to write a social history rather than probing secondary sources, that is, the historical works of Horne, Courrière, and others that trace the Algerian Revolution via political and military events.[26]

When Stora commended Amrane-Minne's "thick book" for breaking the silence surrounding women's participation in the anticolonial struggle, he probably was not thinking specifically of Horne's *A Savage War of Peace*, as he wrote: "Behind the methodological choice to present women's works there is a need for 'the male historian' to avoid reducing Algeria's wars to a single explanation, to find other voices, to suggest some elements that might give an idea of the importance of the mutations caused by these wars in every sphere—the male and the female, in Algeria and in France" ("Women Writing," 79). Yet Stora's words should be read as an important affirmation of Amrane-Minne's historical project, a much-needed revision of Algerian women's war story.

Amrane-Minne's research clearly confirms that that the Algerian War provided unique opportunities for women confronting political oppression to act. As the political scientists Joyce Kaufman and Kristen Williams show in *Women at War, Women Building Peace,* their study of women at war in several conflicts—Sri Lanka, Northern Ireland, the West Bank and Gaza— gender becomes less important than willing bodies in a "people's war" (41). Yet, they conclude that women's participation in a nationalist cause, a powerful motivating force that might mean women's liberation, rarely ends in social transformation (51). This paradigm surely applies to postcolonial Algeria, where political events of the postindependence era—including the Family Code, which restricts women's rights, approved by the National Assembly in 1984, and the *décennie noire,* Algeria's dark decade of the 1990s— confirm the strength of residual patriarchy.[27]

Amrane-Minne is one voice among many to ask, How can women who once rebelled against the colonial system, despite the patriarchal traditions that held them back, and were able to function successfully during a time of great conflict regain that earlier momentum? New strategies are called for. Where and how are women to find them? With respect to new strategies, we find that as new scholarship emerges, historians such as Natalya Vince (whose work I discuss in the conclusion) express gratitude to Amrane-Minne for her historical work, particularly her extensive use of oral interviews, thereby affirming the importance of "bottom-up" engagement in both the development and the understanding of national narratives. Nevertheless, Vince finds that Amrane-Minne does not truly challenge the structuring framework and idiom of the dominant discourse in the text that writes women back into the national narrative (223). Similarly, the historian Mohammed Harbi has criticized Amrane-Minne for what he sees as minimizing both the social conflicts opposing Algerian men and women (conflicts such as forced marriage and conservative male rejection of mixed social interaction) and the political tensions that emerged among *moudjahidate* during the war (preface, 6). Thus, both historians suggest that Amrane-Minne's work provides an important blueprint that can indeed be reworked and enhanced.

In other words, Amrane-Minne's texts, her historical study and her collection of interviews, provide a solid framework—facts, figures, and personal perspectives of former women combatants—that should help readers better contextualize the literary production—novels and memoirs—in the chapters that follow. Yet, we must bear in mind that her work opens the door to further study. By alerting her readers to listen attentively to women's voices, ever aware of their multiplicity, Amrane-Minne suggests a way to approach and interpret narratives, both memoirs and fiction. The Algerian War, as she reminds us, was always a collective endeavor in which a multitude of Algerian women, herself included—many anonymous, many forgotten—played significant roles. If her "thick book" represents both an objective and a subjective endeavor, it is perhaps her personal way of coming to terms with the individual and collective trauma of an extremely violent episode in French and Algerian history. Signing her work Danièle Djamila Amrane-Minne, she embraces the two voices that converge in her work: Danièle Minne, militant, and Djamila Amrane, historian.

2 HERSTORY IS THE WAR STORY

From Assia Djebar's Early Fiction to *L'amour, la fantasia*

Examining the literary representations of contemporary war in three Arab countries in which women have played a significant role—Algeria, Lebanon, and Palestine—the critic Miriam Cooke asserts that whereas the wars of Lebanon and Palestine empowered the women who participated in them, transforming their lives in significant ways, the Algerian War of Independence did not. In her view, Algeria's anticolonial struggle came too soon to serve as a catalyst for significant social change, that is, for the insertion of feminist issues and concerns into the nationalist agenda ("Wo-man, Retelling the War Myth," 186).[1]

Placing gender at the center of an analysis of war that views Algeria quite critically, she cites the Palestinian writer Sahar Khalifa, who, in her novel *Abbad al-shams* (Sunflower), asks: "What happened to Algerian women after independence? [...] They went out into the light and the men left them in the dark. It was as though freedom was restricted to men alone" (qtd. on 186).[2] Calling for a feminist critique of the Algerian War, Cooke challenges historians and writers to contradict the assertion that the anticolonial struggle, although admittedly empowering for some, was not a transformative experience for most Algerian women (184).

Historians have responded to the challenge. As shown in the previous chapter, Danièle Djamila Amrane-Minne's research and Natalya Vince's more recent analyses reveal the difficulty of evaluating Algerian women's individual and collective transformation during and following the liberation struggle. Indeed, Vince, through her interviews with former combatants, found women's participation in the nation-building process to be complex, sometimes difficult to define, and easily misunderstood. Yet, she and Amrane-Minne conclude that the women—some as agents of change, others as witnesses to a political revolution—were transformed in significant ways by a struggle that forced so many to assume new responsibilities.

For a writer's response, I suggest that we turn to Assia Djebar, Algeria's most prominent woman novelist, whose fiction has focused primarily on Algerian women's struggle against both French colonialism and indigenous patriarchy. In a literary career that spanned fifty years (1957–2007), Djebar reached a public far beyond her nation's borders, her election to France's Académie française in 2006 confirming her place among the "immortals" of modern literature written in French. The novelist's untimely death in 2015 marked the loss of a major figure in Francophone literature.

In this chapter, a study of three of Djebar's novels written over two decades, I argue that while the Algerian novelist shares Cooke's feminist agenda, her writings offer a nuanced analysis, for Djebar considers women's empowerment an ongoing process, not limited to one moment in her nation's history. In this regard, the novelist, with an academic background in history, has examined historical archives and conducted interviews with former women combatants, tracing the diverse ways in which Algerian women came to participate in the anticolonial war and collectively contributed to its success. While Amrane-Minne uses historical documentation to chart Algerian women's participation in the liberation struggle and bring women's voices into the war narrative, Djebar pursues the same objective through historically grounded fiction. Her writings grapple with the question that Cooke raises: were women empowered by the war experience?

Djebar's literary career began in the 1950s with the publication of *La soif* in 1957 (published in English as *The Mischief* the following year) and *Les impatients* (The impatient ones) in 1958, novels that focus on young women coming of age in preindependence Algeria. Although written during the early years of the Algerian War of Independence, these works are set in the period before the war began. They depict Algerian women's struggle against the constraints of patriarchy and eschew political engagement. In contrast, *Les enfants du nouveau monde* (*Children of the New World: A Novel of the Algerian War*), published in 1962, and *Les alouettes naïves* (The naïve larks), published in 1967, examine the ways the anticolonial war altered women's lives, guiding them progressively toward active participation in a changing world. Both works depict the psychological awakening of Algerian women that occurred during the war.

Written in 1960, while the Algerian War still raged, and published in the summer of 1962, as Algeria gained its independence, *Les enfants du nouveau monde* depicts a community caught up in the events of the early years of the war. Written as the war drew to a close and published in 1967, *Les alouettes naïves* focuses on several members of a group of Algerian exiles in Tunis during the last years of the war. While the first text introduces one uncertainty, the final outcome of the anticolonial struggle, the second presents another, the burden of nation-building once peace is restored. Yet, these early war novels have not received much critical attention.[3] Translated into English two decades after its initial publication, *Les enfants du nouveau monde* eventually found a reading public in the United States, particularly in university courses focusing on feminism and world literature.[4] *Les alouettes naïves*, however, has had no renaissance in Algeria, France, or the United States.[5]

In contrast, Djebar's fifth novel, *L'amour, la fantasia* (*Fantasia: An Algerian Cavalcade*) is perhaps the most widely read fictional work depicting Algerian women's war story. With a complex and innovative narrative structure that interweaves strands of personal and collective history, the text combines an autobiographical journey with the history of Algeria in two dramatic and painful historical periods, the conquest of 1830 and the independence struggle of 1954, thereby widening Amrane-Minne's historical inquiry. The novel quickly drew the attention of readers and critics at home and abroad, establishing Djebar as a leading North African writer. Published in 1985, it was translated into English the same year, reaching an English-language audience soon after its original publication in France.

Concurring with critics who assert that the lack of attention to the early works results in an incomplete picture of the writer's corpus, I propose to examine the two early war novels along with *L'amour, la fantasia*, tracing the evolution of Djebar's sociopolitical objectives and narrative techniques over two decades, from the early years of independence through the mid-1980s, as I probe the question of Algerian women's empowerment through political engagement. Aware that many critics, as well as the novelist herself, have tended to group all the early novels of the 1950s and 1960s together, considering *L'amour, la fantasia* the beginning of a new literary phase, since it followed a decade during which Djebar turned to cinema to express the trauma of war and the uncertainties of the postcolonial era, I nevertheless put these three works together for the following reasons. A study of several works should help us appreciate more fully the extent and nature of Djebar's evolution as a writer. The earlier texts, in both their political and their aesthetic intent, set the writer on the path she pursued throughout her literary career. In addition, they explore the ways in which women's individual and collective empowerment occurs during periods of extreme social upheaval. Finally, I hope to show that *Les alouettes naïves*, published in the immediate postindependence years, serves as a bridge between the other two novels. Embodying the reflections of a writer who, along with her nation, matured during the long and violent war, and rooted in the writer's own experience, it initiates the autobiographical journey further developed in *L'amour, la fantasia* and subsequent works.

Anticolonial in their political engagement, subversive in their feminist objectives, and aesthetically innovative, the three texts express the writer's belief that Algerian men and women experienced the war of decolonization quite differently. As men struggled to throw off the yoke of French colonialism, achieving their goal after almost eight years of violent conflict and political negotiation, women, the captives of both a colonial structure and an indigenous patriarchy, have had to continue to struggle for agency within their family and society years after their nation achieved political independence from the colonial power. Djebar insists that unless Algerian women, individually and collectively, appropriate voice and authority in private and public realms, the yoke of patriarchy will continue to restrict their lives.

Djebar experienced the Algerian War primarily in exile. A student at the École normale supérieure in Paris when the conflict began, she joined Algerian students in Paris on the strike organized by the FLN in 1956, then went into exile in Tunisia in 1958 with her first husband, Walid Garn.[6] In Tunis she worked as a journalist for the FLN political newspaper, *El Moudjahid*, interviewing Algerians in the refugee camps at the Tunisian border to gather information about the war, while completing a graduate degree in history at the University of Tunis. In 1959 she accepted a position in North African history at the university in Rabat, Morocco, teaching while working with Algerian refugees there.[7] She returned to Algeria following independence to teach in the history department at the University of Algiers.[8]

Never directly involved in military action—she was neither in the maquis nor in prison—Djebar contributed to the war effort primarily as a journalist in exile. Thus, she experienced the conflict from a physical distance, gleaning information through written reports and personal interviews with refugees, combatants, and other informants. For example, some events described in *Les enfants du nouveau monde* are based on information she received from relatives (Schyns, *La mémoire littéraire de la guerre,* 73). Although Blida, a small city southwest of Algiers where the novel takes place, was one that Djebar knew well, having lived there as a boarding student during her years at the French colonial lycée, she no longer lived in that city when the war began. In contrast, *Les alouettes naïves,* with its focus on the lives of Algerian exiles in Tunisia, more closely reflects the writer's personal experiences. Having lived in exile, first in Tunisia and later in Morocco, before returning to Algeria at the end of the war, she drew upon her life experience to construct that fictional work.

Women and War, Part 1: *Les enfants du nouveau monde*

Les enfants du nouveau monde is a realistic chronicle of one day's events in one Algerian city. The date is May 24, 1956, less than two years into the war that will last for almost eight years; the independence struggle is in its embryonic stage. As the narrative unfolds, twenty characters appear, men and women connected to one another by family ties. Through the intricate meshing of their lives, the novel offers readers a panoramic view of a community awakening to the psychological as well as physical demands of the revolution, yet unable to predict its outcome. Significantly, the opening scene focuses on women as witnesses to war, cloistered in their homes, immobile and afraid:

> Il arrive aux femmes qui, dans la fraîcheur de leur chambre, ne bougent pas, de se tendre un instant, les yeux grands ouverts, le regard fixe, avec une palpitation enfantine, et d'imaginer leur mari debout contre un mur, au soleil de midi, secoué sans doute d'une peur qu'il doit s'efforcer de ne point révéler, mais que l'épouse retrouve en lui, le soir lorsque tout est fini, que la montagne reprend sa nudité orgueilleuse. (15)

(In the coolness of their room, the women sometimes don't move; they grow tense momentarily, eyes wide, staring into space, hearts pounding like those of the children as each imagines her husband up against a wall in the sun at high noon, no doubt shaking with a fear that he must make every effort to conceal. But the wife recognizes it at night, when everything is over, when the mountain once again assumes its arrogant nakedness. [3])

Djebar emphasizes women's immobility by depicting them sheltered in their rooms as they watch "la montagne dans les feux de la lutte" (13; the mountain under fire [3]). Here, the novelist immediately draws attention to the gap between male and female experiences, expressing difference in spatial terms: women, from the confines of home, imagine their men facing danger directly in streets patrolled by the French army.

Not only does this passage transmit the immediate effect of the war upon the population, it reveals the reasons for women's inability to act. A rigid patriarchal society that cloisters women, requiring their submission and promoting passivity in the formative years, prevents their emotional and political maturity. Their apparent lack of maturity encourages the critic Bouba Mohammedi-Tabti to conclude that women's gaze substitutes for action; they watch the spectacle of war unfold as if they were spectators at a theatrical performance ("Assia Djebar," 120).

Yet, as the war intensifies, women who first experienced events from a distance and from the protection of their homes become increasingly vulnerable. The community loses Lla Aïcha, an elderly woman killed by stray shrapnel as she sits peacefully in her inner courtyard. Occurring in the early pages of the novel, the incident, which, as the critic Clarisse Zimra explains, was based on a true event recounted to Djebar by her mother-in-law, is a symbol of "war's senseless cruelty, which could reach everywhere and everyone, even the most feeble and the most innocent in the most secure of enclosures" (afterword, 213).

In addition, as the war gains in intensity, with some individuals and families fleeing the war zone, others joining the resistance, women are forced to adopt new strategies, attitudes, and behavior for survival. For example, when men leave home to join the resistance, are imprisoned, or killed, they assume greater authority within their families: "Il se trouve toujours une femme, jeune, vieille, peu importe, qui prend la direction du chœur" (*Les enfants*, 14;

There is always one woman—young, old, it makes no difference—who conducts the choir [2]). Calling attention to the social transformation that is taking place, the critic Gordon Bigelow describes these changes as a social upheaval that "shatters the undergirding of identity and community, launching characters into a cultural free-fall" ("Revolution and Modernity," 20).

Within the context of rapid social transformation, Djebar broadens the social spectrum to include a number of "modern" and "traditional" women, defining the former as women who are mobile and have access to the city, the latter as those who remain cloistered in closed interiors. The novelist warns, however, that boundaries between closed and open spaces are often porous; women militants, in cities or in the countryside, may later find themselves confined to another form of enclosure, to life behind prison walls when captured by the French military.

To present a cross section of Algerian women, Djebar introduces Salima, an imprisoned militant; Hassiba, a young woman about to join the rebels in the maquis; Suzanne, a French intellectual who espouses the anticolonial cause; Touma, a prostitute and traitor to her people and to the nationalist cause; Amna, an Algerian police officer's wife; Chérifa, a militant's wife; and Lila, a university student whose husband has joined the underground. Some choose to participate in the revolution (Salima, Hassiba), and others are thrust into new, sometimes dangerous situations (Amna, Chérifa, Lila). Whether by choice or by circumstance, all are swept up by the winds of political change and required to react to them. Amna, when challenged by her husband to denounce her neighbor, lies to him (never having deceived him before), then warns the militant's wife, Chérifa, of his imminent arrest.

Aware that only she can save her husband, Chérifa immediately sets out across town to warn him and urge him to flee:

> Elle a oublié le danger lui-même; peut-être n'est-ce pas lui, en vérité qui l'a poussée, mais un désir sournois de savoir soudain si elle ne peut être vouée qu'à l'attente dans sa chambre, à la patience et à l'amour. Ainsi, elle a traversé la ville entière, cette présence pour elle aux yeux multiples, hostiles et au terme de cette marche, elle a découvert qu'elle n'est pas seulement une proie pour la curiosité des mâles—une forme qui passe, mystère du voile que le premier regard sollicite, faiblesse fascinante qu'on finit par haïr et sur laquelle on crache—non, elle a existé. (162)

(She'd forgotten the danger itself. In truth, it's perhaps not that which drove her, but rather a gnawing desire to suddenly know whether she could really spend her life waiting in her room, in patience and love. That's why she crossed the entire town, bared her presence to so many hostile eyes, and at the end of her trek discovered that she was not only a prey for the curiosity of men—a passing shape, the mystery of the veil accosted by the first glance, a fascinating weakness that ends up being hated and spat upon—no, she now knows that she has existed. [143])

In this passage, one of the most dramatic and symbolic in the text, Chérifa, a passive bystander to the political events until this moment, rises to the challenge by engaging in political action. Not only does she test her courage by venturing into public space alone but she understands the transformative effect of participating, albeit minimally, in the political struggle: "Toutes ces sensations violentes qui ont alimenté sa volonté de plus en plus tendue et qui, de plus en plus, la découvraient à elle-même, l'ont introduite dans un état second" (162; All the violent emotions that had fed her increasingly strained willpower and that had revealed her temperament, pushed her beyond herself [143]). By crossing town alone to warn her husband, Chérifa opens her world to new sensations and new possibilities. Adopting new behavior to fit the crisis situation, she redefines agency in her terms, thereby affirming her sense of self. It is true that she will not join the maquis with her husband and indeed cannot express to him the desire to do so, but she will return to her home with the resilience needed to carry on alone.

Chérifa's return to her home, which readers may read as a regression, leads Miriam Cooke to conclude that "this has been an empowering experience, but it is not shown to be transformative" ("Wo-man, Retelling the War Myth," 184). However, as Amrane-Minne reveals in her study of women participants in the war, the *moussebilate,* civil militants, who made up 88 percent of the activists, provided crucial support in the form of supplies and/or refuge for the combatants (*La guerre d'Algérie,* 225–27). In my view, the novel leaves us wondering whether Chérifa may become a civil militant engaging in further political actions from her home—transmitting arms, messages, or medicine or harboring militants—given her new sense of agency.

Yet, the signs of male resistance to female agency are apparent. Depicting the interplay between Chérifa, a veiled woman crossing a main square in Blida, and the hostile eyes of her countrymen, Djebar alerts her readers to traditional male resistance to women's freedom of movement in public spaces. In this vein, the city street becomes a metaphor for women's possibilities and limitations. Chérifa gains a new sense of self-worth by venturing into a public space and enduring the stares of Algerian men seated at the café, but Touma dies in the street, murdered by a brother committed to cleansing the shame that her loose behavior has cast upon her family. Since FLN revolutionaries have made this honor killing a requirement for the young man to join their cell, the implementation of an archaic code, as the critic Evelyne Accad notes, represents a disquieting omen for women's rights in postcolonial Algeria ("Assia Djebar's Contribution," 807). Expressing the concern that women's rights remain in jeopardy, Djebar warns her readers that Algerian women face an indigenous patriarchal structure so deeply rooted that it may not change with independence.[9]

Broadening the social spectrum to include "modern" as well as "traditional" Algerian women, Djebar introduces Lila, a young woman whose education and worldliness mirror the writer's world but contrast vividly with Chérifa's life experiences. Yet, the novelist chooses to reveal similarities that attenuate their differences. Lila, like Chérifa, confronts a dangerous political situation not of her making. Once her husband joins the underground, she chooses to live alone. When she provides refuge for her young cousin, a rebel on the run who arrives at her doorstep seeking shelter, she is arrested for harboring a fugitive. She will resist her interrogators in prison, attesting to the same courage that Chérifa has shown. As each woman faces her own test, both mature politically.

Yet Djebar is careful to portray both women's evolution realistically; they awaken to political action in measured steps. Lila has been living alone since her husband left for the maquis; she chose not to follow him, because at the time she did not share his strong political commitment. Chérifa, as we have seen, does not join her husband either; she will wait for his return, albeit now with a greater sense of purpose. Nevertheless, with both women remaining at home while their husbands are in the maquis, we are tempted to ask whether Chérifa and Lila are not yet mature enough for the sacrifices that active participation in the struggle entails, or whether their men are not yet prepared to accept their wives as fellow combatants.

As Djebar's early novels announce themes and depict protagonists that are further developed in later works, we should note that Lila prefigures both Nfissa, the female protagonist of *Les alouettes naïves,* and Isma, Djebar's semiautobiographical protagonist of *L'amour, la fantasia* and *Ombre sultane* (*A Sister to Scheherazade*). Similarly, the relationship between Isma and her father that is portrayed in *L'amour, la fantasia* (further elaborated in *Nulle part dans la maison de mon père*) begins here as an Algerian father proudly walks his daughter to school: "Lila se souvient de son père qui lui portait son cartable et la conduisait, main dans la main, à l'école primaire" (146; Lila remembers that her father used to carry her book bag and, her hand in his, take her to elementary school [129]).[10] Readers of *L'amour, la fantasia* will immediately recognize this scene as the one that opens that text. Thus, this early work of fiction contains an autobiographical element that reappears in Djebar's later novel.

Although some characters, relationships, and events depicted here do recur in later texts, the deep friendship between Lila and her cousin Bachir remains unique. Lila comes to consider her friendship with her cousin as profound as romantic love. After Bachir's death, she recalls with nostalgia their last night in her apartment, talking until dawn: "Parler avec transparence, avec palpitation, au cœur de la nuit, quelles belles heures cela faisait! elle y pensa ensuite, bien plus tard" (200; Speaking honestly, with passion, in the deep of the night—those were beautiful hours she realized, later on, much later [182]). Their relationship, however, does not survive the war: Bachir is assassinated, Lila imprisoned. Is Djebar warning readers that true friendship between a man and a woman can rarely, if ever, survive, or is she acknowledging the terrible cost in human lives of Algeria's war of liberation?

In search of new ways to articulate Algerian women's war story, a narrative involving an unstable and rapidly changing world, Djebar structures a text composed of multiple interconnected fragments. Each chapter, named for a character, begins that individual's story, interrupts it, and continues the narrative in a later chapter. In the same vein, the third-person narrator transitions abruptly from scene to scene, focusing briefly on one character and then rapidly moving on to another. Finally, as characters express their inner thoughts, their reflections form a succession of incomplete fragments, with the rapid sequencing of events contributing to a heightened sense of disjunction and dislocation. As the critic Jane Hiddleston notes, the multivoiced, fragmented narrative creates a feeling of instability and improvisation, producing a collective vision of modern Algerian women whose voices are neither definitive nor fully evolved (*Assia Djebar,* 40).

Clearly, Djebar chooses a narrative strategy that conveys the sense of a revolution in the making. In 1956 Algeria is in the throes of a revolution; men and women caught up in the conflict have not yet fully assimilated an experience that presumably will lead them to greater political and emotional maturity. The fragmented form captures the drama of one moment in history, one day's events reflecting a volatile, rapidly changing political struggle. Having adopted several innovative narrative strategies in this text, Djebar explained that stylistic experimentation such as the multiplicity of characters, the use of flashback, and the Aristotelian unity of time, place, and action were new to her.[11]

By depicting multiple female characters with different points of view, she introduces a gendered perspective that offers a nuanced interpretation of Algerian women's capabilities and limitations and, most importantly, eschews any reductive analysis. Bigelow suggests that the analysis of gender systems that emerges in the novel leads to a more complex analysis of colonial Algeria's cultural practices and historical transformation than the social theorists Frantz Fanon and Pierre Bourdieu provide in their theoretical writings ("Revolution and Modernity," 14). Although they, like Djebar, represent the anticolonial war as a process that destabilizes the foundations of identity and community, the novelist, Bigelow argues, understands most fully the strong claim of imbedded cultural norms upon Algerian society, particularly those related to gender. An insider to the workings of her society, she is far more aware of residual patriarchy than are European or European-trained male theorists. Thus, if the tone of the novel appears optimistic, conveying the belief that the colonized will win the war, this optimism remains nuanced, particularly with regard to women's rights.

Articulating Algerian women's war story by experimenting with narrative strategies such as polyphonic, or multivoiced, discourse and narrative fragmentation, Djebar also introduces contrapuntal representation, a concept the postcolonial critic Edward Said explores in detail in his theoretical study *Culture and Imperialism,* published three decades later. Borrowing the concept of counterpoint from music and using it as a model for approaching history and literary texts allows him to bring together conflicting ideologies such as imperial and counterimperial discourses, viewing them as intertwined and overlapping histories, thereby connecting, rather than separating, two opposing positions (18).[12] By adopting a contrapuntal perspective, Said explains, we can "think through and interpret together experiences that are discrepant, each with its particular agenda and pace of development, its own internal formation, its internal coherence and system of external relationships, all of them coexisting and interacting with others" (32). In this way, he argues, differences can be articulated but need not be resolved.

Probing the musical aspects of Said's theory, the critic Kathryn Lachman emphasizes the musical foundations of counterpoint and the importance it attaches to each voice: "Each voice must be fully realized on its own and able to stand independently. All voices are considered of equal importance; no voice dominates, except momentarily" (164). Applying Said's concept to Djebar's novels, I suggest that this contrapuntal approach begins in *Les enfants du nouveau monde*, with the potentially discrepant relationship between Chérifa, the "traditional" woman, and Lila, the "modern" woman, who express connection and reciprocity as each, in her own way, engages in actions that test courage and resiliency in time of war.

Finally, as Djebar concludes her text, in which various narrative strategies convey the sense of an emerging revolution, she leaves us with the image of Hassiba, the aspiring militant who has come to Blida to meet the liaison who will lead her to the maquis. Arriving at the train station wearing a flimsy white dress and high-heeled shoes, the young woman appears singularly ill-prepared for the harsh life awaiting her in the maquis. Ironically, the image of the beautiful girl dressed in white comes into the view of Lila's cousin, Bachir, moments before he dies, gunned down by the French soldiers pursuing him. The idealistic young revolutionary dies with a vision of beauty, purity, and innocence that harsh reality would not sustain. Thus, Djebar ends the text upon a note of uncertainty as "the children of the new world," some sorely unprepared, others far too idealistic, face the multiple challenges that the liberation struggle has set in motion but not resolved.

Women and War, Part 2: *Les alouettes naïves*

While *Les enfants du nouveau monde* depicts Algerian women awakening to the demands of a political and social revolution, *Les alouettes naïves* continues to chart their evolution in the final years of the struggle. If, in terms of chronology, the text may be considered a sequel to *Les enfants du nouveau monde*, it reflects the themes and style of the previous work as well. Thematically, the novel presents the story of a woman in a period of political turmoil. Stylistically, it attests to the novelist's commitment to experimentation with form, structure, and narrative strategies. The complex narrative involves two narrators—Omar, the protagonist, who tells his story and those of his friends; and a second narrator, who may or may not be the author—and a tripartite temporal division—"Autrefois," "Au delà," "Aujourd'hui" (Past, Timeless, Present)—in which boundaries blur as characters move back and forth between past and present.

In this text, the novelist introduces three protagonists, who, having actively participated in the anticolonial war in Algeria, are now in exile in Tunis. Omar is director of an orphanage for refugee children, Rachid a journalist writing for the FLN newspaper, and Nfissa a social worker tending to Algerian refugees. Through flashbacks, we learn that Omar, arrested in Algeria for his political activity, spent much of the early war years in prison, Rachid fought with the ALN in the maquis, and Nfissa served as a nurse in the maquis. Following a French military attack in which her fiancé was killed and she was captured, Nfissa, like Omar, spent time in prison.

In the first section, "Autrefois," Omar, encountering his close childhood friend Rachid in Tunis, recalls their shared childhood and adolescence. Nfissa, joining her family in Algiers upon her release from prison, recounts her experiences in the maquis and in prison, her narrative interspersed with nostalgic memories of childhood. Hence, Djebar places male and female experiences in relation to each other as the two narratives oscillate between past and present. The second section, "Au delà," marks an abrupt and bold transition as it shifts to Rachid and Nfissa, who, as newlyweds, secure a brief period of time for themselves, apart from the world. Here, Djebar audaciously describes the erotic nature of their relationship as she shows her female protagonist embracing her sexuality. In the final section, "Aujourd'hui," Djebar, focusing again on the couple, depicts their lives in exile. Through flashbacks, she shows them meeting and then marrying in Tunis during the final years of the war. In this final section, Nfissa, married and expecting a child, withdraws from the political struggle to focus on her inner, private world.

Although *Les alouettes naïves* complements *Les enfants du nouveau monde* thematically and stylistically, significant elements separate them. Whereas the first introduces multiple characters as it focuses on a series of events that occur within twenty-four hours on one specific day in one Algerian city, the second widens the temporal and spatial frame to include Tunisia and Algeria, past and present. In addition, Djebar rejects the panoramic sweep of the previous text to "zoom in" on her three protagonists, thereby developing a more profound analysis of characters and the events that shape their lives. Perhaps most significantly, the optimism of *Les enfants du nouveau monde* gives way to a more somber tone as *Les alouettes naïves* probes the psychological effects of a long and violent military conflict. Depicting the trauma, suffering, and disillusionment that individuals and the community have endured, it puts forth the perspective of a writer who, having lived through the years of violent upheaval, is fully aware of the toll the war has taken, individually and collectively, and of the difficulties now facing the newly independent nation. Balancing pessimism with optimism—Rachid's view with Omar's—the novel conveys the weight of an uncertain future upon the individual and the nation.

Djebar has explained that she wrote the work during the immediate postwar years, when the mood of the newly independent nation was indeed one of great uncertainty. Distinguishing this novel from her first three texts, which she admits she wrote rapidly and "dans une fièvre joyeuse" (with joyous excitement), she writes in her reflective essay on her work, *Ces voix qui m'assiègent* (These voices that besiege me):

> Le quatrième, *Les Alouettes Naïves*, par contre, je l'ai écrit plus longuement, de 1962 à 1965: premières années de l'indépendance, à Alger, où je ne faisais que marcher dehors (Alger, ville alors à la fois cosmopolite et de désordre joyeux, *incertain*). (64, italics mine)

> (The fourth, *Les Alouettes Naïves*, in contrast, took me longer to write, from 1962 to 1965: I spent the first years of independence in Algiers, outside, walking [the city of Algiers at the time was both cosmopolitan and in a state of joyous disorder and *uncertainty*].)

Having noted that the narrative techniques—polyphony, fragmentation, and counterpoint—create a sense of instability and uncertainty in *Les enfants du nouveau monde*, we find Djebar using the same techniques in the subsequent work. In this vein, the critic Clarisse Zimra explains that as the two narrators interweave various threads, juxtaposing the public self, an exterior world where men are at war, to the private self, an interior world of women in love, they construct a work in counterpoint ("In Her Own Write," 218). We should add, however, that the boundaries between the gendered public and private realms, the world of men and the world of women, are not always clearly delineated; both men and women participate in the public sphere, the anticolonial struggle, as well as in the private realm, the interior world in which they too experience love and deep emotional bonds with friends and family. In addition, contrapuntal representation in the novel extends beyond the juxtaposition of public and private realms to include home and exile, past and present.

Opening with Omar's description of a refugee camp at the Tunisian border, the text immediately introduces the theme of exile, the experience Djebar came to know during the war and one she investigated for the journal *El Moudjahid*. Omar, the first of two narrators, provides the description:

> Assis près du chauffeur, je regardais enfin les rescapés de la guerre: ils nous faisaient face, tournaient le dos à l'horizon, "les frontières", disaient-ils paisiblement, comme si, dressés devant le ciel, ce n'était pas au bord d'un cratère qu'ils attendaient mais tout contre l'avenir, ce mot riait de certitude au fond de leurs yeux hâves et bibliques. (15)

> (Seated next to the chauffeur, I finally looked at the refugees: they faced us, their backs against the horizon, "the borders," as they said peacefully, as if, set against the sky, they were not waiting at the edge of a crater but against the future, a word filled with certainty emanating from their haggard biblical eyes.)

Omar, as narrator, expresses the sentiment he shares with these refugees in the camp. The borders separating Algeria from Tunisia are more than geographical divisions. As Jane Hiddleston notes, they are transitional spaces for refugees, who "enter a space of exile haunted by the uncertain history of their native land, itself in its moment of creation" (*Assia Djebar*, 46).

Acknowledging her personal satisfaction in writing passages that recall her experiences with refugees at the time, Djebar explains:

Plus de cinq ou six ans après, quand j'ai écrit cette ouverture des *Alouettes Naïves* où ces réfugiés ne sont qu'un arrière-plan, un horizon, j'ai su que je me délivrais enfin de l'émotion, non de *l'attention* (mot plus important) accumulée véritablement ces jours-là. Si bien qu'au fur et à mesure que je continuais mon livre, à chaque fois qu'un des personnages revenait aux frontières et qu'il mentionnait plus ou moins brièvement ces réfugiés, ces insertions étaient voulues comme rappel du malheur et de la tragédie—or, j'écrivais toujours ces passages dans le bonheur parce que je m'en libérais et qu'il me semblait avoir enfin accompli ma tâche vis-à-vis de ces compatriotes dont j'avais bien connu quelques-uns. ("Le romancier dans la cité arabe," 119)

(More than five or six years later, when I wrote this opening chapter of *Les Alouettes Naïves*, where the refugees are only a backdrop, a horizon, I knew that I was finally freeing the emotion, not the *attention* (a more important word), accumulated during those days. As I continued writing my book, each time a character returned to the border and mentioned more or less briefly these refugees, these insertions were deliberate as if to recall unhappiness and tragedy—but I always wrote these passages with a feeling of happiness, because I was freeing myself of them and it seemed to me that I had finally fulfilled my obligation toward these compatriots, some of whom I had gotten to know well.)

Confirming her personal desire to record the refugee experience via this opening scene, the novelist introduces two forms of exile, one experienced by displaced villagers dwelling in the refugee camps, the other by exiled revolutionaries such as Omar and Nfissa, who, having relocated to a foreign capital, long to return home. Nfissa, who fled to Tunisia following her release from prison in Algeria, is depicted experiencing the pain of dislocation and the longing for home as she walks through the streets of the capital: "Seule dans les rues, Nfissa se sentait étrangère, ne savait où aller" (315; Alone in the streets, Nfissa felt like a stranger not knowing where to go).

Edward Said defines exile as "the unbearable rift forced between a human being and a native place, between the self and its true home" ("The Mind of Winter," 49). Said believes, however, that plurality of vision compensates, at least in part, for the psychological dislocation and "gives rise to an awareness of simultaneous dimensions, an awareness that—to borrow a phrase from music—is contrapuntal" (55). Adapting to a new place, a new environment, the exile finds that the new does not replace the old but results in contrapuntal juxtaposition. Following Said's assertion that the exile's world is one in which geographical space (home and exile) and temporal spheres (present and past) are always in contrapuntal juxtaposition, I argue that counterpoint, as an expression of exile, is the structuring element of the novel, with the theme of exile emerging as an autobiographical element. Djebar's exploration of exile in the novel—she had not explored the theme in earlier works—foreshadows the autobiographical project that Djebar will develop further in *L'amour, la fantasia*.

Throughout *Les alouettes naïves,* exile is linked to uncertainty. As the three protagonists struggle to come to terms with the years of violent conflict and face the next phase of Algerian history—the reconstruction of the country following the devastation of war—they express their fears and hesitancies, yet do so in different ways. Omar questions his memory of events, confessing at times to amnesia: "Oui, j'ai tout oublié" (32; Yes, I have forgotten everything). Rachid appears uncertain about the purpose and value of his writing: "Pour moi, écrire ne mène à rien, [. . .] L'écrivain est un homme déchiré, infirme, impuissant" (279; In my view, writing leads nowhere, [. . .] The writer is a conflicted, infirm, and impotent man). Nfissa finds her political commitment weakening. Following her marriage to Rachid, she spends days at home alone, awaiting his return. When he leaves Tunisia to return once more to the maquis in Algeria, she remains behind. As she awaits the birth of her child, she withdraws further into her private world.

If in *Les enfants du nouveau monde,* Djebar charts the emergence of female agency as women like Chérifa discover their courage and resilience, in *Les alouettes naïves* she begins by portraying Nfissa's active involvement in the war, her empowerment through political action, but goes on to probe the young woman's relationship to the men in her life—her father, her fiancé, her husband, and male friends—men who not only nurture, support, and often influence her decisions but, in Algeria's patriarchal structure, may try to claim the authority to control and dominate her. Focusing on one woman's struggle for self-realization, Djebar achieves a complex portrait of a protagonist who, as she moves from the outer to her inner world, becomes increasingly difficult to classify. As Hiddleston explains, readers may see Nfissa reverting to a conventional role, that of wife and mother, or find Djebar's portrait of her protagonist functioning as a symbol of resistance to the "straightforward explanatory narratives" that claim to neatly and clearly define the fictional character, placing her in an ideological category (*Assia Djebar*, 51).

I suggest, however, that we interpret Nfissa's withdrawal from the public to the private realm in one of two other ways: first, as a reminder of Algerian women's struggle in the two spheres, against French colonialism and indigenous patriarchy, the latter expecting her to assume a domestic role; second, as an emotional reaction to the stress of war. Nfissa's harsh experiences in the maquis (particularly the French military attack that killed her fiancé, Karim, and resulted in her capture and imprisonment), followed by exile in Tunisia, where, despite her deep longing for home, she does not contact her family, across the border in Algeria, for fear of placing them in danger, create great stress for her. Private space, therefore, becomes a place of refuge for a wounded soul. And, as home space serves as refuge providing stability and comfort in a present torn by painful and chaotic events, so does the past. For Nfissa, her childhood spent in a protected home, now a distant memory, comes to signify a lost paradise. Holding fast to past memories such as scenes at the hammam, where she accompanied her mother when she was a child, and family gatherings and interactions, she turns to these nostalgic memories to lighten the burden of exile; they grant her refuge and solace.

Yet, as the couple constructs a home together, a refuge against the pain and chaos of the present, Nfissa learns that Rachid lives with his own traumatic war experiences. Intent upon forgetting the past and unable to do so, he eventually shares with his wife the traumatic memory that haunts him. Having witnessed the death of an innocent young girl, killed by his ALN unit because her mother betrayed the Algerian cause, he is haunted with guilt and remorse. Revealing her compassion for the man who has returned from the war zone a deeply troubled individual, Nfissa expresses regret at not having shared Rachid's experience in the maquis: "Si j'avais vécu avec toi ce temps de maquis, j'aurais été ta mémoire" (481; If I had lived with you in the maquis, I would have been your memory). In her mind, the shared experience might have brought their private worlds closer.

Finally, the very title of this text, *Les alouettes naïves*, reinforces the deep sense of uncertainty with respect to the future that is conveyed within. The term refers to the female dancers of the Ouled Naïl tribe, women who had acceptable social status as courtesans in precolonial Algeria but later, in colonial Algeria, were denigrated as *prostituées-danseuses* who served French colonial soldiers. Significantly, French soldiers used the term pejoratively during the liberation struggle as well. When Nfissa is captured with her friend Lila, a French soldier calls them *alouettes* (42).

In her preface to the novel, Djebar explains that she learned from the historian Jacques Berque that the French term *alouette naïve* originated in the mispronunciation of Ouled Naïl, the Arabic name of the tribe, by French legionnaires. Misnaming the dancers, the French colonizer also misconstrues their place and function, seemingly unaware that the Ouled Naïl had once been a powerful tribe of warriors and that their women, whom he views as a sexual commodity to satisfy his desires, had in fact possessed significant autonomy.

When Rachid, in his thoughts, refers to his wife as "mon alouette naïve," recalling the expression the French legionnaires applied to the female dancers of a bygone era, it is not clear where he wishes to situate her:

"Mon alouette naïve," pense-t-il, se rappelant soudain cette expression que les légionnaires appliquaient aux prostituées-danseuses de son pays, de celles qu'il a connues lui-même autrefois, symbole à la fois d'une déchéance extérieure et d'une lumière en elles tout à fait anonyme. (482)

("My naïve lark," he thinks, suddenly recalling the expression that French legionnaires gave to the prostitute-dancers of his country, those he had known in an earlier time, symbol of both an exterior degradation and a light within that was completely anonymous.)

Is Rachid adopting the precolonial sense of the term, defining the Algerian woman as a free creative spirit who, through her dancing, had developed an indigenous art form, or, as the critic Christine Quinan asks, is he recalling "a foreboding moment in a long history of the use and abuse of the Algerian female body by imperial powers" ("Veiling Unveiled," 738)? Most importantly, is Rachid, the committed revolutionary, revealing his male desire to control?

Leaving us to ponder these unanswered questions, Djebar cautions her readers that the promise of a new order may indeed be an empty promise and that for Algerian women the struggle must go on: "Car je sais d'avance—vieux préjugé?—que la guerre qui finit entre les peuples renaît entre les couples" (*Les alouettes naïves*, 481; For I already know—an ancient prejudice?—that the war that has ended between nations reemerges within couples).[13] Yet, she also reminds us that women emerging from the liberation struggle, like the Nailiyat of the past, defy simple categorization. Empowered through their war experiences, although admittedly battle weary, Nfissa and her sisters are prepared to appropriate their own narrative and reject inappropriate labels, simplistic categories, and false stereotypes.

Women and War, Part 3: *L'amour, la fantasia*

Approaching *L'amour, la fantasia* as the third stage of a writing project that places Algerian women in the war story, we find the writer broadening her historical scope of inquiry and introducing a more complex narrative structure. With the first work limiting its spatial-temporal scope to twenty-four hours in one city and the second tracing the lives of three protagonists from the beginning to the end of the liberation struggle, the third places the war within the larger narrative of French colonial history and incorporates autobiographical fragments of the writer's life into the Algerian women's war story.

In contrast to the opening paragraphs of the previous texts, which bring readers immediately into the war, *L'amour, la fantasia* begins with the author's childhood memory of her initiation into the colonial school system: "Fillette arabe allant pour la première fois à l'école, un matin d'automne, main dans la main du père" (11; A little Arab girl going to school for the first time, walking hand in hand with her father [3]). Thus, she chooses to begin with a personal experience that she considers not only extremely important but highly ambiguous. Writing more than four decades after the event, she expresses the belief that Western acculturation, a process that resulted in her acquisition of the colonizer's language and access to public space, the determining factor in her development as an artist and intellectual, also led to her exclusion from many aspects of traditional woman's world. Thus, she equates the experience as one of gains and losses.

Several Maghrebian male writers have also acknowledged ambiguity vis-à-vis their experience in French colonial schools. Kateb Yacine, in *Le poly-*

gone étoilé, equates his educational experience with being thrust into "la gueule du loup" (181; the jaws of the wolf). Abdelkébir Khatibi also expresses uneasiness with French language and culture as he, like Djebar, brings autobiographical fragments into *La mémoire tatouée*, a work that combines autobiographical fragments with poetry and parable. Yet Djebar defines her experience as distinctly female gendered. Having been liberated from the female enclosure of her Algerian sisters through Western education, the novelist reaches maturity haunted by the weight of exile. If the sentiment of exclusion leads Djebar to reestablish links with the maternal world from which she felt distanced—but in fact a realm she never lost—when she grasped her father's hand when he walked with her to school, it also encourages her to probe her nation's history, from the colonial conquest through the Algerian War, which began in her early adulthood. Throughout her literary career, she will examine Algerian history in multiple ways and in multiple texts.[14]

Delving into French colonial archives in preparation for her novel *L'amour, la fantasia,* she discovers accounts of the military campaigns in the 1830s: official reports, correspondence between officers, letters officers and soldiers sent home to their families. Among these records, Baron Barchou de Penhoën's description of the battle of Staoueli, with its depiction of Algerian women on the battlefield, directly engaged in anticolonial resistance, draws her attention. In a highly visual scene of violence that could easily inspire Orientalist painters of the period, the French colonial officer portrays two women on the battlefield, one mutilating a fallen soldier:

> L'une d'elles gisait à côté d'un cadavre français dont elle avait arraché le cœur! Une autre s'enfuyait tenant un enfant dans ses bras: blessée d'un coup de feu, elle écrasa avec une pierre la tête de l'enfant, pour l'empêcher de tomber vivant dans nos mains; les soldats l'achevèrent elle-même à coups de baïonnette. (Qtd. in *L'amour, la fantasia*, 28–29)

> (One of these women lay dead beside the corpse of a French soldier whose heart she had torn out! Another had been fleeing with a child in her arms when a shot wounded her; she seized a stone and crushed the infant's head to prevent it falling alive into our hands; the soldiers finished her off with their bayonets. [18])

Although Barchou's report affirms women's participation in anticolonial resistance, it is clearly biased, depicting these women as part of a savage horde. The French military officer makes no distinction between the actions of the two women he describes. Whereas the first admittedly appears savage—ripping out a soldier's heart—the second, a mother who chooses to sacrifice her child rather than surrender the child to the enemy, is a noble, tragic, stoic figure.

Djebar cites Barchou's passage in *L'amour, la fantasia,* then rewrites the scene:

> Ces deux Algériennes—l'une agonisante, à moitié raidie, tenant le coeur d'un cadavre français au creux de sa main ensanglantée, la seconde, dans un sursaut de bravoure désespérée, faisait éclater le crâne de son enfant comme une grenade printanière, avant de mourir, allégée—, *ces deux héroïnes entrent ainsi dans l'histoire nouvelle.* (29, italics mine)

> (These two Algerian women—the one in whom rigor mortis was already setting in, still holding in her bloody hands the heart of a dead Frenchman, the second, in a fit of desperate courage, splitting open the brain of her child, like a pomegranate in spring, before dying with her mind at peace—*these two heroines enter into recent history.* [18])

Reinterpreting Barchou's text, she notes the same details—the bloody heart, the child's fractured skull—but considers the women's actions to be acts of resistance to French colonial occupation, not savagery. In addition, she connects these two women to the militants of Algeria's anticolonial war. For her, these nineteenth-century Algerian women, neither passive bystanders nor secluded odalisques of a harem, foreshadow Algerian women's more recent *moudjahidate,* the women combatants of the Algerian War.

As she rewrites the violent episode, Djebar establishes a relationship between the French colonial archives and her own writing that the critic Anne Donadey terms "palimpsestic" ("Rekindling the Vividness of the Past," 885), referring to the process by which one written text is superimposed on another, the first so imperfectly erased that traces remain visible (Genette, *Palimpsestes,* 451). Donadey describes Djebar's writing process as one of "overreading" or "reading women back in," explaining that Djebar first "reads" women back into history and then "writes" over the colonial documents she has unearthed from French colonial archives to create a palimpsest.[15] Studying Djebar's use of the palimpsest in the text, Donadey concludes that the process of scratching off one inscription to impose another is a violent act, hence a fitting metaphor for colonization, whose intent is to obliterate the history and culture of the colonized.

Alerting her readers to the actions of the forgotten women of Algerian history, Djebar, like Amrane-Minne, constructs a counternarrative to those that have ignored women's militancy in Algeria's resistance to colonialism. Reflecting upon her role as a writer and historian in the project to restore Algerian women to their proper place in history, she states: "Écrire ne tue pas la voix mais la réveille, surtout pour ressusciter tant de *sœurs disparues*" (*L'amour, la fantasia*, 229, italics mine; Writing does not silence the voice but awakens it, above all to resurrect my vanished sisters [204]). Having proven via Barchou's text that the "soeurs disparues" were active participants in early resistance against the French, she becomes a "spéléologue de la mort" (86; spelunker of death) as she continues to probe historical documents of the period. This is particularly apparent when she reconstitutes the horror of two separate incidents of *enfumade* that occurred during the early years of the French conquest.

In 1845 two French officers, Lieutenant Colonel Aimable Pélissier and Lieutenant Armand Jacques de Saint-Arnaud, ordered their men to set fire to caves, asphyxiating the tribes that used them as refuge. After uncovering the mass tomb—approximately fifteen hundred corpses of men, women, and children who died of asphyxiation—Pélissier followed his actions with written testimony. Saint-Arnaud, on the other hand, never returned to the site of the *enfumade* of the Sbeah tribe he had massacred, and the confidential report that he supposedly sent to French military headquarters mysteriously disappeared. Whereas the first incident of *enfumade* entered the annals of French history, unleashing a polemic in Paris because of its violent nature, the second, successfully silenced in France, was relegated to oral history, known only to the victims' descendants. Djebar, a bilingual historian versed in French and Arabic, is able to probe both written and oral sources to elucidate her nation's history.

Ironically, as the novelist revives the violent chapter of colonial history, she finds herself paying tribute to the members of the invading colonial army whose reports, letters, and memoirs allow her to break the silence surrounding the brutality of the colonial conquest. She writes that Pélissier's report allows her to inscribe upon it "la passion calcinée des ancêtres" (93; the charred passion of my ancestors [79]). Armed with the report and the tools she has acquired, the ability to read and analyze it, she is able to bring the massacre to the attention of her readers and the public at large.

Bearing the weight of her ancestral legacy, Djebar inserts her own voice and presence into colonial history. She states, "Je suis née en *dix-huit cent quarante-deux,* lorsque le commandant de Saint-Arnaud vient détruire la zaouia des Beni Ménacer, ma tribu d'origine" (243, Djebar's italics; The date of my birth is eighteen hundred and forty-two, the year when General Saint-Arnaud arrives to burn down the *zaouia* of the Beni Menacer, the tribe from which I am descended [217]), and adds, "Avant d'entendre ma propre voix, je perçois les râles, les gémissements des emmurés du Dahra" (243; Before I catch the sound of my own voice I can hear the death-rattles, the moans of those immured in the Dahra mountains [217]). Thus, the novelist not only assumes Algeria's historical legacy but confirms its importance to her development as a writer. As her appropriation of the colonizer's language and her knowledge of the history of colonial conquest allow her to unearth hidden history and interpret the findings, her commitment to narrative experimentation encourages her to bring historical elements into her innovative fiction. Adopting a contrapuntal structure that sets events of the colonial conquest in relation to autobiographical fragments in the first two parts of the novel, she then introduces multiple women's war testimonies in the sections that follow.

The war testimonies, first-person narratives that, in the critic Winifred Woodhull's view, offer a "liberatory dimension for women" (*Transfigurations of the Maghreb,* 82), bring several women's stories into focus. Zohra Sahraoui, a widow, explains that she was severely punished by the French military for sheltering Algerian combatants; they burnt her house down.[16] Having recorded the narrative recounted to her in dialectical Arabic, the writer translates Zohra's words into French, translating verbatim current popular expressions. For example, she writes "La France est venue et elle nous a brûlés" (133), adopting the term *Francia,* which in dialectical Arabic indicates both the French nation and its people, to capture the tone and flavor of the original.

The war narratives include the testimony of Chérifa, who as a young girl in the maquis witnessed her brother's death—he was shot and killed as they fled from a French military patrol—and then hid in a tree for two nights before retrieving his body for burial.[17] Here, Djebar is careful to retain the style that often characterizes the oral interview. Although the moment described may be very dramatic and emotionally charged, the words and the tone of the report do not always convey the informant's emotions. For example, when Chérifa recounts her capture, she begins by recalling the defiant words she shouted at the French soldiers: "Tirez ai-je dit, Cela m'importe peu! Je suis une fille, je ne suis pas une femme complète, mais je laisserai derrière moi des hommes! . . . chacun d'eux tuera cent d'entre vous! Tuez-moi!" (153; "Shoot," I said. "It makes no difference to me! I'm a girl, I'm not a grown woman, but I'll leave men behind me! . . . Each one of them will kill a hundred of yours! Kill me!" [135]). At first, she finds the words with which to defy her captors, words that express her anger and reveal her courage. Yet, as she recounts the beatings and torture that followed, her testimony becomes stark, laconic, subdued: "Ils apportèrent une cravache. Ils me frappèrent. Ils branchèrent l'électricité de leurs appareils. Ils me torturèrent" (153; They brought a whip. They beat me. They switched on the electricity for their machines. They tortured me [135]). The understatement is particularly striking when, following a long session of torture, she simply states, "Ce fut particulièrement éprouvant" (155; It was particularly hard [137]). Djebar notes in this regard: "J'ai remarqué que plus les femmes avaient souffert, plus elles en parlaient par une forme concise et à la limite presque sèche" ("Entretien," 202; I noted that the more the women had suffered, the more they spoke about it in a very concise, almost dry manner).

Although resolutely stoic and defiant before her captors, Chérifa admits to weeping in despair when back in her cell, after the emotionally charged event (*L'amour, la fantasia,* 154; *Fantasia,* 135). Thus, she shares her intimate emotions with the novelist, and by extension with the reader. Consequently, as Chérifa "tells" war and Djebar "writes" war, an important collaboration takes place between the informant and her scribe. Here, Djebar illustrates the historian Alessandro Portelli's assertion that oral history involves the creation of relationships between narrators and narratees, on the one hand, and between past events and present dialogic narratives, on the other. Stressing the importance of the first relationship, Portelli adds that the individual who takes on the task of remembering and the responsibility of telling requires the presence of the narratee, the person who will listen to the story and pass it on (*The Order Has Been Carried Out*, 14–15).[18]

Through the relationship between the narrator and the narratee in *L'amour, la fantasia*, Chérifa's individual testimony enters the collective corpus of Algerian history; her narrative effectively brings the experiences of rural women, largely illiterate, often quite young, to the printed page. Moreover, as the narratee (who is also the novelist) connects the former combatant to the historical struggle, she attests to the "powerful sense of agency" that the war experience has granted her narrator (Hiddleston, *Assia Djebar*, 75). Finally, as Portelli cautions, oral history is not just the collection of stories but concerns their interpretation and representation. It involves the researcher's selection of sources and active role in the interview and concludes with the comments of the authorial voice and the meanings implicit in the final process of editing and montage (*The Order Has Been Carried Out*, 18). For Djebar, as well as for the historians Amrane-Minne, Vince, and Portelli, the interpretive dimension of the text falls on their shoulders. It is their responsibility, for the text appears under their name.

By engaging in the dual process of rewriting colonial history from the perspective of the colonized female subject and eliciting oral testimony from her Algerian sisters, Djebar assumes two distinct projects. The first entails rewriting past documents; the second brings women's voices into the pages of history. Thus, one involves the writer's active intervention—she rewrites Barchou's report—while the other requires minimal intervention but an attentive ear. In search of truth and authenticity, Djebar must listen carefully, transcribe accurately, and translate faithfully the words of her informant. Yet, how faithful is her translation? Despite her efforts to adopt a style that is as close to the original oral narrative as possible, Djebar acknowledges the limits of language and admits to Chérifa: "Ta voix s'est prise au piège; mon parler français la déguise sans l'habiller" (161; I have captured your voice; I disguised it with my French without clothing it [142]). The novelist's use of the French language has created a barrier to the immediacy and intimacy she hoped to achieve. As Donadey aptly notes in this regard: "The dialogue between women in Djebar's work inscribes itself precisely in the interstices between sisterhood and appropriation, in the shuttling between 'speaking for' and 'speaking very close to'" (*Recasting Colonialism*, 53).

If, by delving into oral history to affirm Algerian women's participation in the liberation struggle, Djebar becomes increasingly attuned to Algeria's oral tradition, her affirmation of women's role in the process of oral transmission confirms what she already knew. Female elders in her own family, as in so many Algerian families, had always assumed the role of oral historian and family genealogist. As a child, she learned from her grandmother of the exploits of her ancestors Mohammed Ben Aissa El Berkani and Malek Sahraoui El Berkani: the former fought with Emir Abdelkader against the French in the 1840s; the latter died in a rebellion against the French in 1871.[19]

Most importantly, as Djebar records, transcribes, and translates oral narratives of the more recent anticolonial struggle, she comes to value orality and its significance to her development as a writer: "Je pense que le plus important pour moi est de ramener le passé malgré ou à travers l'écriture, 'mon écriture' de langue française. Je tente d'ancrer cette langue française dans l'oralité des femmes traditionnelles" ("Entretien," 201; I think that what is most important for me is to bring back the past despite my use of the French language and yet through my use of it. I try to anchor this language in traditional women's orality). By intertwining the complex, dense, highly literary language that defines her voice with oral narratives of her sisters who engaged in combat, Djebar achieves a unique and extremely well crafted study of women at war.

In conclusion, we see that Djebar, beginning with *Les enfants du nouveau monde*, shows that the war introduced a range of challenges and possibilities to women. First huddled in their homes, afraid and immobile, they then emerge to face the challenges of a new order, their country in the throes of war. Returning to Cooke's assertion that Algeria's anticolonial struggle came too soon to serve as a catalyst for significant social change, I conclude with the critic's own reflection on the significance of the war for the individual. Writing that wars provide "multiple discursive spaces in which individuals can find, retain, and interpret agency," Cooke concludes: "New individuals are empowered, and their empowering and centering decenters others" ("Wo-man, Retelling the War Myth," 180). In other words, war destabilizes the foundations of identity and community, opening the way to new possibilities. Although Cooke's reflections apply to postmodern wars, those that came after Algeria's war, I argue that they apply to the Algerian War of Independence as well. Djebar's early war novels predict that woman's role in the nation-building process that followed would be, as the historian Natalya Vince concludes, complex, sometimes difficult to define, and easily misunderstood. Nevertheless, each individual who participated in the anticolonial struggle and survived—albeit often with emotional, if not physical, scars—emerged empowered through this deeply transformative process.

3 MAPPING THE TRAUMASCAPE

Yamina Mechraka's *La grotte éclatée*

> The legacy of trauma is, as a rule, imprinted onto the lives of survivors and perpetrators, descendants and eyewitnesses—people who, in various roles, shared and were directly implicated in single or serial traumatic events.
> —MARIA TUMARKIN, *Traumascapes*

With a simple phrase—*Arma virumque cano,* "I sing of arms and the man"—the Latin poet Virgil begins the *Aeneid,* one literary work among the many that attest to the power of the war story. Celebrating the Trojans' victory in battle, the epic also expresses pain and loss, describes death and destruction, and ultimately questions whether violence leads to lasting peace. Through the ages, war has inspired literature written by its survivors and descendants, as well as by the historians and writers who come to the study of violent conflict from varying geographical, cultural, and temporal spaces. Like Virgil, they not only sing of victory in battle, they explore the dark side of war.

Yamina Mechakra's novel *La grotte éclatée* (The shattered cave), published in 1979, takes us to this dark side. Choosing as her protagonist a young nurse who tends to the wounded in the war zone of the Algerian maquis, the novelist shows that not only do landscapes of war present visible scars of conflict but they attest to invisible traces as well. If the visible scars—blighted landscapes, wounded and mutilated bodies of combatants and civilians, bones of the dead—are powerful reminders of war's destructive force, so are the psychological wounds and emotional trauma that form the scars we cannot see.

The sociologist Maria Tumarkin applies the term *traumascape* to places marked by violence, war, and trauma. In her text *Traumascapes: The Power and Fate of Places Transformed by Tragedy*, she defines the traumascape as a "distinctive category of place, transformed physically and psychically by suffering, part of a scar tissue that now stretches across the world" (13). Including in her study natural disasters and political upheavals—earthquakes and tsunamis, as well as the Holocaust, the Rwandan genocide, and the anticolonial wars of Vietnam and Algeria—she argues that these places are not mere backdrops to modern-day tragedies but provide a key to understanding them.

Describing trauma as an overwhelming experience, Tumarkin explains that people are so disoriented by such an event that they can never fully comprehend what they have experienced or witnessed. Moreover, the ways in which they usually experience the world and make sense of their own place in it are shattered. Drawing the distinction between trauma, which is purely psychological, and the traumascape, which involves spatial coordinates, sites and spaces, she explains that they are connected: the traumascape, a physical setting, remains a haunting reminder of the traumatic event, the "unfinished business" (12) that, although internalized, has not been put to rest.

She writes: "Because trauma is contained not in an event as such but in the way this event is experienced, traumascapes become much more than physical settings of tragedies: they emerge as spaces, where events are experienced and re-experienced across time. Full of visual and sensory triggers, capable of eliciting a whole palette of emotions, traumascapes catalyse and shape remembering and reliving of traumatic events. It is through these places that the past, whether buried or laid bare for all to see, continues to inhabit and refashion the present" (12). Calling attention to the haunting that occurs afterwards, Tumarkin follows the theoretical path of the trauma theorist Cathy Caruth. As I noted in the introduction to this study, Caruth, working with Freudian concepts, describes trauma as a wound.[1] She also provides us with a clear definition of trauma: "In its most general definition, trauma describes an overwhelming experience of sudden or catastrophic events in which the response to the event occurs in the often delayed, uncontrolled repetitive appearance of hallucinations and other intrusive phenomena" (*Unclaimed Experience*, 11). Within this framework, she refers to trauma as an "unclaimed experience" that, because of its unassimilated nature, continues to haunt the survivor, imposing itself repeatedly in the survivor's nightmares and repetitive actions.

In this chapter, I adopt Tumarkin's term *traumascape* to designate the war-torn landscape that characterizes Mechakra's novel, and I employ Caruth's concept of trauma as an "unclaimed experience" to describe the protagonist's state of mind. As we follow Mechakra's protagonist negotiating her way through a territory scarred by the violence of war, it becomes increasingly clear that her experience involves troubled inner and outer landscapes, psychological trauma and the physical reality of a war-torn land.

Mechakra comes to Algerian literature as a survivor and victim of the Algerian War. Her father was arrested several times during the war and she recalls being terribly shaken, if not traumatized, when, as a child, she witnessed French soldiers tossing the corpses of badly mutilated Algerian soldiers into the street close to her home (Mokhtari, *Yamina Mechakra*, 36).[2] Born in Meskiana, a town in the Aurès Mountains, in 1949, she spent her childhood and adolescence in her native region, later pursued a career in medicine, obtaining her medical degree and psychiatric training in Constantine, and returned to her hometown to practice psychiatry before assuming a position at Drid Hocine, a psychiatric hospital in Hussein Dey, a suburb of Algiers, where she worked until retirement. Mechakra published two novels in her lifetime, *La grotte éclatée* and *Arris*, a sequel to the first work, which appeared two decades later, as well as a short story, "L'éveil du mont" (The mountain awakens), published in 1979. The novelist's untimely death in 2013, following a long illness, provoked an outpouring of sympathy for her and appreciation of her literary work.[3]

In *La grotte éclatée* Mechakra presents her readers with a fictional nurse's diary that spans the years of the Algerian War. Re-creating events of the war, which occurred when she was too young to take part but old enough to later recall with anguish, she sets her protagonist on a journey that begins in the maquis, where the young nurse tends to sick, wounded, and dying combatants. Situating most of her text in the Aurès Mountains, where the war began in 1954, Mechakra introduces several autobiographical elements. She depicts a protagonist who, like herself, lived in this mountainous region in eastern Algeria, where the population is predominantly Chaouia, her Berber ethnic group.[4] Both the novelist and the unnamed narrator are health professionals, one a doctor, the other a nurse. They both experience the trauma of war, the novelist as a child and the protagonist as a young adult, and both confront mental illness. Mechakra, a psychiatrist by profession, treats the mentally ill; her protagonist struggles with madness as a result of the trauma she has endured.

An Orphan's Tale

Mechakra's protagonist begins life as an outsider to her own culture. She is an illegitimate child born to an Algerian mother and her lover, both of whom abandoned her. Moved between orphanages and foster homes, the child is eventually educated by nuns in a Catholic orphanage. As she recounts her life story, the narrator, who remains nameless throughout the text, reveals that having neither family nor a family name that would confirm her roots in Algerian society, she enjoys a certain freedom: "Très jeune je connus le mépris et la pitié des noms dotés, très jeune je pris goût à mon sort et dégustais mon indépendance, ma vie sans attache" (33; As a young child I faced the scorn and pity of the pedigreed, at a very young age I enjoyed my fate in life and enjoyed my independence, my life without ties). At the same time, however, she struggles with an identity fraught with ambiguity: "Chez les uns on m'appelait Marie ou Judith, chez les autres Fatma. Je portais mes prénoms comme des robes et mes saints comme des couronnes" (33; Some called me Marie or Judith, others Fatma. I wore my first names like dresses and my saints like crowns).

Reaching adulthood "sans fiche d'état civil" (34; without an identity card), belonging to neither the European nor the Algerian community, she seizes the opportunity to secure acceptance and self-worth by participating in the anticolonial struggle. Offering her services as a nurse, for the nuns had provided her with rudimentary medical training, she joins the nationalist cause, convinced that it will lead to her social integration in a new Algerian society: "J'avais compris qu'il était grand temps de vivre et qu'un nom n'avait point d'importance" (29; I had come to understand that it was indeed the time to live, that a name had no importance). Hence, she views those struggling for an independent Algeria as representing the interests of the marginalized and believes that they will aid her in her personal quest for community and belonging.

With the identity quest as a key element, the novel's plot and structure recall the orphan tale of traditional folk narrative. As both a traveler and a seeker, the orphan embarks upon a journey that leads to and through various physical and emotional trials and returns to the point of departure having gained insight and maturity. As in the orphan tale, the outward journey presented in the novel involves a series of transformative experiences. In this text, the heroine's decision to join the independence struggle sends her into the war zone, specifically to the cave that becomes her home and refuge, where life-changing events occur. There she creates a new family with a husband, a child, and friends who share the sheltered space. The idyllic period is brief, however. Her husband dies of his combat wounds before the child is born. A napalm attack by French military forces subsequently destroys the cave, killing her friends and seriously wounding her child and herself. Evacuated to a psychiatric hospital and then to a refugee camp, both across the border in Tunisia, she returns to Algeria at independence, prepared to start life anew in the village she left during the war.

Charting the journey from the traumascape to the hospital and the refugee camp in Tunisia and back to Algeria at independence, Mechakra places her protagonists in several distinct settings: the cave that serves as a shelter and a hospital, where she tends to the wounded; the psychiatric hospital, where she recuperates following the cave's destruction; the refugee camp, where she bonds with other displaced Algerians; the site of the destroyed cave, where she comes to terms with her past trauma. With this structure in mind, I posit the hypothesis that despite the novel's experimental style—narrative fragmentation and poetic prose—it can be considered a work of realism, or more specifically, traumatic realism. I borrow the term *traumatic realism* from Michael Rothberg, a critic of Holocaust literature, who applies it to literary representation of extreme events, explaining that the writers of traumatic realism undermine conventions of storytelling without entirely forgoing narrative or its ability to document history (*Traumatic Realism*, 227).[5]

Adopting this critical lens, I find that as a narration of daily life in the war zone, Mechakra's novel is a historically accurate, albeit fictional, journal of a young Algerian nurse deeply traumatized by the events of the war. In this regard, the text introduces dates, places, and events that correspond to many

Algerians' authentic experiences of the anticolonial war: young women served as nurses in the maquis; rebel camps were bombed; the wounded were treated in hospitals; individuals and families displaced by war lived in refugee camps; survivors of cataclysmic events have revisited the sites of trauma and tragedy. From this realist perspective, the dates that punctuate the text—from November 1955 to July 5, 1962 (the official date of Algerian independence)—reinforce one's sense of reading a personal diary of the period in which an experience shared by other young Algerian women in the maquis has been faithfully recorded. Some recorded their testimony, their names and exploits entering history; others remain anonymous to this day, their courageous actions lost to history. And as with their male compatriots, some survived the war, while others did not.

Within this historical framework we find as well that the novelist, trained in psychiatry, faithfully transmits the sensations, meaning, and consequences of the traumatic event. More precisely, the trauma that haunts the narrator disrupts her narrative through sudden flashbacks that elicit seemingly disconnected images, narrative fragmentation that captures her sense of disrupted time, and inconsistencies that reflect a dislocated memory. Thus, we find some conventions of narration, but not all, undermined. In this regard, ARRIS, the village that marks the beginning and the end of the narrator's trajectory, is grounded in reality; it is a town in the Aurès Mountains that has existed for centuries and is of historical significance.[6] The birthplace of Mostefa Ben Boulaïd, one of the historic figures of the Algerian Revolution, and the site of rebel activity during the liberation struggle, it is home to forty thousand inhabitants. Visitors to Arris these days are greeted with an imposing monument honoring Ben Boulaïd, as well as a memorial to the victims of the Algerian War.

Placing the text within the framework of traumatic realism, I bear in mind the reflections of the critics Zineb Ali-Benali and Rachid Mokhtari. Ali-Benali asserts that the novel is concerned with the traces of the history of the war; consequently, the ways events are experienced and the memories they engender are more important than the events themselves (*Diwan d'inquiétude et d'espoir,* 102). Mokhtari, in turn, considers *La grotte éclatée* a testimony to war's irreparable trauma, not a chronicle of Algeria's military exploits (*Yamina Mechakra,* 164).

Healing the Wounded, Mourning the Dead

Bringing her readers into the rural war zone, Mechakra reminds them that much of the anticolonial war was fought in rural areas. By depicting her protagonist as a nurse, she develops the theme of woman as healer in a world in which violence is ever present and inflicted indiscriminately upon the innocent and the defenseless as well as upon the armed enemy. We may recall that the political theorist Jean Bethke Elshtain, in her study *Women and War*, defines history's gender gap in terms of women as "life givers" and men as "life takers," noting as well that in time of war men occupy one space, the battlefield, women another, the safe and secure home (161). She finds an exception to the rule in the "ferocious few" (163), legendary women warriors, such as Joan of Arc, who cross the gender divide. Adopting soldiers' garb and their weapons, these women enter the battlefield. Had Elshtain studied the history of the Maghreb, she would have found yet another example of the ferocious few in the legendary Berber queen La Kahina, who, as Kateb Yacine acknowledges in his preface to Mechakra's *La grotte éclatée*, appears to have historical links to the Aurès Mountains.[7] The protagonist in the novel, however, fits into a different category: she saves lives in the war zone.

Choosing a protagonist who tends the wounded, Mechakra foregrounds the role of woman as protector of life and limb. Nurses help restore shattered bodies and minds to health; they do not take lives. The critic Pamela Pears views Mechakra's protagonist's role in the war as a form of traditional activism, noting that a nurse remains primarily a caretaker who follows orders and performs a supporting role (*Remnants of Empire*, 64). Similarly, Elshtain includes nurses in the group of noncombatants, stating that in the complex logistics of twentieth-century warfare, nursing allowed women to get close to military action "of which they are not an active part" (184). In her view, these "angels of mercy," whose function is to "soothe, heal, tend, and offer solace" (183), play a traditional role. Similarly, Mokhtari links the nurse's role to the myth of ascetic patriotism (*Yamina Mechakra*, 25). Clearly, the nurse's image and her contribution to the anticolonial struggle contrast with the portrait and actions of the urban combatant, the revolutionary figure breaking with the traditional roles and conventional stereotypes commonly attributed to Algerian women. I argue, however, that both forms of militancy were important and numerically significant. Of the 10,949 women officially recognized as former combatants, 1,744, or 16 percent, were nurses in the maquis (Taleb Ibrahimi, "Les Algériennes," 207).

To fully grasp the importance of the nurse's role in the Algerian War, we must ground their participation in the war historically, contextualizing it within the temporal frame 1955–1957, the period the historian Neil MacMaster has called the dynamic phase of women's direct engagement in the Algerian War (*Burning the Veil,* 316). During this period—which corresponds to the three years that Mechakra's protagonist is in the maquis—women were urban guerrillas, nurses, ancillaries, and providers of logistic support to the Algerian army.

MacMaster and Amrane-Minne assert that this mobilization emerged as a response to the dire situation facing male combatants in the cities and the countryside, and not as a central policy decision on the part of the FLN leadership.[8] However, as MacMaster explains, the FLN made skillful use of the heroic symbol of female warriors, appearing to champion the position of women while, in reality, subordinating them to male control. He takes as one example the case of Nafissa Hamoud, the first woman doctor to join the maquis. Although highly experienced, she was not promoted to chief doctor in her district, Wilaya III; a less experienced, male doctor was given the position that should have been hers (321). Similarly, despite their dangerous exploits, the *fidayate* were never placed in positions of authority; they carried out the orders they were given (317).

Most importantly, this "dynamic phase" of women's involvement came to a rather abrupt end. If in the early years of the war, late 1954 through 1958, the ALN had been able to create safe zones, including infirmaries in the mountain villages, they could not sustain them. Once the French army began to pursue aggressive military campaigns in the countryside, attacking rebel camps in the maquis more frequently, all who served—women as well as male combatants—were highly vulnerable. In addition, conservative voices within the FLN were always opposed to women's direct participation in the war zones and sought to have them removed from the maquis. Although it is unclear which of the two factors was decisive, in late 1957 and early 1958 the FLN withdrew all but a few highly skilled women from the rural war zones, sending them to Tunisia and Morocco for safety. Women who had gained a sense of purpose and self-esteem in the face of danger and hardship found themselves abruptly excluded from the maquis and, as MacMaster sadly notes, from roles of responsibility within the FLN as well (334).

To further probe the history of nurses in the maquis, we may turn to both written and oral testimony: chronicles published during the war in journals such as *El Moudjahid* and oral interviews collected by historians, Amrane-Minne in the 1980s and Natalya Vince two decades later.[9] One of the first published accounts, a series of articles entitled "Le journal d'une maquisarde" (The diary of a female combatant) appearing in *El Moudjahid* from June 22 through August 31, 1959, presents a chronological account of a young woman's experiences in the early years of the war, including her activities as a nurse. This chronicle, which the critic Christiane Chaulet-Achour has called a *récit-matrice*, a foundational text, is one that, she asserts, gives us key images of the female combatant's world: surviving enemy attacks, caring for the wounded, transporting medical supplies, attending political meetings, educating village women in matters of hygiene (*Noûn*, 77). The text also conveys the sense of solidarity among the combatants, the importance of the medical training the medical staff had received before coming to the rural combat zone, and a detail that looms large in Mechakra's novel, the key role of the cave, the clandestine site that serves as both the place to hold strategic military and political meetings and the shelter for combatants, medical personnel, and wounded soldiers.[10]

Oral and written narratives reveal that the women's work in the war zones required medical training. Hence, many nurses had trained in urban clinics and hospitals. In her study of Algerian women's participation in the war, Khaoula Taleb Ibrahimi cites a memoir that, like the *El Moudjahid* series, sheds light on the role of nurses in the maquis. Drifa, who had joined the maquis as a high-school student in Sétif, writes:[11]

> Pratiquement, toutes les élèves infirmières de Sétif sont montées au maquis. Parce que c'était plus facile pour elles: elles avaient quelque chose de précis à faire. Quand elles proposaient leurs services, elles avaient quelque chose à offrir: soigner, tandis que les autres se sentaient inutiles. ("Les Algériennes," 208)

(Virtually all the student nurses in Sétif went into the maquis. It was easy for them: they had something specific to do. When they proposed their services, they had something to offer: medical aid, the others felt useless.)

Once in the maquis, these women, many of them young, urban, and middle class, found the experience of living in rural Algeria quite challenging; many were encountering rural poverty for the first time. In addition, they often came into conflict with socially conservative army officers and the male rank and file, who saw them as a threat to the traditional gender roles and rigid sexual segregation practiced in the countryside. Yet, Drifa appears to have met only well-intentioned combatants. She states:

> Nous avons été très bien accueillies. Il existait entre eux et nous un esprit de camaraderie remarquable. Bien sûr, il y avait bien quelques grincheux qui n'admettaient pas notre présence . . . Il étaient agressifs et je me suis parfois accrochée avec eux. Le lieutenant nous demandait d'être souples et patientes. Mais ce fut l'exception quand même. (210)

(We were very well accepted. Between them and us there was a remarkable spirit of camaraderie. Of course, there were some grouches who didn't want us there. They were aggressive, and I often tangled with them. The lieutenant asked us to be flexible and patient. But they were really the exception.)

Yamina Cherrad, a former nurse interviewed by Amrane-Minne, confirms Drifa's account, acknowledging that the men were initially hostile to the young women recruited for medical service but soon came to admire them for their courage and dedication to their work and to the nationalist cause (*Des femmes*, 55). The various oral and written narratives reveal that the women not only had to show courage in the face of trying situations, they had to maintain a strict code of moral behavior as well.

In addition to confronting poverty and misogyny, nurses constantly had to deal with a lack of medical supplies, assist in operations, or perform them under extremely difficult conditions, frequently losing their patients. The maquis was a place where the medical staff, doctors, and nurses were often tending to the dying and burying the dead rather than restoring the wounded to health. They witnessed the death of combatants and fellow nurses. As Amrane-Minne's interview with Malika Zerrouki reveals, the memory of the loss of a fellow nurse clearly caused pain even years later. In this same interview, Zerrouki acknowledges the recurrent feelings of helplessness in the face of combatants' mortal injuries, which were very difficult to live with at the time and continue to haunt her years later (*Des femmes*, 90–91). "Weepers over war's inevitable tragedies" (Elshtain, *Women and War*, 4) who provided crucial support to male fighters, these women worked under extremely difficult physical and psychological conditions, and young girls were forced to mature very quickly.

Returning to the distinction between "traditional" and "nontraditional" activism discussed earlier, questions emerge about whether the nurses were part of fighting units and were armed. Taleb Ibrahimi's informant, Drifa, states that in her region no girl ever used a gun ("Les Algériennes," 210). MacMaster writes that although the ALN avoided training women as combatants, the FLN propaganda organization distributed photographs to the international media of women soldiers in the maquis carrying automatic rifles, though they were not necessarily prepared to use them (*Burning the Veil*, 318). He cites as an example a photograph of Kheira Bousafi holding a rifle. The young woman explains in her interview with Amrane-Minne that a male soldier lent her his weapon for the photo, adding: "Les filles n'étaient pas vraiment armées, parfois un petit revolver, il n'y avait pas assez d'armes" (*Des femmes*, 51; The girls were not really armed, sometimes a small revolver; there weren't enough weapons for us). Thus, we find that accounts vary: some women were armed, others were not. Most significantly, none appear to have been trained to join fighting units, and the FLN-ALN never considered troops of women combatants in their military plans (MacMaster, *Burning the Veil*, 318).

This brief overview of the nurse's role during the Algerian War reveals that the distinction between the "ferocious few" and the "noncombatant many," the traditional and nontraditional women activists, remains somewhat ambiguous. In this regard, MacMaster, who argues that the weight of the patriarchal ideology that held sway in the FLN throughout the war cannot be underestimated, asserts that women whose war experiences would presumably prepare them to claim equality and assume positions of political power in postcolonial Algeria were clearly undermined during the liberation struggle by decisions made by their brothers in arms. Yet, whether or not we consider the nurse's role a traditional one, in their memoirs or in interviews with historians former women combatants who worked in that capacity in the maquis expressed the conviction that their war experiences had brought about significant social, political, intellectual, and spiritual transformation, on the part of both the individual and the collective. Khadidja Belguembour, a former nurse interviewed by Natalya Vince, states it quite well: "What I experienced was so beautiful and clean that it needs to be conserved jealously. It mustn't be touched" (*Our Fighting Sisters*, 220).

Combining Realism with Poetry

Turning to Mechakra's novel *La grotte éclatée*, we find the text reiterating much of what memoirists and Amrane-Minne's and Vince's informants described: on the one hand, the hardships related to a war fought by a rebel army; on the other hand, the difficulties faced by young women thrust into a predominantly male universe. Oral and written testimonials and fiction depict young women worn down by the physical demands of forced marches and famine as well as by the psychological strains of frequent confrontation with death. Graphically described in Mechakra's novel, the harsh conditions remind us of the record of long night marches recorded in Amina's journal (Amrane-Minne, *La guerre d'Algérie*, 66). Mechakra's protagonist struggles to keep up with her companions on mountain trails and drinks a jackal's blood to keep from starving to death. Her body betrays the physical strain: "Je songeais un instant à la femme chauve que j'étais, aux yeux rougis par les longues veilles" (26; I thought for a moment of the bald-headed woman I had become, my eyes reddened by long night vigils).

When Mechakra's protagonist describes the death of a maquisard—"Il avait les yeux grands ouverts, la poitrine ensanglantée. Il haleta quelques instants et s'éteignit dans mes bras" (37; His eyes were wide open, his chest covered with blood. He gasped for a few seconds and then died in my arms)—she echoes the experience recounted by informants, nurses watching helplessly as wounded combatants died. Her description, like theirs, is verbally terse and highly visual.

As we read *La grotte éclatée* in conjunction with Amrane-Minne's interviews, we encounter striking parallels between Mechakra's fictional novel and Yamina Cherrad's testimony. Both young women volunteer as nurses in the early years of the war, marry combatants who lose their lives in the struggle, and are left widowed with children to raise. In Mechakra's text, the protagonist's romantic interlude, which leads to marriage and motherhood but unfortunately ends with the loss of her spouse, occurs in a fictional world; it is an authentic experience for Yamina Cherrad.

Examining the parallels further, we find both women supervising infirmaries and, for a period of time, being the only woman in the all-male camp. In 1958, a year of heavy fighting in the maquis, Cherrad's infirmary in the Constantine region and Mechakra's fictional infirmary in the Aurès Mountains were destroyed by French military attacks.[12] In addition, they both care for young boys wounded by artillery fire, establishing close ties with them. Cherrad takes in a young boy whose leg she amputated; he remains with her for several years before returning to his family. Mechakra's narrator develops similar bonds with Salah, a young amputee who joins her reconstituted family in the cave.

The most striking similarity between the two narratives, however, is the account both women give of the physical and psychological challenges they face when amputating the limbs of wounded soldiers. Cherrad recalls: "Toujours avec la scie, sans anesthésie. Il fallait les tenir, c'était dur, cela les faisait souffrir, bien sûr" (*Des femmes*, 59; Always with a saw, without anesthesia. We had to hold them down, it was hard, and they suffered, of course). Mechakra's protagonist, in turn, remembers: "La scie criait, les hommes hurlaient de douleur et ma tête bourdonnait.—L'Algérie entière coulait par la blessure" (38; The saw cried out, men screamed in pain and my head pounded. All Algeria flowed out through the wound). In both instances, the conditions are the same: physical trauma for the men, psychological trauma for the nurses who tend them.

Yet, as we compare the two brief descriptions of amputations performed on wounded soldiers, we find Amrane-Minne's informant giving a brief but comprehensive description of the event as she remembers it and Mechakra's narrator providing both a description and an interpretation. With the sentence "All Algeria flowed out through the wound," the writer, speaking through her fictional protagonist, gives symbolic value to her narrative that is not present in Cherrad's account.[13] The novelist transforms raw experience into fiction via a selective process that involves choosing facts, sites, and characters that have symbolic value and take the description to a metaphorical level common to literature but not to oral testimony.

Examining the relationship between testimonial literature and fiction, Christiane Chaulet-Achour asks whether the fictional character could be "written" without a real-life model, a courageous individual who had embarked on the perilous journey, risking life and limb. Her answer is no. Fiction, she states, needs to draws upon authenticity; it needs a "real" person experiencing a "real" event (*Noûn*, 91). Nevertheless, if war stories cannot be written without an original lived experience, testimonial literature, once it has been archived—and perhaps put on a dusty library shelf that is rarely visited—lives on through the fiction it inspires.

A question remains. Could Mechakra and Amrane-Minne have read each other? The dates of publication of Mechakra's novel, 1979, and Amrane-Minne's collection of interviews, 1994, tell us that the novelist would not have read Cherrad's testimony. If Cherrad had read Mechakra's novel prior to her interview with Amrane-Minne in the 1980s, she probably would not have been influenced by it; she had her own story to tell. Indeed, parallels between Cherrad's testimony and Mechakra's novel confirm that the novelist was historically well documented and suggest that she may very well have interviewed former combatants, either formally or informally. Clearly, Mechakra had an excellent grasp of her nation's anticolonial struggle despite having had no direct experience of life in the maquis.[14]

As Mechakra's narrator recounts the war, she describes the physical hardships graphically but also infuses her narrative with poetry, some of which is imbued with nationalist fervor. Finding her place in the world through her participation in the liberation struggle, she expresses her newfound sense of belonging in a praise song, bringing lyricism to a distinctly harsh universe:

Je t'aime peuple sanglant coulé dans mes veines.
Je t'aime fils candide au regard déchiré.
Je t'aime enfant modelé dans la terre glaise d'un matin
Effacé. (30)

(I love you, people whose blood flowed in my veins.
I love you, candid son with a ravaged look.

I love you, child modeled in the clay of a morning
Erased.)

Repetition—"Je t'aime," "Je t'aime," "Je t'aime"—and the choice of the familiar object pronoun *te* convey the strong bond that she, the marginalized figure, now feels toward her people.

Turning to the poetry that emphasizes the ravages of war, Mechakra evokes landscapes of death and destruction with prose that is impressionistic, symbolic, and filled with poetic images:

> Des os claquent, s'entrecroisent. Se recherchent. Les gorges de Kherrata suintent de gouttes de rosée. Un silence de cimetière plane. La terre éclatée retient précieusement quelques gouttes de pluie. Des vautours debout sur les crêtes rougies s'incrustent dans un décor qui surgit du jour. (112)

> (Bones rattle, cross one another. They seek out one another. The Kherrata gorges ooze drops of dew. A cemetery's silence pervades. The shattered land holds on preciously to several raindrops. Vultures standing on the reddened crests dig themselves into a decor that appears in the day.)

As bones rattle, reminding the reader of the *danse macabre*, the dance of death of medieval times, the drops of dew and rain, symbols of hope and regeneration, mark the contrast with the crests reddened with the blood of the fallen where vultures wait to feast on the dead.

Combining poetic images—some expressing hope and nationalist sentiment, others projecting an apocalyptic vision of the nation at war—with a realistic account of life in the war zone, Mechakra offers readers a text that blends realism, symbolism, and surrealistic elements in a way that leads Kateb Yacine, in his preface to the work, to consider her text a prose poem rather than a novel and to praise it as such: "Ce n'est pas un roman, et c'est beaucoup mieux: un long poème en prose qui peut se lire comme un poème" (7; It is not a novel, and it is much better: a long prose poem that can be read as a poem). As I have previously suggested, the poetic elements may heighten or lessen the harsh reality of life in the traumascape while conveying the individual's sense of joy, sorrow, and at times mental confusion.

The Cave: Reality and Metaphor

An archetype of the maternal womb, the cave appears in myths of origin and rebirth as well as in initiation rites in a variety of cultures and recalls prehistoric times, when men and women lived in caves.[15] It is a specific reference for Muslims, who recall that the prophet Muhammed received his first revelation from the angel Gabriel in Hira, a cave in the Jabal al-Nour, a mountain not far from Mecca. In Mechakra's novel, the cave emerges as both a real and a symbolic element, thereby joining other Algerian texts in which it appears as an important reference. The cave metaphor, as the critic Christa Jones explains, represents the struggle for identity and subjectivity construction in the literature (*Cave Culture in Maghrebi Literature*, 1).

Representing a physical refuge, the cave as metaphor in several of these works suggests a return to the protected and protecting maternal space of the womb. For example, in Mouloud Mammeri's novel *L'opium et le bâton*, set during the Algerian War, the protagonist, wounded in an ambush, retreats to a cave to recover from his wounds. He later emerges from the subterranean refuge transformed, having experienced physical and psychological healing. Mohammed Dib's *Qui se souvient de la mer*, a novel that expresses the horror of war through science fiction, depicts a city threatened by a calcifying plague and a family saved by the narrator's wife, who leads her husband and children to underground shelter as the city above them disintegrates into rubble. In this work, a woman's ability to find a way to safety allows the family to survive the apocalypse.

In Kateb Yacine's *Nedjma*, however, the symbolism is somewhat ambivalent. The cave is the mysterious place where the enigmatic Nedjma is conceived and where one of her mother's lovers, possibly her biological father, is killed. As such, it evokes not only the womb but also eroticism, incest, and murder. Assia Djebar's references to the cave in her works are also varied. They are symbolic in her film *La nouba des femmes du Mont Chenoua*; the cave becomes a place of female bonding as the rural women of Mount Chenoua gather together to perform traditional dances and rituals in a dark, humid, and mysterious grotto in the mountains, a refuge lit by the candles the women have placed there. Yet, the references are historical in *L'amour, la fantasia*, in which she recalls the infamous incidents of *enfumade*, asphyxiation by fire, that took place in the nineteenth century as France sought to pacify Algerian tribes that took up arms against them. When, in 1845, two French military officers, Pélissier and Saint-Arnaud, ordered their men to set fire to caves the tribes used as refuge, the caves became the Algerians' tombs. Significantly, the transformation of the cave from refuge to tomb also occurs in *La grotte éclatée* more than a century later, when Algerians once again fight the colonizer.[16]

In *La grotte éclatée*, the cave as a subterranean refuge for the wounded combatants is an ambivalent space, representing restoration and renewal for some, the end of life for others. Moreover, as a refuge for the wounded, it regroups those weakened, wounded, and defeated in battle. Within this context, the nurse-narrator wages her war, not against an enemy on a battlefield, but against death, the grim reaper claiming the lives of the men she is struggling to save. An ambivalent space for the soldiers she tends, it is ambivalent for her as well. There her child is conceived and born, and her husband dies. Most significantly, the cave becomes home space as the narrator constructs a family around her: Arris, the combatant she marries; Arris, the son conceived and born in the sheltered space, named after his dead father; Salah, the paraplegic boy; Kouider, the elderly nomad who guards the cave's entrance.

By giving birth to her son in the cave, the narrator acknowledges a new sense of power: "Je me sentais aussi forte que la vie, que l'inconnu, que le sort. Je suis vie, j'ai donné la vie" (85; I felt as strong as life, as the unknown, as destiny. I am life, and I have given life). With these words, she "domesticates" the formerly male space, the site of strategic political, military, and medical operations, offering a counternarrative to the violence, death, and destruction of war.[17] Hence, in Mechakra's novel the cave takes on multiple meanings. Readers may view it symbolically, as the matrix of mother earth with its connotation of hope and rebirth, and/or realistically, as the strategic site where the wounded are treated, the able-bodied soldiers and medical staff are sheltered, and, finally, the heroine creates improvised home space. The narrator's transformation of the cave into a domestic space offers evidence of her resiliency, her ability to "make a home out of the cracks."[18]

Although the cave provides shelter to the maquisards for an extended period of time, it proves vulnerable to French artillery. The French military attack on the rebel military camp not only destroys the cave, killing everyone but the narrator and her infant son, but shatters the survivor's world. The narrator survives the bombing, but her child is terribly maimed, losing his sight and his legs, and she bears physical scars, the loss of one arm, burns on her legs, and emotional scars as well.

In one short paragraph the narrator describes the physical destruction, and in the two sentences that follow, her emotional state after the attack:

> L'automne. Nouveaux bombardements sur la frontière. Je ne me souviens de rien.... Notre grotte éclata... Je la vis se remplir de fumée puis plus rien... Quand je me réveilla je n'avais plus qu'un bras, mon fils gisait au pied de Kouider méconnaissable: le napalm avait eu le dernier mot. Des arbustes nous servirent d'asile. Salah était enseveli sous les décombres.
>
> Un vide glacé m'habitait. J'étais inerte de tout mon corps, de tout mon être. (92)

> (Autumn. New bombings on the frontier. I don't remember anything.... Our cave exploded.... I saw it fill up with smoke, then nothing more.... When I came to, I had only one arm, my son was lying at the feet of Kouider, who was unrecognizable: napalm had had the last word. Some bushes protected us. Salah was buried under the ruins.
>
> I was filled with a cold empty feeling. My entire body, my whole being, was numb.)

With Tumarkin's and Caruth's analyses of trauma as the theoretical framework, we find that the narrator's description of the napalm attack resembles the testimony of many traumatized survivors. Her memory of the event, like the memories of other traumatized individuals, lacks precision. Her numbness corresponds to the physical and emotional state of a soldier whose emotional paralysis Caruth describes: "The experience of the soldier faced with sudden and massive death around him, for example, *who suffers this sight in a numbed state,* only to relive it later on in repeated nightmares, is a central and recurring image of trauma in this century" (*Unclaimed Experience,* 11, italics mine).

The Road to Recovery

From the Greek word meaning "wound," *trauma* refers both to the original experience and to the resulting physical and psychological injury that shatters the individual's sense of self and security in the world. A crucial aspect of the injury, as trauma theorists maintain, is the difficulty of articulating the experience. Yet, language, as the psychotherapist and Holocaust survivor Dori Laub asserts, can heal the survivor. Urging victims of trauma to articulate their experience as part of the healing process, he writes: "There is, in each survivor, an imperative need to *tell* and thus to come to *know* one's story, unimpeded by ghosts from the past against which one has to protect oneself. One has to know one's buried truth in order to be able to live one's life" ("Truth and Testimony," 63). In other words, the unconscious repetition through which trauma is initially expressed—the flashbacks, nightmares, and multiple signs of emotional stress—must be replaced by a conscious language. The critic Leigh Gilmore explains, however, that this expression needs to emerge "in structured settings" (*Limits of Autobiography*, 7).

If we view Mechakra's text as the "structured setting" in which the narrative unfolds, and the narrative as the constructed memory of the traumatized individual, we find that the destruction of the cave, an event that occurs midway through the narrative, leads the protagonist to experience and interpret reality differently than before. She depicts her life as a series of fragmented episodes conveyed to the reader through fragmented scenes and dialogues, flashbacks, and poetic verse combined with prose. As Pamela Pears acknowledges, the narrator "deals with literally fragmented bodies, possesses a somewhat fragmentary memory, and loses her son in an accident that will forever fragment her life" (*Remnants of Empire*, 64).

Although the critic Désirée Schyns asserts that the novelist portrays her protagonist's madness symbolically (*La mémoire littéraire de la guerre*, 95), I argue that the prose, anchored in reality, and the highly symbolic poetry combine to describe the protagonist's fragile emotional state. In my view, this stylistic hybridity aptly conveys the disorientation and profound sense of loss that a traumatized individual would experience in these circumstances. In this vein, we find the protagonist struggling to reach the truth. Because she cannot always tell what is real from what is false, we readers come to question her reliability as a narrator. Her unreliability is most apparent when, while convalescing in the psychiatric hospital in Tunisia, she shows definite signs of madness. Unable to distinguish the real from the imaginary, she speaks to her psychiatrist about a statue whose remains she carried as a pebble in her pocket and eventually lost in the souk. Are we to interpret the statue as her shadow, a calcified reflection of her former self?

Living in a world that lacks clarity and coherence, the nurse-narrator informs her psychiatrist that her entire world is a pure invention: "Mon fils, inventé—La grotte, inventée—L'orphelinat, inventé—Moi, inventée—Vous, inventé—La guerre, inventée" (96; My son, imagined—The cave, imagined—The orphanage, imagined—Me, imagined—You, imagined—The war, imagined). Blocking out reality, she attempts to avoid memories of the world she lost and the painful truth that this world is gone forever. It is not surprising that she imagines her dead son growing in his coffin (119).

Yet, following her unsuccessful efforts to forget the past, the narrator comes to the understanding that the memories of those she loved—Arris, Kouider, Salah—are there to sustain her through this very dark period in her life. She not only brings her friends, Salah and Kouider, back through memory but imagines them as she would like to have known them: Salah as a young boy walking on strong legs; Kouider, a youthful twenty-year-old, happily in love. Her imagination offers solace and becomes a useful means for surviving in difficult times. While escape through imagination provides temporary solace, community offers healing. Asserting the importance of community to the healing progress, the psychologist Kai Erikson writes that traumatized people tend to withdraw into a "protective envelope," living in a place of "mute, aching loneliness, in which the traumatic experience is treated as a solitary burden" ("Notes on Trauma and Community," 186). When trauma is shared, he explains, it can create a sense of community, which lessens the burden. In this regard, we find that Mechakra's protagonist, who withdrew psychologically into a space of solitude in the psychiatric hospital, where she appeared unable to share her trauma with anyone—those who had been her emotional support were now dead and her child severely handicapped—finds comfort in a community of displaced persons like herself in the refugee camp. Despite the difficult conditions in terms of food and lodging, the camp is an open, fluid transitional space that promises new possibilities for the future through spiritual kinship. There individuals who have lost family, friends, and shelter struggle to survive and to find meaning in their lives. Through encounters with women who tell her their stories, she finds the support she needs and begins to rebuild her life.

It is important to note that Mechakra's narrator listens attentively to other women's life narratives just as she had listened closely to the male combatants who shared past memories and future aspirations with her in the maquis. In the maquis with the men, she learned of Kouider's dream of fraternity and justice, as well as his love for Zehira, thwarted by oppressive tribal traditions. In the refugee camp, she learns of Rima's forced marriage, imposed by the same oppressive patriarchal code. Commenting on the women's narratives, the narrator states: "Elles m'avaient dit leur naissance, leur jeunesse, leur nuit de noce, leur premier enfant et leur veuvage. J'avais écouté. Elles en savaient, des choses" (126; They spoke to me of their birth, their youth, their wedding night, their first child, and widowhood. I listened. They knew a lot of things). Thus, her healing process involves listening rather than sharing her personal experience with others. She does, however, eventually share it with her readers.

Is it possible that the narrator's reticence to reveal her life story reflects her sense of distance from women who have not shared her experience in the male world of the maquis? Her personal experiences—and her psychological wounds—are rooted in her participation as a nurse in the fighting zone. The women in the camp reveal emotional wounds that stem from indigenous patriarchy. Their narratives reflect a struggle against a patriarchal system that has controlled their lives, their sorrow often rooted in forced marriage and the physical and emotional scars they bear because of this authoritarian practice.

Mechakra's protagonist, however, has not been bound by the rules of traditional patriarchy. The illegitimacy that denies her a place in traditional society has allowed her to escape patriarchal constraints; she is able to choose her husband freely. Moreover, by coming of age in the world of men in combat in the maquis and later experiencing life among women in the refugee camp, she comes to know two worlds that are separated by gender but linked by the forces of oppression, both colonial and indigenous.

Using fiction to describe the impact of the Algerian War upon the nation's women, Mechakra, like Assia Djebar, emphasizes the importance of women's not only speaking against the injustices imposed upon them by indigenous patriarchy but also listening attentively to one another. As the text becomes explicitly feminist, we recall that Mechakra's focus upon women's issues begins early in the novel. In the opening pages, she called attention to women's unique forms of expression and creativity:

Langage pétri dans les nattes tressées au feu de l'amour qui flambe depuis des siècles au cœur de mes ancêtres et dans mon cœur vers lequel souvent je tends mon visage gelé et mon regard humide pour pouvoir sourire. Langage pétri dans les tapis, livres ouverts portant l'empreinte multicolore des femmes de mon pays qui, dès l'aube se mettent à écrire le feu de leurs entrailles pour couvrir l'enfant le soir quand le ciel lui volera le soleil: dans les khalkhals d'argent, auréoles glacées aux fines chevilles, dont la musique rassure et réconforte celui qui dort près de l'âtre et déjà aime le pied de sa mère et la terre qu'elle foule. (13)

(Language created in the mats woven by the fire of love, which for centuries has burned in my ancestors' hearts and in my heart, fire toward which I often turn my frozen face and teary gaze to be able to smile. Language formed in carpets, open books carrying the multicolored imprint of the women of my country, who at daybreak begin to write of the fire in their wombs to cover their child in the evening, when the sky takes away the sun; in the silver *khalkhals*, chilled rings on their slender ankles, whose music calms and comforts the child sleeping near the hearth, who already loves his mother's foot and the earth she treads.)

With this introductory paragraph, the novelist draws upon the language and cultural elements of her female lineage, ancestors who expressed their creativity through traditional handcrafts—baskets, rugs, embroidery, and pottery—as well as music, their ankle bracelets tinkling as they walk. Paying tribute to traditional arts, which engage women's hands differently than they do the writer's, she is aware that these various art forms—like her poetry and prose—fulfill the individual's creative impulses.[19]

Studying Mechakra's text, Pears observes that one traditional art form, the wool carpet, becomes a metaphor for the author's literary project, the weaving together of multiple women's voices. When joined, these individual voices create a sense of community. It is interesting to note in this regard that museum curators confirm the novelist's reflection on the relationship between traditional forms of expression and literature. In her introduction to a catalog of an exhibition of traditional Algerian women's handcrafts, the curator Marie-France Vivier compares women's traditional craft to the art of written expression: "On peut considérer qu'il s'agit d'une 'écriture' qui manifeste la conscience d'autonomie des femmes et laisse entrevoir le savoir ésotérique dont elles sont dépositaires dans la société traditionnelle" (15; We can say that it represents a form of "writing" that attests to women's autonomy and shows their mastery of esoteric knowledge in traditional society).[20]

Exploring the relationship between artisanal production and literary expression, Pears notes as well that the novelist does not oppose tradition to modernity but emphasizes women's common bonds (*Remnants of Empire*, 66).[21] These bonds extend to the liberation struggle, for as historical accounts reveal, Algerian women—urban, rural, poor, or middle class—struggled together to liberate the nation despite experiencing the war in many different ways. For example, Amrane-Minne's historical findings clearly indicate that noncombatants played a crucial role by providing fighting units with food, lodging, medicine, and laundry, transporting messages and weapons, visiting family and friends in prison, and holding vigils at the prison gates. Although their support was not sufficiently recognized at the time, it has become evident to historians and the public at large that it was extremely important to the nationalist struggle.

Significantly, as a comprehensive women's narrative emerges in *La grotte éclatée*, a symbolic shift occurs, transforming the narrative metaphorically from the first-person singular to the first-person plural. This shift from *I* to *we* is crucial to the narrator's empowerment, enabling her to recognize her importance as both an individual and a member of a nation moving toward a new postcolonial identity. Acknowledging this shift from the individual to the collective, Chaulet-Achour finds that the novel, which began as one woman's experience in a war-torn world, provides textual space for multiple voices to express a variety of thoughts, feelings, and desires.[22]

The Long Road Home

Although the protagonist constructs a "home out of the cracks" during the time she dwells in the refugee camp, as she had in the cave, this home proves temporary. Eventually each refugee leaves the camp to embark upon the long road home. Yet, for many displaced persons, including the narrator, the concept of home is fraught with ambiguity. Where is the place called home?

In her essay "Bodies on the Move: A Poetics of Home and Diaspora," Susan Stanford Friedman reflects on the ambiguity associated with the phrase *there's no place like home.* She writes: "'There's no *place* like home' means home is *the* best, the ideal, everything that elsewhere is not. Places elsewhere can never bring the same happiness as home. Alternately inflected, the phrase turns into its opposite. 'There's no place like home' also means that no place, anywhere, is like home. Nowhere is there a place like home. Home is a never never land of dreams and desire. Home is utopia—a no place, a nowhere, an imaginary space longed for, always already lost in the very formation of the idea of home" (192). These remarks call attention to the psychological situation of all diasporic individuals and communities, who experience the pain and/or exhilaration of leaving home and homeland and, as "bodies on the move," construct identities "in motion" (205). Their home is often a distant place, and homecoming a dream deferred.

In Mechakra's novel, the protagonist, like the orphan in the folktale—and legendary Ulysses—finds the voyage home challenging. It involves making a symbolic return to the traumascape, the site of the shattered cave, a journey she must make as a lone survivor, although she is accompanied by the poet Hamoud and Rima, two friends she made in the refugee camp. The men she knew in the maquis have all perished, either from their battle wounds or from the bombing that obliterated the cave. And her infant son has died as well. Returning to the site, she finds it marked by a calcified tree that bears witness to the ravages of war—"un arbre nu et déchiré, mort debout, au pied duquel dormaient ma grotte et mes amis" (171; a barren and broken tree, dead but still standing, at whose base my cave and my friends lay sleeping). Thus, nature has provided a tombstone for those entombed in the rubble of the shattered cave.

In her study of traumascapes, Tumarkin remarks upon the magnetic attraction of these tragic sites for their survivors: "Soldiers return to battlefields, former concentration camp inmates walk through the camp gates again. Few modern images are as iconic as the vision of survivors returning to the site of their trauma" (*Traumascapes,* 133). A powerful reminder of tragedy, Tumarkin explains, they evoke emotions ranging from pain to enchantment and involve both the memory of a lost past and a commitment to the future. As substitutes for gravesites in the absence of victims' bodies, they are very powerful reminders of loss (85). As she examines the variety of situations that give rise to the traumascape, including wars and natural disasters, the sociologist asks: Are the survivors who choose to return seeking a way to reconcile with their past? Has time masked injuries that have never healed? (133). She finds no clear answers. The therapeutic benefits of returning to the site co-exist with the danger of re-traumatizing the survivor (153).

In Mechakra's text, her protagonist's return to the site where the cataclysmic event occurred appears to be beneficial. Hanging her belt on the dead tree and picking up a small clump of earth to take away with her to her village, she performs two ritualistic gestures that symbolize fertility and renewal. Suggesting that the narrator is ready to start life anew, these gestures encourage readers to conclude that Mechakra chooses to end her novel on a positive note, a firm belief in the future. In this regard, the critic Valérie Orlando finds that by reclaiming the past—the lost land and people—and by constructing a new heterotopia, the novel attempts to make whole a society ravaged by colonialism and its subsequent war of liberation (*Algerian New Novel*, 258). Thus, Mechakra's answer to the question of how and where the individual—and the Algerian nation—will find the strength to move toward the future appears to necessitate her protagonist's return to the ancestral land. Approaching ARRIS, the village she claims as her home, the narrator speaks her final words:

> Je dis ma foi en demain, clouée sur ma poitrine.
> Je dis ARRIS mon pays et ses moissons
> ARRIS mes ancêtres et mon honneur
> ARRIS mon amour et ma demeure. (172)

> (I speak my faith in tomorrow, nailed to my chest
> I say ARRIS my country and its harvests
> ARRIS my ancestors and my honor
> ARRIS my love and my home.)

These words clearly express joy—"ARRIS my love and my home"—and faith in the future—"my faith in tomorrow." They encourage the critic Simone Rezzoug to call Mechakra's work a novel of enduring hope (*Écritures féminines algériennes*, 87).

Nevertheless, Mechakra leaves her readers with two troubling images: a blind, crippled child who dies of his wounds; a tree destroyed in the napalm attack. Like the shattered cave, both can be understood in realistic and symbolic terms, as the "real" consequences of war and their symbolic representations. Commenting on the Algerian painter M'hammed Issiakhem's painting *Les Aveugles* (The blind ones), which appears on the jacket of the second edition of Mechakra's novel (2000), Orlando links the painting to the novel, interpreting the heroine's blinded baby as a symbolic representation of Algeria's blindness. In the postindependence era, she asserts, Algeria neither kept the promises made to women who fought for their country's independence nor respected the traditions of its rural people.[23]

I would add that the child's death must be interpreted as a further sign of the nation's inability to nurture and protect its citizens, both present and possibly future generations. The tree, which as a live, growing organism represents fertility, renewal, and nature's bounty, is yet another casualty of the war. As a dead tree, it can only symbolize the destructive power of war even though, in this instance, the enemy was responsible for the destruction.

Thus, despite the narrator's faith in the future, the various reminders of war's violence—her scarred body, her traumatic memories, and her experience of the devastated landscape and human losses—all warn of difficulties ahead. They may lead readers to question whether Mechakra's optimism expressed in the last pages of the text is illusory. Not only does the novelist leave the reader with an inconclusive ending but throughout her text she challenges the myth of the mighty warrior. Unlike the poet Virgil celebrating the Trojans' triumph in battle, Mechakra never evokes victorious battles; her text speaks only of the dark side of war. Early in the text, her narrator exclaims: "Nous ne sommes pas des héros mais des condamnés!" (27; We are not heroes but the condemned!). Written a decade after independence and published in 1979, *La grotte éclatée* leaves its readers wondering how the traumatized individual, and indeed, the Algerian nation as a whole, would find solace, healing, and the will to move toward the future following the terrible devastation of war.[24] Neither myth nor symbol of revolution, Mechakra's heroine remains a daring voice of dissidence in a scarred and troubled world.

4. WOUNDED MEMORIES

Maïssa Bey's *Entendez-vous dans les montagnes...*

من جبالنا طلع صوت الأحرار ينادينا للاستقلال
ينادينا للاستقلال، لاستقلال وطننا
—"Min Djibalina"

Allons enfants de la Patrie,
Le jour de gloire est arrivé!
. . . .
Entendez-vous dans les campagnes
Mugir ces féroces soldats?
—"La Marseillaise"

The conquest of Algeria in 1830 defined one era in Franco-Algerian relations, the 1954–62 war of independence the other. Since the first brought French settlers to Algeria and the second resulted in their departure, both determined the complex relationship between the two nations. As the preceding chapters have shown, Africa's first successful anticolonial war continues to draw the attention of social scientists, who provide us with critical data and objective analysis, and writers, who put a human face to events.[1] In addition, they reveal that those who write about the Algerian War—a war of national liberation for the colonized, a struggle to maintain the status quo for the colonizer—recognize that the trauma of that war produced indelible, albeit often invisible scars, affecting individuals and the collective psyche of France and Algeria. As the historian Benjamin Stora put it, "Pour les Français, une 'guerre sans nom'; pour les Algériens, une 'révolution sans visage': un des plus durs conflits de décolonisation de ce siècle n'a vraiment jamais été 'assumé' des deux côtés" (*La gangrène et l'oubli*, 8; For the French, it was a 'war without a name'; for the Algerians, a 'revolution without a face': neither side has really come to terms with one of the most difficult conflicts of decolonization of the twentieth century). In this same vein, the historian Todd Shepard writes that "the Algerian War was the most traumatic case of decolonization in the French Empire" (*Invention of Decolonization*, 4).

Probing the war's traumatic effects upon individuals—and by extension, on the Algerian nation—in the preceding chapter, devoted to Yamina Mechakra's *La grotte éclatée*, we noted that the Greek word *trauma* means "wound." It is in this sense that the trauma theorist Cathy Caruth describes trauma as a wound that "addresses us in the attempt to tell us of a reality or truth that is not otherwise available" (*Unclaimed Experience*, 4). Significantly, in both the historical and literary realms, works inspired by the Algerian War adopt the trope of the unhealed wound to characterize its effects. For example, the historians Mohammed Harbi and Benjamin Stora write: "La Guerre d'Algérie [. . .] réveille sans cesse de vieilles blessures qui n'en finissent pas de cicatriser" (*La guerre d'Algérie*, 9; The Algerian War [. . .] continues to open old wounds that never heal).

For Maïssa Bey, the metaphor of the unhealed wound is inextricably linked to her personal history. The novelist's father, an FLN militant, was arrested, tortured, and executed by the French security forces in the early years of the liberation struggle. Bey was a six-year-old child at the time of her father's death. Her novella *Entendez-vous dans les montagnes . . .* explores the war's repercussions, the haunting and persistent effects that have been characterized as unhealed wounds by those who experienced the war as well as by those who examine it through a critical lens. As Bey revisits the Algerian War, she, like Mechakra, asks: How does an individual, a community, or a nation negotiate between the story of the unbearable nature of an event and the story of the unbearable nature of surviving it? In other words, can the survivor's wounds heal?

Both Mechakra and Bey experienced the war as children. Hence, they are both members of a generation that sometimes witnessed or experienced traumatic events they could barely understand. Returning to the war as an adult, Mechakra presents her readers with a fictional narrative that does not reflect her own experiences. Bey, in contrast, uses a fictional framework to bring to light a personal family narrative, her father's story and her own relationship to it. In recognition of the difficulty of Bey's task, I entitle this chapter "Wounded Memories," applying the term to traumatic recollections of the liberation struggle that have been denied or repressed, thereby increasing the survivors' psychological pain.[2] In my view, the term is appropriate given that the trauma evoked in Maïssa Bey's *Entendez-vous dans les montagnes . . .* (Do you hear in the mountains . . .), published in 2002, is rooted in a historical blank—both personal and collective—surrounding the torture and death of the novelist's father. Thus, while Mechakra depicts the immediacy of war in her novel, Bey offers a different perspective, exploring the war's traumatic effects in terms of occulted memory and personal loss.

Revisiting the Algerian War from the perspective of Algeria's undeclared civil war, Bey presents three individuals—an elderly Frenchman, a middle-aged Algerian woman, and a young Frenchwoman—each with an Algerian past, who meet on a train as they travel through France sometime in the 1990s. The Algerian woman has left her country, seeking refuge in France from the violence of the civil war at home. Their journey, which will lead all three to reformulate their relationships and attitudes to the past, and by extension to the present, serves as a symbolic place of memory for two of them: the Algerian woman, daughter of an FLN militant tortured and killed by the French during the Algerian War, and the Frenchman, a former French soldier who may be implicated in the Algerian's torture and death. The third, the young Frenchwoman, will come to understand her colonial heritage.

Viewed as an allegory of Franco-Algerian relations across generations, the narrative becomes a tale of one generation's need to come to terms with the Algerian War and their children's struggle to reach the truth regarding the events of that war. By setting her three protagonists—all strangers to one another—on a train trip across France, the novelist introduces the voyage as a journey to self-understanding as well as a reflection upon the philosophical issues of morality, justice, and freedom. Moreover, as the politically engaged writer delves into her nation's history, the trope allows her to posit the importance of literature as a significant form of resistance to injustice and tyranny. Hence, Bey's text is open to multiple interpretations.

Inspired to write during the turbulent 1990s, Bey has emerged in recent years as an increasingly important literary voice. Her corpus to date—eight novels, two plays, two collections of short stories, and numerous essays—focuses on critical periods of Algeria's history: the French conquest of Algeria in 1830; the Algerian War of Independence, 1954–62; the undeclared civil war between the Algerian government and Islamic fundamentalists, 1992–2002; present-day Algeria. In her first novel, *Au commencement était la mer* (In the beginning was the sea), published in 1996, which she situates in the period of the 1990s, she addresses the issue of Algerian women's rights during the dark decade of internal strife. *Pierre sang papier ou cendre* (Stone blood paper or ashes), published in 2008, delves further back into history, recalling the events of June 1830, when the French fleet invaded Algeria. *Puisque mon coeur est mort* (Since my heart is dead), of 2010, examines the effects of the undeclared civil war upon victims' families. *Hizya*, published in 2015, deals with the frustrations of youth in present-day Algeria. The 2002 *Entendez-vous dans les montagnes...*, the focus of this chapter, revisits the Algerian War during *la décennie noire*, the dark decade, 1992–2002.

From Samia Benameur to Maïssa Bey

Born in 1950 in Boghari (Ksar-el-Boukari), a village south of Algiers, Samia Benameur was a high-school French teacher in Sidi Bel Abbes, the city in western Algeria where she still lives, when, in the mid-1990s, she began publishing her work, adopting the pen name Maïssa Bey. Writing during the period of Algeria's undeclared civil war, she was well aware of the dangers she faced, yet she continued to speak out against violence and repression, chose to stay in Algeria, and refused to wear the veil. She did, however, assume a pen name to protect herself and her family. Selecting Maïssa, a first name her mother favored, and Bey, the surname of her maternal grandmother, the novelist turned to her maternal lineage to establish a public identity. Thus, she chose to honor her mother, who after her husband's death raised her five children alone (*A contre-silence*, 32).

To her mother's courage and determination in the face of hardship, her father added the dimension of political activism. A schoolteacher in Boghari, Yagoub Benameur was an FLN militant during the Algerian War. In a short memoir entitled "Mon père, ce rebelle" ("My Father, the Rebel") the novelist details her father's political activity. A political officer in the FLN beginning in 1955, he raised funds, delivered weapons, and organized meetings held at his father's farm. This logistical support for the men in the maquis went undetected because of his role as a village schoolteacher. As Bey notes, it was hard to imagine that this dedicated civil servant would be capable of driving his wife and children to visit his parents' farm on a Sunday afternoon in a car with a trunkload of weapons destined for the maquis ("Mon père, ce rebelle," 80–81; "My Father, the Rebel," 27). Yet, his political activities were eventually revealed, and he was arrested. It is unclear whether the French authorities became suspicious of him or a villager denounced him to the authorities.

Arrested at home in February 1957, Benameur had neither legal representation nor a trial. The dossiers confiscated by the police at the time of his arrest may have proved his affiliation with the FLN and sealed his fate. The false reports that appeared in the local press after his death described him as "un dangereux fellagha abattu par les forces de l'ordre alors qu'il tentait de s'enfuir" ("Mon père, ce rebelle," 80; the dangerous *fellagha* slain by security forces while trying to escape [27]). His body was never returned to the family for burial.

In a short text entitled "Fragments" Bey recalls the night of her father's arrest:

> Je suis tirée de mon sommeil au milieu de la nuit. J'entends des bruits de pas. Des voix. J'ouvre les yeux. Il y a des hommes dans la maison. Trois ou quatre ou peut-être plus. Je ne les connais pas. Je ne les ai jamais vus. Ce sont des soldats. Ils portent un uniforme vert et un gros ceinturon. Ils vont d'une pièce à l'autre. Ils ne nous parlent pas. Ils ne nous regardent pas. Toutes les lumières sont allumées. Ma mère est en chemise de nuit. Elle porte mon petit frère dans ses bras. Il dort, lui. Mon grand frère est debout, à ses côtés. Je ne vois pas mon père. Les soldats ouvrent toutes les portes. Tous les tiroirs. Même ceux du bureau de mon père. Ils jettent par terre tout ce qu'ils y trouvent. [. . .] Ils emportent les dossiers de mon père. Il va remonter, c'est sûr. Mais il tarde trop. [. . .] Longtemps, j'attends mon père. (73)

(I am pulled out of my sleep in the middle of the nights. I hear footsteps. Voices. I open my eyes. There are men in the house. Three or four, or maybe more. I don't know them. I have never seen them before. They are soldiers. They wear a green uniform with a big belt. They go from one room to the other. They don't speak to us. They don't look at us. All the lights are on. My mother is in her nightgown. She has my little brother in her arms. He's asleep. My big brother is standing next to her. I don't see my father. The soldiers open all the doors. All the drawers. Even those in my father's study. [. . .] They throw everything they find on the floor. They take all of my father's dossiers. I'm sure that he is coming back upstairs. But he is taking too much time. [. . .] I wait for my father for a very long time.)

Although readers may be surprised by the terse style the author adopts to depict an event that is emotionally charged, the minimalist style suggests that words fail to fully convey the trauma experienced by the child, and by her mother and siblings, at this moment. By presenting the event from the child's perspective, Bey recovers the tragic moment, which she recalls and transmits in detail, yet with a significant gap. Awakening after the police have taken her father away, she does not witness his arrest. As the child patiently anticipates her father's return, it is clear that she is unable at this time to fully comprehend the significance of the event, which will continue to haunt her in her adult life.

In this same text, the novelist returns through memory to the empty classroom following her father's arrest. Here, she evokes his death as a collective tragedy as well as a personal loss. Her father was the community's schoolteacher; his loss extends beyond the family. She writes:

> Je suis dans la classe de mon père. La salle est vide. Il n'y a pas d'élèves. Il n'y a pas de maître. La blouse grise de mon père est restée accrochée au portemanteau près de la porte. Je respire son odeur. Je referme la porte. Je quitte la classe. Je quitte l'école. Je quitte l'enfant que j'ai été. ("Fragments," 74).

> (I am in my father's classroom. The room is empty. There are no students, no teacher. My father's gray smock hangs from the coatrack near the door. I smell the scent. I close the door. I leave the room. I leave the school. I leave behind the child I once was.)

Although she uses the same terse style, her perspective is that of an adult aware of a defining moment in her life. The sense of protection and security that her father had represented for her and the community is gone. The transformation from a world of security to one of extreme precariousness, from peace to war, is reinforced by the juxtaposition of two scenes: an opening scene in which the child is pushed on a swing by the all-protecting father and the final scene of the empty classroom. The father's tragic disappearance puts an abrupt end to a childhood.

Places, whether private or public, are always complex constructions of personal and interpersonal experiences. Thus, by reliving the police raid that occurred one night in the family home and then returning to the classroom, where she draws the reader's attention to an artifact, the gray smock that the schoolteacher—her father—will never again pick up from the coatrack, Bey draws upon two memories anchored in places that held great importance for her as a child, home and school, both irreparably transformed by her father's death. If, as the sociologist Eugene Victor Walter notes, meaningful places are containers of experience that capture events and store them symbolically, they not only store meaning about the past but also provide roadmaps for the future. Inextricably linked in the child's mind to the memory of her father, these places represent Yagoub Benameur's legacy to his daughter, influencing her later development as an educator, writer, and political activist.

I introduce these two autobiographical fragments as signposts leading to Bey's fiction, suggesting that just as her father's militancy and personal sacrifice shaped the politically engaged writer's world, his martyrdom became the unhealed wound that emerges in multiple ways in her fiction. At the same time, these fragments reveal the incomplete nature of her memories. Asleep in her room when her father was arrested, and too young to fully understand the importance of the event, she experiences a double absence, the loss of the parent and the incomplete memory and knowledge surrounding the event. Significantly, the recollection of the empty classroom allows her to acknowledge her father's death as a collective as well as personal loss. Finally, Bey's restrained style, which the critic Etienne Achille associates with the literary voice that Albert Camus adopts in *L'Étranger* (*The Stranger*), emerges clearly in the narrative of her father's arrest.[3]

As we examine Bey's autobiographical writing, Alison Rice's study of contemporary Francophone Algerian women writers, *Polygraphies*, provides analytical guidelines. Rice finds that much of these women's writing, while autobiographical, does not conform to traditional autobiography. First, she emphasizes its collective nature: "Allowing the personal to punctuate the literary work is not meant to call attention to the individual in an egotistical move but is instead a measure that enables the writer to express the experiences of *many:* the polyphonous nature of the text is striking, even when the solitary subject seems to be the focus. Each person is inextricably connected to others, and the text cannot help but sing of those others and allow them to sing through the literary work as sources of inspiration" (1). Calling attention to the plurality of voices and stories present in a single-author text, Rice also notes how the writers bring together fact and fiction, thereby interrogating notions of truth. Quoting the Algerian-born philosopher and critic Jacques Derrida, who writes that "not all literature is of the genre or the type of 'fiction,' but there is fiction in all literature" (*Acts of Literature,* 49), Rice claims that autobiographical texts "move us beyond the opposition between the truthful and the duplicitous" (6). She adds: "What happens in the literary work of fiction, then, is not a claim to the truth but an effort to question unequivocal truth by transforming the text into a space where multiple truths lie, where subtle complicated truths prove to be all the more convincing precisely because of this paradoxical structure" (6). Studying Bey's text, we will find it reflecting both aspects of nontraditional biography, the plurality of voices expressing multiple truths and the interweaving of fact and fiction. As her protagonists evoke memories of Algeria, the novelist combines fiction with historical truth, adopting the concept of novelistic liberty that Assia Djebar puts forth in her novel *La femme sans sépulture* (Woman without a tomb) to compensate for historical blanks.

Grappling with life stories that will forever remain incomplete, both writers use their imagination to fill in the blanks. Djebar cannot get to the "whole truth" regarding the last days in the life of the martyred combatant Zoulikha because neither written records nor oral testimony exist. Similarly, Bey cannot delve further into the events of her father's disappearance. She can only interrogate memory, hers and others, and read signs, documents and photographs that she includes in her text. Whereas in Djebar's novel the protagonist, Zoulikha, speaks to her daughter, and by extension to her readers, in four fictional monologues that reach them from beyond the tomb, Bey uses visual elements, a photograph of her father and official certificates that bear his name, to signal his presence in the fictional narrative. However, as the critic Névine El Nossery states in her analysis of the relationship between the photograph and the text, the photograph and other accompanying documents serve as evidence of the father's existence, yet "their inclusion in a fictional narrative challenges the possibility that such an intricate and multi-layered reality can be accurately represented in any genre" ("Fictionalisation of History," 279). El Nossery finds the ambiguous relationship between fact and fiction a recurring theme in Bey's work. This ambiguity is further emphasized in the text via the movement between singular first- and third-person pronouns, a narrative device that allows the novelist to keep the necessary distance from a subject that is so intimate and personal. Assia Djebar uses the same narrative strategy for the same purpose in her novel *L'amour, la fantasia*, as does Eveline Safir Lavalette in her memoir *Juste Algérienne: Comme une tissure*.

Reading the Other

Setting her protagonists on a long train ride across France to the port city of Marseilles, Bey introduces the well-worn theme of the unexpected encounter that we find in literature and film, from Agatha Christie's *Murder on the Orient Express* to Alfred Hitchcock's *Strangers on a Train*. In this vein, as the postcolonial theorist Sara Ahmed explains, encounters are meetings that involve surprise and conflict. Probing the effect of the relationship between encounters with others and identity, she writes: "Identity itself is constituted in the 'more than one' of the encounter: the designation of an 'I' or 'we' requires an encounter with others. These others cannot be simply relegated to the outside: given that the subject comes into existence as an entity only through encounters with others, then the subject's existence cannot be separated from the others who are encountered" (*Strange Encounters*, 7). In other words, the face-to-face meetings with others that we all experience help shape our individual identities. Bringing a temporal element into the discussion, Ahmed insists that the encounter that occurs in the present "reopens past encounters" (8). Indeed, the past weighs heavily on the present in Bey's text; the Frenchman and the Algerian woman, two individuals separated by nationality, age, and gender, are connected by a common but conflicted history, the Algerian War. Their surprise encounter on the train will test Ahmed's premise that each will be transformed by the chance meeting with the other.

Finally, a crucial aspect of the chance encounter involves the subject's "reading" of the other. This process most often begins with the visual scrutiny of the gaze before involving language as the individual seeks to determine common bonds and/or differences between the self and the other. As Ahmed explains, "When we face others, we seek to recognize who they are, by reading the signs on their body, or by reading their body as a sign" (8). In this way, these acts of reading the other, as she argues, "constitute 'the subject' in relation to 'the stranger' who is determined to be 'out of place' in a given place" (8). In Bey's text, the Algerian woman is "out of place," as she travels beyond the borders of her homeland, whereas the two French nationals in the train compartment are traveling to destinations in their home country.

Examining the opening scene closely, we find that the Algerian woman, seeking solitude, chooses an empty compartment and begins to read her book. The Frenchman, who enters next, sits opposite her, offers no greeting, and appears to ignore her presence. Shortly before the train departs, a young girl enters the compartment. Seeing an elderly man and a middle-aged woman, she decides that the journey will be a calm one and claims her seat. Neither the man nor the woman acknowledges her presence, and she does not acknowledge theirs. As the train leaves the station, the reader is left to wonder whether there will be any interaction among the three strangers on the train.

Glancing up at the Frenchman before the young girl enters the compartment, the Algerian woman describes him as a white-haired man in his sixties, with light eyes, sharp features, a face lined with wrinkles. First, he causes her to think of her father. Then, a passage from the book she is reading, Bernhard Schlink's *The Reader*, superimposes itself upon her description of the passenger.

> *Je l'observais avec ses cheveux gris, ses joues toujours mal rasées, les rides profondes qu'il avait entre les sourcils et qui couraient des ailes du nez au coin de la bouche. J'attendais. (Entendez-vous dans les montagnes . . . , 10)*

> (I studied him, his gray hair, his face, carelessly shaven as always, the deep lines between his eyes and from his nostrils to the corners of his mouth. I waited. [*The Reader*, 141])

Set off in italics in Bey's book to distinguish it as a "borrowed excerpt," the passage describes the German narrator's father, thereby bringing a textual reference to Schlink's novel directly into Bey's. Just as an unexpected encounter on the train will transport the Algerian traveler back in time to her nation's liberation struggle, the novel she is reading on the train will take her back further in time, to World War II, and to a different space, Hitler's Germany.[4]

Depicting a protagonist who, as a reader, chooses a book that takes her to an earlier era and a different geographical space, the novelist introduces an autobiographical element, her own passion for reading. An avid reader, Bey has stated that reading has been a great source of inspiration for her: "Ce que je sais des hommes, de l'univers, de moi-même, je l'ai appris dans les livres, et donc par l'intermédiaire du langage écrit" ("Faut-il aller chercher des rêves," 20; What I know about people, the universe, myself, I learned through books, and thereby by means of the written language). In her autobiographical essay *L'une et l'autre* (One and the other), she states that through the many books she has read, her horizons have widened and her vision has broadened without her leaving home (26). She attributes this passion for books and reading to her father's influence. Teaching her to read at a very young age "dans la langue de l'autre" (26; in the language of the other), the French colonizer's language, he opened a window for her on a wide and varied world, as Djebar's father, also a teacher in the French colonial school system, did for her.

Alison Rice notes that intertextuality is a crucial aspect of Bey's work, reflecting the writer's perception of literature as a web of connections and dialogues: "Inspired by the words and truths of the beings in books before her, she is acutely aware of the possibility that her writing will spark similar reactions in her readers and provide a sense of solidarity among them" (*Polygraphies*, 48). Indeed, in her autobiographical essay Bey refers to a rather large number of writers she has read, including Jean Cocteau, Édouard Glissant, and Milan Kundera. Yet, in the novella she focuses exclusively on one key text, ironically or perhaps prophetically entitled *The Reader*.

Reading and Misreading *The Reader*

The important intertext *The Reader* depicts a love affair between a young German high-school student and his neighbor, a woman in her mid-thirties, a liaison that proves to be literary as well as sexual. Each time the lovers meet, Michael, the adolescent, reads a classic work of literature aloud to Hanna. Knowing nothing about his mysterious neighbor except that she lives alone and works as a tramway conductor, he later "misreads" her sudden departure from the city—and his life—as his fault. Seven years later, Michael, now a university law student, attends a trial of former Nazi SS guards as part of a law-school seminar and discovers that Hanna, his former neighbor and lover, is one of the defendants. The women on trial are accused of leaving their Jewish prisoners to die in a burning church during the war. Hanna is blamed for writing a letter that attempts to hide their culpability. At the trial, Michael realizes that Hanna is illiterate, a secret that has determined many of her life choices. Hence, she could not have written the document that condemns her. Yet, his guilt for having loved a war criminal keeps him from divulging this information, which would have significantly lightened her sentence, to the presiding judge. During Hanna's years in prison, Michael sends her audiotapes of literary works that he records for her; she uses these tapes to teach herself to read. With literacy comes knowledge; her ability to read allows her to delve into the history of the Holocaust and understand more fully the tragic consequences of her actions. Upon her release from prison she commits suicide.

Although this brief synopsis does not do justice to the complex novel, it suggests links between the two texts. Through chance encounters, Michael and the Algerian woman (who remains unnamed throughout Bey's text) meet older individuals who are guilty of war crimes. Yet, the personal lives of the older generation reveal human dimensions that the younger generation cannot ignore. In addition, both encounters set in motion a series of "misreadings." Unaware of Hanna's secrets—her illiteracy and her Nazi past—Michael misreads her behavior toward him during their affair. Similarly, the Algerian woman, unaware at first that the man in the train compartment is a former French soldier who may have tortured and killed her father during the Algerian War, "misreads" him as well. Reading Schlink's novel, she finds that the French traveler bears a resemblance to Michael's father, but the physical similarity obscures their differences. Neither a Nazi nor a Nazi sympathizer during the war, Michael's father is a "good German." A philosophy professor who has studied Hegel and Kant, he believes in freedom and human dignity, as affirmed by the second quotation from Schlink's text. Michael recounts: "Lorsqu'il parla, il me fit un exposé sur la personne, la liberté, et la dignité, sur l'être humain comme sujet et sur le fait qu'on n'avait pas le droit de le traiter en objet" (*Entendez-vous dans les montagnes . . .* , 34; "When he spoke, he instructed me about the individual, about freedom and dignity, about the human being as subject and the fact that one may not turn him into an object" [*The Reader*, 141]). The philosopher, however, speaks in abstractions; he does not offer specific advice that would help his son make the best moral choices.

The third and final quotation from *The Reader* that Bey brings into her text deals squarely with the issue of individual culpability. Spoken by a middle-aged Alsatian who drives Michael to the site of a former concentration camp in Alsace, these words describe Nazi criminal behavior as a form of indifference:

> Non, je ne parle pas d'ordres reçues et d'obéissance. Le bourreau n'obéit pas à des ordres. Il fait son travail. Il ne hait pas ceux qu'il exécute, il ne se venge pas sur eux, il ne les supprime pas parce qu'ils le gênent ou le menacent ou l'agressent. Ils lui sont complètement indifférents. (*Entendez-vous dans les montagnes . . .* , 17)

> (No, I'm not talking about orders and obedience. An executioner is not under orders. He's doing his work, he doesn't hate the people he executes, he's not taking revenge on them, he's not killing them because they're in his way or threatening him or attacking him. They're a matter of such indifference to him that he can kill them as easily as not. [*The Reader*, 151])

Thus, through this chance encounter the young student finds a chilling explanation of the executioner's mind-set and actions: he is motivated by neither hatred of his victim nor misplaced obedience but simply by indifference to the plight of another human being.

Taken together, the three quotations establish the link between the Holocaust and the Algerian War and provide information for the successive generations attempting to decipher the past in order to better understand the present. If the first quotation initiates the theme of misreading as the Algerian woman mistakes the "good German" for the "not-so-good Frenchman," the second puts forth abstract ideals of freedom and dignity, in contrast to the third, which blames indifference for so much human suffering and injustice in the world.

Bey brings Schlink's philosophical novel into her text in a way that tempts the reader to engage in further investigation. Providing her readers with neither the author's first name nor the publishing house nor the year of publication of the text, she sets the three quotations off with italics and quotation marks but gives no page references to the French edition she cites. Neither contextualizing the quotations nor providing information concerning the content of the German novel, she challenges her readers to conduct their own research in order to establish the relationship between the two works and thereby gain a fuller understanding of her text. Finally, as she extends moral issues of culpability beyond the Algerian War of Independence to include World War II, she encourages her readers to embark upon a path that she herself has taken, a journey through books. Although her knowledge of the Algerian War is personal and direct, the knowledge of World War II that enters her text comes from her reading and research.

Situating the events of the Algerian War between two other violent conflicts, World War II and Algeria's undeclared civil war, Bey introduces multiple collective memories that suggest a concept the critic Michael Rothberg terms *multidirectional memory*; she thus brings together Holocaust and postcolonial studies. Concerned that various memories might compete with one another, that the Holocaust might eclipse other historical moments, particularly decolonization, Rothberg writes: "Against the framework that understands collective memory as competitive memory—as a zero-sum struggle over scarce resources—I suggest that we consider memory as multidirectional: as subject to ongoing negotiation, cross-referencing and borrowing; as productive and not privative. [. . .] This interaction of different historical memories illustrates the productive, intercultural dynamic that I call multidirectional memory" (*Multidirectional Memory*, 2). To show that the emergence of Holocaust memory and the historical process of decolonization are not separate but overlapping processes, Rothberg references various texts and films, drawing specific attention to the writings of Charlotte Delbo. A member of the French Resistance and a survivor of Auschwitz, Delbo, in addition to publishing a series of memoirs of Auschwitz, published *Les belles lettres* (1961), a compilation of letters published in the French press opposing the Algerian War.[5] Bringing the Holocaust and decolonization together, Delbo opened the way for writers such as Didier Daeninckx, Nancy Huston, Leïla Sebbar, Mehdi Lallaoui, and Maïssa Bey, who would also bring together memories of World War II and Algeria's anticolonial war.[6] Bey, in addition, adds another historical layer to "multidirectional memory," the violent undeclared civil war, 1992–2002, which compels her Algerian protagonist to seek a safe haven against violence in France three decades after her father and his fellow combatants fought a long and difficult anticolonial war.

Through this process of historical overlapping, we see that the fictional characters in the two historical contexts—Nazi Germany during World War II and Algeria during the liberation struggle—suffer trauma and its aftermath, haunting persistent memories that impact upon their present reality. In the case of Michael and the Algerian woman, they belong neither to the first generation, those who were adults during the traumatic period, nor to the second, those born after the events that marked their parents' generation and who inherit memories from their families and the culture at large. They are members of the "1.5 generation," a category developed by the critic Susan Suleiman in her study *Crises of Memory and the Second World War* to describe those who were young children during war and sometimes witnessed traumatic incidents they could only barely comprehend. They differ from the second generation, which the critic Marianne Hirsch calls the "postmemory" generation, who are haunted by memories they inherited but did not experience directly.[7] Born after the events, the latter find their connection indirectly, through stories told by family members and in photographs and documents that families have kept. Born during the events, the "1.5 generation" nevertheless shares with the following generation a preoccupation with events they must struggle to understand.

In Bey's text, the shared bonds among individuals who experienced war as children is quite evident when the Algerian woman finds herself physically and psychologically disturbed by Schlink's novel:

> Elle ne se sent pas très bien. [...] C'est peut-être à cause de ce qu'elle vient de lire. De ce qui est raconté dans le livre, qu'elle a choisi au hasard en passant dans une librairie, non, pas vraiment au hasard, mais pour quelques passages lus en le feuilletant, des questions posées par cet homme qui interroge son père pour comprendre le passé. (16)

(She does not feel very well. [...] That may be because of what she has just read. From what is said in the book that she selected randomly while in a bookstore, no, not really randomly, but for several passages she read while perusing it, questions this man asks his father in order to understand the past.)

It is clear from this passage that the woman has deliberately chosen a book that is of personal significance to her because it interrogates the past. In *The Reader*, Michael is able to question his father to learn about Germany's past. Bey's protagonist, however, cannot. Having lost this connection following the death of her father, she experiences the loss as an unhealed wound. Nevertheless, two unexpected encounters on the train, one with the former French conscript, the other with the young French girl, will be transformative in this regard. The former soldier will provide her with a clearer understanding of the traumatic events of 1957. Her encounter with the young French girl will allow her to pass the historical legacy on to the next generation so that the history will be neither lost nor forgotten.

Sharing a Troubled History

As the two voyagers travel through France, the Algerian woman and the Frenchman both return through memory to Algeria. First recalling the Algerian landscape she left behind as she looks out on the French countryside, the Algerian woman then remembers her father as she studies the face of the Frenchman sitting opposite her. He, in turn, brings back his memories of Algeria, the country where he did his military service during the Algerian War. As her memories seem to be activated visually, by the sights that surround her, his appear to be linked to sound as well: first his French combat unit singing "La Marseillaise" and then, as he listens to the train wheels squeaking on the rails, the sound of the *gégène*, the portable electric generator used by the French military to torture the Algerian captives. Hence, before they begin the conversation that will reveal a common past, each engages individually with memories of a geographical space that is of great significance to them both. This shared past, which is experienced quite differently by the two travelers is reflected in the novella's title, which borrows from both France's national anthem, "La Marseillaise," with its line "Entendez-vous dans les campagnes" (Do you hear in the countryside), and Algeria's most popular revolutionary song "Min Djibalina," with its line "From our mountains came the voice of the free."

The Frenchman and the Algerian woman might remain locked in their own thoughts and perhaps never communicate with each other were it not for an unforeseen disruption. When a distraught woman passenger bursts into their compartment announcing a robbery that she is convinced was carried out by Arabs, her racist comment leads to the conversation between the two previously silent individuals. Through this conversation, the Algerian woman learns that the Frenchman, a conscript during the Algerian War, had been part of a unit assigned to Boghari, her hometown, in 1957, the year of her father's death. She comes to realize that he may well have had some part in her father's death; he may even have been her father's executioner.

As their conversation continues, it becomes clear that while the woman carries the wound of a shattered childhood, the man lives with the guilt of having witnessed and participated in military operations he cannot morally justify. Significantly, as he ruminates on the past in an interior monologue, he adopts the trope of the unhealed wound to described his own troubled memories:

> C'est comme si on avait ouvert des vannes pour laisser couler la boue, toute la fange d'un passé qui s'avère soudain très proche et encore sensible. Comme si en passant le doigt ou en palpant une cicatrice ancienne dont les bords s'étaient refermés, croyait-on, on sentait un léger suintement, qui se transforme peu à peu en une purulence qui finit par s'écouler de plus en plus abondamment, sans qu'on puisse l'arrêter. (43)

> (It is as if we had opened the floodgates to let the mud flow, all the filth of the past, which suddenly seems very close and still sensitive. As if by lightly touching or pressing on an old scar whose edges you thought had healed, you felt a light secretion that slowly turned into pus that flowed more and more abundantly and could not be stopped.)

Describing his Algerian past in terms of mud, filth, and a festering sore, he reveals that he suffers from the trauma of war. Like the nurse in Mechakra's *La grotte éclatée*, the former soldier has experienced life in the traumascape and carries the scars. Just as many American men and women who have served in the armed forces struggle with the psychological illness that the medical profession now terms post-traumatic stress disorder or PTSD, he lives with a war wound. And like those who witnessed atrocities, were unable to stop them, or engaged in unjustifiable killing, he suffers from a syndrome that therapists today refer to as "moral injury." To the symptoms of PTSD, which include depression, anxiety, and disquieting flashbacks, moral injury adds the burden of guilt, grief, regret, shame, and alienation.[8]

As Bey's text explores traumatic memory, a critical difference emerges between the soldier's and the Algerian woman's recollections of the past. The Frenchman has very vivid, albeit traumatic memories of the Algerian chapter in his life, a period that continues to haunt him. In contrast, the Algerian woman, having experienced the trauma of war as a child, finds it difficult to assemble the various fragments of that early period in her life into a complete picture. She recalls several brief images yet is unable to truly remember her father. His physical being—his voice, his movements, even his smell—elude her. Hence, photographs and documents serve as her much-needed memory support; they help her recover fragments of a past that in large part escapes her. In contrast, the former soldier, struggling with memories that are too vivid, too painful, finds that the past overwhelms him. Both individuals live with unhealed wounds that they can only treat by coming to terms with a painful past.

Although the Algerian woman wishes to learn more about her father's assassination and may be able to do so in conversation with Jean, the former soldier, she wants Marie, the young girl who also shares the train compartment, to learn about this period in history, which neither the girl's grandfather, a pied-noir who left Algeria at independence, nor French history textbooks have communicated to her. Marie is primarily a bystander to the dialogue between her two fellow voyagers, but as a descendant of pieds-noirs she too is connected to the complex relationship between France and Algeria.

Following the conquest of Algeria, the pieds-noirs created barriers to harmony and understanding rather than bridges between the various communities as they dispossessed the colonized of their rights and their land. As the historian Benjamin Stora explains, the pieds-noirs' systematic exclusion of the indigenous Algerian population from their land and from equal legal status, that is, French citizenship, eventually fueled the nationalist movement that led to the war. Not only did the pied-noir population create an elitist society in which they held the power and the economic advantage but they augmented this population with European settlers from Spain, Italy, and Malta to whom they systematically granted French citizenship and land taken from the Algerian people. Thus, as the colonial elite stripped the indigenous people of their land and their rights, relegating them to an inferior status, they encouraged and facilitated the social and economic promotion of European settlers in Algeria, a situation that the colonized sorely resented. As Stora states, "Le refoulement foncier et le déracinement culturel de la population 'indigène' hors des territoires les plus riches, construisent un système de dépossession de l'identité" (*L'Algérie*, 23; The land dispossession and cultural uprooting of the indigenous population from the richest territories created a system of identity dispossession).

It is understandable that Marie's grandfather chooses not to share this important history lesson with his granddaughter; it does not put French colonization in Algeria in a favorable light. He does, however, speak to her of the beauty of the Algerian landscape, engraved in his memory. As Marnia Lazreg notes, this concept of the beauty of the land "anchored imperial identity in a tangible space implicitly deemed worth fighting for" (*Torture and the Twilight of Empire*, 175); it therefore projected the colonialist ideology. Thus, through this chance meeting on the train, the young girl gains knowledge of Algerian history that complements, if it does not completely offset, her family's colonialist narrative. We see, then, that the voyage, with its multiple possibilities—a journey to self-understanding; an exploration of Algerian history; a search for answers to the broad philosophical issues of morality, justice, and freedom—is indeed a transformational journey for the pied-noir's granddaughter, Marie, as well as for the other two travelers.

The Haunting Specter of Torture

The early years of this millennium witnessed the publication of several important works of fiction and nonfiction that raise the issue of torture by the French military during the Algerian War. In 2001 Louisette Ighilahriz's written testimony detailing her abuse at the hands of French paratroopers (a testimonial narrative that I examine in chapter 6) and retired French general

Paul Aussaresses's memoirs, in which he admits to having tortured Algerians, describes the methods used, and offers neither regrets nor apologies, both appeared.[9]

In her study *Torture and the Twilight of Empire: From Algiers to Baghdad* (2008), Marnia Lazreg defines torture as "the deliberate and willful infliction of various degrees of pain using a number of methods and devices, psychological as well as physical, on a *defenseless*, and *powerless* person for the purpose of obtaining information that a victim does not wish to reveal or does not have" (6). Her carefully documented analysis asserts that torture and terror were the weakened colonial power's final efforts to retain Algeria, with France's sense of imperial identity stifling most qualms of conscience. Part of the process of justifying immoral actions involved the concept of subversion, shifting from the notion that wars of decolonization are caused by injustices and inequalities inherent in the colonial system to a denigration of the FLN militants, labeling them subversive insurgents, rebels, and terrorists. Within this ideological framework of imperialism, Lazreg asserts, the workings of conscience are mediated by identity. In a war of decolonization, when imperial identity is separated from national identity, the rejection of torture becomes possible.

Examining Bey's novella, we find that while the torture of an Algerian schoolteacher suspected of collaborating with the FLN is at the core of the text, testimony concerning the victim's final hours remains sorely incomplete; the one witness who could speak up, the former soldier, remains silent. Hoping to learn the details from the soldier, who, if not an active participant, was at the very least a witness to her father's torture and execution, and challenging him to bear witness, to divulge what he saw and heard, the victim's daughter is first met with his defiance as he exclaims: "Personne n'est sorti indemne de cette guerre! Personne! Vous entendez!" (65; No one got out of this war unharmed! You must understand, no one!). Only at the end of the text does he acknowledge his presence at the fateful event, stating somewhat haltingly: "Je voulais vous dire... il me semble... oui... vous avez les mêmes yeux... le même regard que votre père. Vous lui ressemblez beaucoup" (72; I meant to tell you... it seems to me... yes... you have the same eyes... the same look as your father. You look a lot like him). With these words, he admits his connection to her father and his tragic demise without clearly assuming responsibility or avowing any culpability. Yet, if he was not the executioner, he was at the very least an accomplice to a war crime.

In her reading of this scene, Alison Rice assumes that the Frenchman's hesitant speech betrays profound emotion, revealing a loss of control and "an acute regret for having hurt the other" (*Polygraphies,* 124). In Rice's view, this acknowledgment of their shared history reflects a desire on his part to shed light on a situation that has hurt them both. Similarly, Siobhán McIlvanney states that the ellipses that occur in this passage, and indeed throughout the text, indicate the challenge faced by the characters in achieving "dialogic consensus" ("Fictionalising the Father," 213) as they search for words to express their relationship with the violent past that has marked them. The critic adds that if the difficulty of putting the past into language is owing to the inexpressible horror it contains, it is heightened by the presence of the (implicated) Other: "The hesitancy and vacillations characteristic of Bey's dialogue in *Entendez-vous...*, and evidenced in her title, are further fuelled by an acute awareness of the presence of the listener/reader and a sensitivity to his/her own difficulties in confronting a traumatic past, while simultaneously signaling a (communicative) space which s/he is invited to inhabit" (213). In other words, Bey's readers may not share the novelist's specific experience, but the process of reading her text allows them to engage in a participatory act that elicits a sympathetic response from those struggling with their own "wounded" memories.

By ending with the Frenchman's words, the text may leave the reader wondering whether these are indeed the final words spoken between the travelers or whether the two will continue their dialogue, finally unearthing the hidden history that the victim's daughter has been seeking all these years: the eyewitness account of the torture and death of her father. At the end of the novel, however, the historical blank remains. Yet, through a series of interior monologues—passages woven through the text that are set off in italics—the former soldier discloses a significant amount of information to the reader that he does not share with the Algerian traveler. For example, he recalls his captain's order to consider every Algerian suspect guilty of the crime for which he or she has been arrested, thereby justifying torture and execution. He remembers his encounter with the prisoner whose features, build, and glasses match those of the man in the photo that precedes the written text. And he recalls in detail the interrogation of the prisoner by an officer. As the officer prepares to leave the room, allowing the prisoner to decide whether he will cooperate with his interrogators or face torture, he, the prisoner, and the soldier in the room hear a terrible scream. At this moment the prisoner raises his head and looks directly at the soldier. Meeting the prisoner's gaze and thereby recognizing his humanity, he accepts some responsibility for the prisoner's fate. From this moment, the soldier will not be able to carry the imperial burden nor participate in the prisoner's fate—nor accept it—with an easy conscience. He now bears a moral wound.

Nevertheless, Jean, the former soldier, remains either unwilling or unable to uncover the crucial hidden history in its totality. Hence, we may conclude that the historical blank that must be recovered in order to heal the wounds of war, both his and hers, will remain buried in the presumed executioner's tortured mind. Clearly, the narrative gap, the torture session that is not described—transmitted neither verbally nor via an interior monologue—creates ambiguity with respect to the soldier's role in the schoolteacher's death. He may have neither witnessed nor participated in it, or he may have completely repressed it. Returning through memory to the scene, he recalls the commanding officer's words ordering him and a fellow soldier to remove the body following the victim's death, as well as their compliance with his orders. As they dump eight bodies in a clearing in the forest, he withdraws into silence, a defense against a growing sense of culpability. He masks the moral wound with silence that gives way, in part, during the face-to-face encounter with the victim's daughter.

If the encounter has a transformative effect on the presumed executioner, what significance does it hold for the victim's daughter? Having visualized her father's executioner as some sort of monster when she was a child—"un peu à l'image des bourreaux représentés dans les livres et les films d'histoire" (39; a little bit like the pictures of executioners in books and historical films)—she now finds her vision transformed. As the long night's train journey comes to an end, she realizes that an executioner remains undistinguishable from other men and women, "que les bourreaux ont des visages d'homme, [. . .] ils ont des mains d'homme, parfois même des réactions d'homme et rien ne permet de les distinguer des autres" (70; that executioners have men's faces [. . .] men's hands, sometimes even men's reactions, and nothing distinguishes them from others). The possibility of "doing torture," to borrow Lazreg's term, and thereby committing irreparable harm exists within us all.

Fleeing to Exile

As it delves into Algerian history, Bey's text, as we have already noted, is multidirectional. It leads back to World War II but also depicts the present reality of the dark decade, 1992–2002. In an uncanny repetition of history, Algeria during that violent period found itself in a situation that in some respects resembled the French colonial era as Algerian leaders faced an Islamist-led guerrilla movement that challenged the government's legitimacy. The FIS having won the first round of the 1991 parliamentary elections against the established FLN, the government canceled the second round, provoking an undeclared civil war that pitted the government and the army against the Islamists. The increasing violence that would eventually claim the lives of more than 120,000 people forced many secular French-educated individuals into exile. Within this context, the relationship between "home," the familiar and secure space, and "away," the strange and unfamiliar space, was altered by the political events that robbed citizens like Bey's protagonist of a secure and protected space. Home was not "a mythic space of desire in the diasporic imagination" (Ahmed, *Strange Encounters*, 89), for it was filled with danger. Indeed, the protagonist draws parallels between her father's French killers, of the past, and those Algerians currently committing atrocities on their own people, recognizing that previous victims have become the present perpetrators of evil: "Ce ne pouvait être que des monstres . . . comme ceux qui aujourd'hui, pour d'autres raisons et presque aux mêmes endroits, égorgent des enfants, des femmes et des hommes" (38–39; They had to be monsters . . . just the same as those who today, for different reasons but in more or less the same locations, slit the throats of children, women, and men).

By sending the Algerian woman on this journey to France, Bey introduces the intertwined themes of rupture and exile. Leaving home, with its predictable patterns, for the unknown, the protagonist assumes the role of stranger in a foreign land even though she speaks the French language perfectly and was born in Algeria when it was still considered part of France. She is quick to note the irony of her situation; the daughter of a militant Algerian national who gave his life to free his country from the colonial power, she finds herself seeking refuge in that very geopolitical space to escape the violence at home as Algeria descends into civil war. In this regard, she does not identify herself as either a migrant or an exile, but rather as a refugee in need of temporary refuge, "seulement un répit" (31; only a respite).

Having left Algeria, albeit temporarily, she resists speaking of her country to her fellow travelers. However, through his focus on the past—the Algerian War, in which he served—and not on the present civil unrest, the Frenchman draws her into his memory space, the conflicted past they share. Yet, as past and present come together through this unexpected encounter, the woman may indeed be better equipped to deal with her present reality, her life as a political refugee in France. In other words, if she unconsciously feared the dramatic encounter that the trip to France would make possible, the meeting has now taken place; she may now move on to face new challenges.

Writing as Resistance

The journey as metaphor allows the writer to reflect on the role of politically engaged literature in combating dangerous and misguided ideology. This is most evident when the Algerian woman interprets the situation in which she finds herself—in a train compartment with two strangers—as the setting for a TV talk show and comments with some irony:

> Et voilà! La boucle est bouclée! Une petite-fille de pieds-noirs, un ancien combattant, une fille de fellaga. C'est presque irréel. Qui donc aurait pu imaginer une scène pareille? Cela ressemble à un plateau télé, réuni pour une émission par des journalistes en quête de vérité, désireux de lever le voile pour faire la lumière sur *"le passé douloureux de la France."* (40, italics in the original)

> (That's it! We have come full circle! A granddaughter of pieds-noirs, a war veteran, a daughter of a *fellaga*. It's almost unreal. Who could have imagined such a scene? It looks like a TV show, everyone brought together for a program led by journalists in search of the truth, eager to lift the veil, to shed light on "the painful past of France.")

Commenting on the constructed and therefore somewhat artificial, nature of the plot the novelist has set in motion, Bey's protagonist cautions readers to be mindful of the fact that only in fiction (including carefully orchestrated public performances such as those we are accustomed to seeing on television) would it be possible for a presumed executioner, a member of the victim's family, and a descendant of the colonizing power to meet face to face. Indeed, the improbability of this encounter is reinforced by the introduction of theatrical elements reminiscent of seventeenth-century French theater. We find, for example, the three unities of French classicism—the unities of time, place, and action—which, as McIlvanney notes, give the novel a sense of immediacy and claustrophobia ("Fictionalising the Father," 207), encouraging critics to view the text's construction as a three-act play (Achille, "Des Arabes, j'en suis sûre!," 253).

Yet, as the protagonist points to the limits of fiction, Bey's writings affirm literature's power to effect change. In a work in which individuals are transformed by key encounters, the novelist confirms the power of the pen in the struggle to keep the world a just and ethical place. Fiction may be a refuge from painful reality, past or present, but the politically engaged literature that the critic Barbara Harlow terms *resistance literature* has been considered by writers, readers, and the public at large to be an effective means to fight evil and injustice. As the Algerian novelist Tahar Djaout wrote shortly before his death at the hands of Islamic terrorists in Algiers in 1993:

> Le silence c'est la mort
> Et toi, si tu parles tu meurs
> Alors, dis et meurs.
>
> (Silence is death
> And you, if you speak out, you die
> So, speak and die.)[10]

By setting her novel during the dark decade of the civil war, when Islamic fundamentalists were brutally silencing writers such as Djaout, who opposed their religious and cultural policies, Bey affirms the importance of the literature of resistance and the power of the pen.

Nevertheless, by embarking upon her literary career during the period of civil strife and remaining in Algeria throughout the turbulent years, the novelist experienced further trauma. She was deeply shaken by the violence that surrounded her, particularly the death of her friend and colleague Salah Chouaki, shot in his car on his way to work in September 1994. The assassination was very difficult for her to deal with and marked a turning point: "After his death, I began to write my first novel" (Bey, "Interview," 16). We may conclude that the assassinations of the novelist's father and, much later, her close friend, occurring in two critical periods of Algerian history, not only shape this text but lay the groundwork for Bey's later writing and continued political engagement. Indeed, the novelist's political activism led her to establish Paroles et Écriture, an association founded in 2001 to promote women's writing. Adapting the format of *ateliers d'écritures* (reading and writing workshops), the association encourages Algerian women to find inspiration in their life stories and to use writing as a tool for empowerment.[11]

Convinced of the importance of life writing, she reflects upon the emotional impact the writing of *Entendez-vous dans les montagnes...* had upon her. Commenting upon the experience in the diary she kept in 2002, the same year the novella was published and as the years of civil strife drew to a close, she writes:

> Toujours la même émotion en découvrant la forme achevée que prend un texte que l'on a écrit et qui ne nous appartient plus. Une émotion plus forte encore cette fois, parce que j'y retrouve l'image et la présence de mon père. Ce livre est sorti de moi avec une douleur plus grande que celle que j'ai dû éprouver à la mort de mon père, puisque j'étais trop jeune pour réaliser vraiment ce qui nous arrivait. Cela fait plusieurs années que je tourne autour de "ça", retardant le moment d'affronter, de regarder en face, de mettre en mots une scène que je pourrais qualifier de primitive, au sens freudien du terme, dans le mesure où toutes mes représentations du monde réel, tous mes questionnements ont pris leur source dans cette scène mille fois vécue dans mes fantasmes. ("Faut-il aller chercher des rêves," 40)

> (I always feel the same emotion when confronting the finished form of a text I have written and know it is no longer solely mine. This time the emotion is even stronger because I find the image and the presence of my father. I wrote this book with greater pain than the pain I felt at my father's death,

because I was too young to understand what was happening to us. For years I circled "it," putting off the moment to tackle it, to face it, to put into words what I should call a primal scene in the Freudian sense of the term, in the sense that all my representations of the real world, all my questioning, stems from this scene lived a thousand times in my imagination.)

With these words, Bey emphasizes her personal relationship to the text, which allowed her, through fiction, to address her unhealed wound. In this journal she further explains that a key moment for her in the text occurs as the Algerian woman, taking leave of the Frenchman at the train station, turns to thank him for having carried her suitcase (41). For Bey, the respect for civility and politeness in these exceptional circumstances is both necessary and inevitable. In life and in art, the return to protocol and social convention between the two individuals illustrates the contradiction inherent in social relations, revealing that while formalities continue to characterize Franco-Algerian relations, they mask wounds and misunderstandings, on the one hand, and facilitate continuing dialogue and cooperation, on the other.

In conclusion, the text shows that when the victim and the perpetrator speak with each other, listen attentively to each other, and thereby learn from the mistakes and indeed the crimes of the past, then, and only then, will the wounds heal.[12] Grounded in a traumatic incident, this text, which proposed using memory to unearth hidden history, must be viewed as an affirmation of the importance of communication between individuals, communities, and nations. In this regard, the critics Susan Ireland and Patricia Proulx find that Bey, in her portrayal of the characters' mutual reconciliation with the past, creates a space of shared memory ("Cultural Trauma and Narrative Recovery," 120). As they suggest, through the staged confrontation between victim and executioner, an event made possible in the realm of literature, and perhaps nowhere else, a possible model for reconciliation appears.

Perhaps most important in this admittedly staged process is the understanding on the part of the protagonist that the desired recovery of the narrative gap—the torture and death that are never brought back through memory—is, in the final analysis, less important than the act of communication that binds the two strangers on the train. Having grappled since childhood with a sense of loss and uncertainty about the fate of her missing father, the Algerian woman finds that "même si tout n'est pas dit, même si une douloureuse palpitation la fait encore frémir, *quelque chose s'est dénoué en elle*" (69–70, italics mine; even if everything hasn't been said, even if a painful throbbing still makes her shudder, something within her has been set free). With this new sense of freedom, and a new relationship to the past, healing can begin. With healing occurring in the realm of fiction, Bey's text leaves us to ponder whether the protagonist's reality has become the writer's as well.

5 COLLECTIVE TRAUMA, COLLECTIVE MEMORY

Leïla Sebbar's *La Seine était rouge* and *Une enfance dans la guerre: Algérie, 1954–1962*

While France and Algeria produced national narratives of the Algerian War of Independence that have at times elided, hidden, or silenced significant events and historical figures, Algerian women's narratives, fiction as well as oral and written testimony, have succeeded in creating a counterdiscourse. Bringing in voices from the margins, uncovering hidden histories, silenced stories, and forgotten combatants, they provide a much-needed corrective to official versions of events as well as to the epic narratives and romantic fictions that all wars tend to inspire. In this regard, Leïla Sebbar—novelist, essayist, and editor of collections of autobiographical sketches—has become an increasingly important voice in postcolonial literary studies and a significant contributor to this counterdiscourse.

The daughter of an Algerian father and a French mother, both teachers in the French colonial school system, Sebbar was born in Aflou, a small town in western Algeria, in 1941. She spent her childhood and adolescence in Algeria, much of it during the war, and her entire adult life in France. Despite the geographical distance separating her from the land of her birth, her literary work reveals a constant and persistent preoccupation with Algeria: its colonial past, its postcolonial present, and its traces in France. Reflecting on her literary corpus, written over a thirty-year period, she acknowledges the profound effect the Algerian War has had on her writing. In a radio interview conducted in 2017, she stated: "La guerre est au cœur de ce que j'écris;

la guerre est toujours là" (The war is at the heart of my writing; the war is always there).¹

Following the publication of several novels, short stories, and essays exploring the themes of history, memory, exile, and identity, Sebbar appropriates the Algerian war story with the publication in 1999 of *La Seine était rouge* (*The Seine Was Red*), a novel that probes the massacre of Algerians in Paris on October 17, 1961, and its cover-up. In the years following that publication, she has continued to delve into Algerian history, most recently, in 2016, with *Une enfance dans la guerre: Algérie, 1954–1962* (A childhood in war: Algeria, 1954–1962), a collection of written testimonies of men and women who, having experienced the Algerian War as children, draw upon these memories.

In this chapter, a close reading of these two texts that form part of Sebbar's literary corpus but represent different genres—one a work of historical fiction, the other a polyphonic collection of autobiographical vignettes—we find the writer exploring the interrelated themes of collective trauma and occulted history as she brings oral and written testimony into the process of anamnesis, the recovery of historical memory. At the risk of straying somewhat from the subject of this book—Algerian women and the independence struggle—I include these texts for two reasons. First, the novel *La Seine était rouge* is a reminder that the Algerian War was carried out in France as well as in Algeria. Second, *Une enfance dans la guerre* is a form of reference for writers such as Yamina Mechakra and Maïssa Bey, whose experience of war in their childhood marked their adult works. Indeed, the previous chapter, a study of Maïssa Bey's novella *Entendez-vous dans les montagnes . . .* , explored the quest of those who were children during the violent conflict to come to terms with the war of liberation and its legacy. In this regard, Sebbar shares Bey's concern; both writers present protagonists who, as children during the liberation struggle, were too young to fully comprehend the complexity of the situation in which they found themselves; they return to the traumatic events as mature adults, having acquired the necessary analytical skills and historical underpinning.

Moreover, Sebbar, like Bey, writing during the dark decade of Algeria's undeclared civil war, also focuses on the Algerian War, revisiting the events of October 17, 1961, the violent Sunday night in Paris that has come to be known by writers, historians, and critics, as the "Battle of Paris."² Finally, as the two writers situate their texts in the 1990s, with flashbacks to the Algerian War, and refer as well to World War II, they both engage in the complex relationship of past and present that the critic Michael Rothberg terms *multidirectional memory,* which brings various historical moments to bear upon one another.

Writing from the Crossroads

Sebbar first came upon the literary scene in France as a fiction writer, with novels of Algerian immigration, most notably the Sherazade trilogy, *Shérazade, 17 ans, brune, frisée, les yeux verts* (1982); *Les carnets de Shérazade* (1985); and *Le fou de Shérazade* (1991). Her protagonist, Shérazade, is the rebellious, inquisitive and intrepid teenage daughter of impoverished Algerian immigrants living in one of the many housing projects on the outskirts of Paris. Significantly, the adolescent has had no direct experience of the Algerian War and knows very little about it. Her lack of knowledge is not surprising since, as the critic Anne Donadey points out, until a 1983 edict introduced the history of decolonization into the French secondary-school curriculum, students of Maghrebian descent, like Shérazade, did not learn about the Algerian War in the classroom (*Recasting Colonialism,* 19). In Sebbar's text, Shérazade, a high-school student who has run away from home and dropped out of school, is a voracious reader who develops an interest in Algerian literature and a taste for Orientalist painting; both literature and art fuel her interest in the ancestral homeland. Yet, despite her intention to revisit Algeria, she never makes the journey. For Sebbar's protagonist, Algeria remains largely imaginative space.

Examining these early texts that depicted the world of marginalized North African immigrants and their descendants, most of whom were born in France, critics saw the novelist using the craft of writing to lessen her personal sense of exile.[3] Sebbar confirms this view in an epistolary exchange with the Canadian writer Nancy Huston, *Lettres parisiennes: Autopsie de l'exil,* in 1986. In this text Sebbar identifies herself as a *croisée,* a hybrid at the intersection of European and North African cultures:

> Je suis là, à la croisée, enfin sereine, à ma place, en somme, puisque je suis une croisée qui cherche une filiation et qui écrit dans une lignée, toujours la

même reliée à l'histoire, à la mémoire, à l'identité, à la tradition et à la transmission, je veux dire à la recherche d'une ascendance et d'une descendance, d'une place dans l'histoire d'une famille, d'une communauté, d'un peuple, au regard de l'histoire et de l'univers. (138)

(I am there at the crossroads, serene at last, finally in my place, for I am a *croisée*, a hybrid in search of connection, writing within a lineage, one that is always the same. It is tied to history, to memory, to identity, to tradition, and to transmission, by which I mean the search for ascendants and descendants, seeking a place in the history of a family, a community, a people, with regard to history and the universe.)

As the correspondence between Sebbar and Huston sheds light upon the struggle of exilic writers to find their place in the world, it encourages Sebbar to express a personal and authentic self. Writing to Huston, she confides, "Et puis, pour moi, la fiction c'est la suture qui masque la blessure, l'écart, entre les deux rives" (138; And so for me, fiction is the suture that masks the wound, the distance between the two shores), using an extended metaphor to explain that the two shores of the Mediterranean are separated not only by an extensive body of water but by a divided history and that for her, fiction eases the pain of a fractured identity.[4] Coming of age in a colonial society deeply divided and then at war, the daughter of the colonized and the colonizer considers herself an outsider, if not an outcast, rejected by both warring camps (*Une enfance*, 243).

Yet, within this political upheaval Sebbar finds her home space in literature, writing within a lineage "tied to history, to memory, to identity, to tradition, and to transmission." Drawn to the process of recovering and reinterpreting colonial history, she joins postcolonial historians such as Benjamin Stora and Raphaëlle Branche in opposing the collective amnesia surrounding the events of the Algerian War.[5] By focusing on the events that took place in Paris on October 17, 1961, she reminds her readers that the war extended beyond Algeria's geographic boundaries to Metropolitan France. In this regard, Ali Haroun refers to the French branch of the FLN, La Fédération de France du FLN, as "La Septième Wilaya," the Seventh Military District; the other six were located in Algeria.[6]

The Fateful Day: Sunday, October 17, 1961

On October 17, 1961, the Fédération de France du FLN organized a peaceful demonstration of Algerians in Paris to protest a curfew imposed on them by the head of the Paris police at the time, Maurice Papon. An increase in FLN attacks against the police in Paris during the summer of 1961 had given Papon an excuse to impose a curfew that kept Algerians off the streets from 8:30 p.m. to 5:30 a.m., thereby limiting the movements of those he considered to be FLN sympathizers and supporters. Occurring during the final months of the Algerian War, the protest march turned violent as the Paris police attacked the demonstrators who had come to the capital from the shantytowns, primarily on the northern outskirts of the city, and working-class neighborhoods such as La Goutte d'Or and Belleville and attempted to demonstrate peacefully. Men had brought their wives and children; many families were dressed in their Sunday best to march on a rainy Sunday evening. None were armed. It is now estimated that thirty thousand Algerian men, women, and children took part in the demonstration (Einaudi, *La Bataille de Paris*, 183).[7]

The Fédération de France (the FLN in France) had called the march for several reasons. First, it sought to challenge the curfew as a way to demonstrate their support among Algerian laborers in France. Second, the organization opposed the curfew because it made the collecting of funds from the immigrant Algerian community in France more difficult.[8] Finally, the Fédération de France was convinced that by demonstrating strength in Paris it would improve its standing politically within the FLN, particularly since, as the historian Joshua Cole points out, factions within the organization were competing for power as the war was drawing to an end ("Remembering the Battle of Paris," 24). Unfortunately, the Fédération de France was not prepared for the level of violence the police would use on unarmed men, women, and children or for the ability of the police to cover up the violent repression.

According to various accounts, the estimated number of Algerians killed varies between two hundred and three hundred people (Haroun, *La 7e wilaya*, 322; Einaudi, *La Bataille de Paris*, 14; Laronde, "Effets d'histoire," 142). Many of the dead perished in the Seine. Others disappeared, their bodies dumped in the woods around Paris. More than eleven thousand were rounded up and held in stadiums. Of those, many were deported to Algeria, where they remained prisoners in camps until the end of the war or were sent back to their home villages (Jones, "Les fantômes d'une mémoire meurtrie," 92). The police did not limit their assaults to male demonstrators. The historian Jean-Luc Einaudi dedicates his text to Fatima Bédar, a fifteen-year-old Algerian girl who drowned in the Canal Saint-Denis.[9]

Emphasizing the historical importance of the brutal repression, the historians Jim House and Neil MacMaster conclude that it was probably the largest "peacetime" massacre in Western Europe, for at the time France did not acknowledge the Algerian conflict to be a war ("Une journée portée disparue," 267). Yet, despite the extent of the violence, French authorities were largely able to keep the massacre out of the newspapers at the time by giving the press false information, minimizing the number of casualties, and not admitting to the number of Algerians arrested and deported. The critic Michel Laronde has called this cover-up an *acte forclos*, an action deliberately placed beyond the realm of official history by institutionalized silence ("Effets d'histoire," 147).

Significantly, the official silence that enveloped the violent repression of October 1961 in France did not endure. As House and MacMaster explain, an underground countermemory of the massacre soon emerged, nurtured over the years by immigrant communities in France, groups for whom the family was a major vector of memory transmission. By the mid-1980s, numerous works of fiction and nonfiction, films and documentaries, were circulating.[10] In addition, La Marche pour l'égalité et contre le racism (labeled by the media the Marche des Beurs), which took place from October 15 to December 3, 1983, in response to a series of racist crimes against North Africans during the summer, not only expressed the concerns of Algerian immigrants and their descendants in France but drew national attention to their problems as well. Rallying to the cry "Vivre ensemble avec nos différences" (Live together with our differences), the demonstrators concluded a six-week march in Paris, where President Mitterand welcomed a crowd of one hundred thousand young demonstrators. This event was viewed as a powerful statement, a critical counterpoint to the violent repression of the 1961 demonstration of their parents' generation ("Les fantômes d'une mémoire meurtrie," 94; Laronde, *Autour du roman beur*, 22). Finally, in 1999, the year that Sebbar published her novella, the French prime minister, Lionel Jospin, announced on May 5 that the French government would facilitate access to public archives dealing with the events of October 17, 1961, and on June 10 the French National Assembly recognized the eight-year war of liberation as the Algerian War.

A university student in Aix-en-Provence in 1961, Sebbar first wrote about the October 17 massacre for a special issue of *Actualité de l'émigration hébdo* in 1990 to commemorate the twenty-ninth anniversary of the tragic event. At the request of the editor, Abdelkader Djeghloul, a sociologist at the University of Oran, she contributed a short memoir to the issue, a text that served to retrieve the fateful day from her memory and help her understand its impact.[11] In a letter she writes:

> Je n'étais pas à Paris lors du 17 octobre 1961. J'étais à Aix en Provence, où j'ai oublié l'Algérie, cette amnésie a duré longtemps. La France c'était la liberté. Vivre enfin sans la peur de la guerre, sans surveillance, sans protection. L'Algérie a fait retour après les deux révolutions culturelles de Mai 68 et du Mouvement des Femmes auxquels j'ai participé.
>
> (I was not in Paris on October 17, 1961. I was in Aix-en-Provence, where I forgot Algeria; this amnesia lasted a long time. France was freedom. I was finally able to live without fear of war, without surveillance, without protection. Algeria entered my consciousness again following the two cultural revolutions in which I participated, May 1968 and the Women's Movement.)[12]

Sebbar's contribution to the journal, a short text entitled "La Seine était rouge," charts chronologically the stages by which she retrieves the event from memory: 1961, 1976, 1986, 1997.

She begins the text by expressing sentiments of distance and unease in Aix-en-Provence, where, sequestered in her student room that fateful day, she hears a voice on the radio announcing the October 17 demonstration, and recalls:

> Moi je suis seule, recluse, et dans ce fauteuil d'où je ne bouge pas, j'écoute l'histoire violente et mémorable qui est en train d'avoir lieu en même temps que je suis assise là. (96)

(I am alone, reclusive, and seated in this armchair from which I don't stir, I am listening to the violent and memorable history that is taking place while I am seated there.)

In 1976, fifteen years after the event, while examining a newspaper photo in which women in the Algerian countryside are waving an Algerian flag at the end of the war, she finds the image bringing back the sounds and voices associated with the anticolonial struggle and begins to write about Algeria. In 1986, a second photograph, one in which an Algerian woman is waving her country's flag, this time in an urban setting, releases the memory of the fateful day when she, a student in Aix-en-Provence, heard a news report of the demonstration in Paris. As the essay reveals the importance Sebbar accords, on one hand, to the passage of time, and on the other, to sound and image in the process of restoring memory, the publication marks the beginning of her search for transparency regarding the violent response of the Paris police force, a quest that leads her to construct the novel as an anamnesis, or collective memory.

A Community Remembers

Sebbar's emphasis upon collective memory mirrors the collective nature of her literary project; she is one of several novelists to examine the massacre and the silence that first surrounded it. In fact, at the beginning of *La Seine était rouge* she acknowledges several other writers, French and Beur (French nationals born in France to North African immigrant parents), who preceded her in this endeavor: Didier Daeninckx, Nacer Kettane, Mehdi Lallaoui, Georges Mattei.[13] Situating herself among this group, she is the first to use the historical event as the entire subject of a novel (Donadey, "Retour sur mémoire," 190).[14]

Entitling her novel *La Seine était rouge*, Sebbar defines the theme of her text: the violent repression that turned the river red with the demonstrators' blood—metaphorically, if not physically. She is fully aware that since many survivors had been severely beaten, lost family members, or been sent to internment camps in Algeria, the massacre caused individual and collective trauma within the Algerian immigrant community in France, particularly in Paris. Thus, many victims who could bear witness to the event were unable—or unwilling—to talk about the traumatic day, thereby threatening the links of historical transmission. Their silence is not surprising; in his study of collective trauma, the sociologist Kai Erikson writes that traumatized individuals withdraw into a "protective envelope," a place of loneliness and isolation ("Notes on Trauma and Community," 186). He adds, however, that when trauma is shared, it can serve as a source of bonding for the community, thereby alleviating some of the individual pain and promoting healing for the individual and the community (186).

Sebbar comes to the historical event with her own legacy of family silence, her father having continually postponed speaking to her of his experiences during the Algerian War. Accused of belonging to a network that distributed medical supplies to the FLN, Mohammed Sebbar was arrested in 1957 and held prisoner for several months, an incident his daughter recounts in *Je ne parle pas la langue de mon père* (I do not speak my father's language), a collection of essays published several years after the novel appeared. Although neither he nor his French wife was deeply involved in the resistance, they supported the struggle for independence and had friends and colleagues among FLN militants.[15] Moreover, as the principal of a school for Arab children, Mohammed Sebbar was a potential target of colonial extremists.

Given her father's silence, it is not surprising that she would choose to structure her novel as a quest narrative in which a trio of young protagonists embarks upon a journey in search of answers to a historical event that their elders refuse to give them or at least postpone. As already noted, by situating her text in late 1996, with flashbacks to October 17, 1961, as well as references to 1943, when the Vichy government rounded up French Jews in Paris, deporting them to Nazi concentration camps, Sebbar, like Bey, brings three historical events to bear upon one another—World War II, the Algerian War, and Algeria's undeclared civil war of the 1990s. She, like Bey, introduces the concept the critic Michael Rothberg terms *multidirectional memory*, a key structuring element of Bey's novella as well as her own. Significantly, Rothberg discusses Sebbar's text in his critical study, noting that not only does the novel evoke multiple historical conflicts—World War II, the French War in Indochina, Napoleon's invasion of Egypt, May 1968, and Algeria's undeclared civil war of the 1990s—but it concerns itself with "the very structure of collective memory" (*Multidirectional Memory*, 298).

Despite the brevity of her text—138 pages in the original French edition,

116 in the English translation—Sebbar offers her readers a complex narrative that alternates time frames, interweaves multiple narratives, and takes her readers to a variety of memory sites throughout Paris. Set in motion by a young girl's quest for historical truth, the text involves three main characters, none of whom had been born when the events of October 17, 1961, took place: Amel, a sixteen-year-old teenager who is the daughter of Algerian immigrants; Omer, a twenty-seven-year-old journalist living in exile in France because of the internal strife and violence in Algeria in the 1990s; and Louis, twenty-five, the son of a French couple who supported the Algerian cause. Through her choice of protagonists, Sebbar focuses on the three principal groups for whom anamnesis is crucial: Algerian immigrants and their descendants in France, Algerians fleeing strife at home, and French partisans of Algerian independence.

The three individuals contribute in different ways to unearthing hidden history. As Amel's personal quest for historical truth inspires Omer, he joins her in reinscribing historical plaques that mark memory sites throughout Paris. Louis's film, a documentary about the October massacre, includes Amel's mother's testimony. The film gives the young girl the historical information that her mother, Noria, has been withholding from her about the event. Significantly, the trio's bonds of friendship originate in their mothers' connection to one another; the three women and Lalla, Amel's grandmother, had become close friends during Algeria's liberation struggle.

After evoking the tension between one generation committed to silence and a later one in search of anamnesis, Sebbar resolves it in part when Amel and Noria engage in the process of unlocking the past. It must be noted, however, that Noria gives her account of the events of October 17, 1961, by speaking directly into Louis's camera. Facing the eye of the camera, she re-creates scenes of trauma and evokes her personal, painful sense of loss. Noria cannot yet speak directly to her daughter about the massacre, but she can bear witness via a different medium. Here, Sebbar shows that when crucial dialogue between individuals fails, in this case communication between a mother and daughter, the message can nevertheless be articulated through other means. In the final analysis, what matters most is the message, not the means of transmission. As for Amel, with Louis's film available to her, she obtains the information she has been seeking without violating her mother's secrecy. Finally, by acknowledging the importance of documentary films to the process of breaking the silence surrounding the massacre, the novelist pays tribute to the filmmaker Jacques Penijel, whose 1962 documentary *October à Paris* was censored by the French authorities before it could reach the public but was shown twenty-five years later at Papon's trial in Bordeaux.[16]

Breaking the Silence, Bearing Witness

Beginning the text with the sentence "Sa mère ne lui a rien dit ni la mère de sa mère" (13; Her mother said nothing to her, nor did her mother's mother [1]), Sebbar privileges orality, affirming the importance she accords to capturing the spoken word. Acknowledging Algeria's rich oral tradition, which is passed down through generations of women, she foregrounds female links of transmission, of women speaking to women. Even though the opening phrase appears to signal a break in the line of transmission, it is only a temporary break. Lalla tells Amel that she is waiting for the appropriate moment to share the painful story with her. By informing Amel that the disclosure of important information calls for maturity, the grandmother imparts her wisdom to her granddaughter.[17] We may interpret Lalla's reticence as affirming her belief that her words will cause suffering both to her and to her granddaughter when she relates what she experienced and witnessed that day. Yet by delaying the moment, Lalla, like Sebbar's own father, may take her unspoken testimony to the grave, leaving Amel, and by extension the reader, with a significant historical blank.

As the text charts the quest undertaken by Amel, Omer, and Louis to unearth hidden history, the novel interrupts their trajectory with two forms of testimony. Multiple voices—French policemen, harkis (their Algerian collaborators in the French police force), Algerian demonstrators, French supporters of the Algerian cause, and bystanders—give their perspective on the past events. Amel's mother, Noria, presents an extended recollection of the historic day, related in six segments. Thus, through a collective process of diverse eyewitness accounts, Sebbar shows how differing points of view come into play as one recovers hidden history. With thirty-seven chapter headings that alternately name places in Paris, eyewitnesses, the three protagonists, and their mothers, Sebbar models the structure of her text after Einaudi's *La Bataille de Paris;* the latter details the events of October 17, 1961, noting each place where a violent encounter between the police and the demonstrators occurred, the time it occurred, the name of the witness, and either a brief description by the historian or an eyewitness account (99–180).

In contrast to these adult male voices, Noria's testimony is more personal. A victim of the tragic event, she evokes the fear she experienced as a child that day and the greater distress she felt upon learning of her father's arrest. Most importantly, she provides the perspective of an adult looking back on a childhood experience. Is she a reliable witness? What did she understand at the age of seven? What has she forgotten in the intervening years? Indeed, Noria admits to a faulty memory: "J'ai oublié de te dire ... Louis, quand on raconte, on oublie, tout vient dans le désordre, je ne peux plus dire exactement l'emploi du temps de ce soir-là" (113; I forgot to tell you ... Louis, when you tell a story, you forget, everything comes back pell-mell. I can't quite recall the precise order of events that evening [89]).

Despite her disclaimer, Noria proves to be a perceptive eyewitness. Her account includes details that a child would remember—the green and white ribbons in her hair, her first look at the Saint Michel fountain—as well as her observation of Algerians being arrested—"J'ai vu ces hommes debout, les mains en l'air, à côté du bus, les policiers avec des matraques" (61; I saw men standing with their hands in the air, next to the bus. The police had billy clubs [43])—and her glimpse of a dead body on the sidewalk (86; 66). She communicates what she sees clearly even if she lacked the maturity at the time to analyze the events of the day with accuracy and precision. Moreover, Noria prefaces her account of these acts of violence with that of an earlier event, the assassination of her uncle in the weeks preceding the demonstration. A member of the Mouvement national algérien (MNA), rival political party to the FLN, he was a victim of the internecine Algerian struggle that became part of Algeria's hidden history, a conflict Sebbar does not wish to overlook. Significantly, when Noria, as an adult, asks her father whether he knew that his brother was a member of a rival political faction, he refuses to answer her question. Just as her own daughter, Amel, cannot persuade her to speak directly to her of the massacres, she fails to break her father's silence surrounding events of the Algerian War.

Why are the Algerians silent? First, having experienced traumatic events, men and women often do not want to transmit a legacy of pain and suffering to the next generation. Second, the experience was a clear defeat for the

Algerians, particularly for the FLN organizers, who were completely unprepared for the violent response of the Paris police. Finally, because Algerian culture teaches men and women to distinguish between public and private events, male and female space, the women demonstrating alongside the men in the political demonstration considered their role to be primarily supportive, their own realm being the private world of domestic space. Hence, they leave the narrative largely to men.[18]

Yet their experience of participating in the march and its violent repression by the Paris police results in political awakening. Several days later, on October 20, the Fédération de France called Algerian women to hold another protest march. As Noria recalls, the group of several hundred women marched to Saint Anne Hospital, in the proximity of La Santé Prison, where Algerians were held (128; 104).[19] Protesting with her mother and the other women shouting slogans—"Libération de nos époux et de nos enfants" (128; Freedom for our husbands and children [104]); "À bas le couvre-feu raciste" (128; End the racist curfew [104]); "Indépendance totale de l'Algérie" (128; Full independence for Algeria [104])—Noria is both participant and witness to the emergence of Algerian women's political voice. By recovering her mother's testimony, Amel comes to understand her mother's evolution.

Using a narrative strategy that emphasizes the bonds between mother and daughter, Sebbar ends each chapter preceding Noria's testimony except the last with the sentence "Amel entend la voix de sa mère" (32, 57, 111; Amel hears her mother's voice [27, 40, 87]) or "Amel entend sa mère" (83; Amel hears her mother [63]). Then, as Amel and Omer wait for the plane that will take them to Egypt, where they will join Louis, the sentence changes to "*On* entend la voix de *la* mère" (126, italics mine; *They* hear *the* mother's voice [102]), emphasizing the transformational effect of Noria's testimony on her daughter and her friend. Yet, it is also possible to read the sentence as "*We* hear *the* mother's voice," thereby bringing the community at large, including Sebbar's readers, into the process of anamnesis. Thus, this fictional account, like Bey's, suggests that a collective narrative of the past is possible. Just as the critics Susan Ireland and Patricia Proulx find Bey's protagonists, the former French soldier and the Algerian woman, creating a space of shared memory through dialogue ("Cultural Trauma and Narrative Recovery," 120), the critic Anne Donadey considers the shift from "*her* mother" to "*the* mother" the signal that as Noria comes to emblematize the mother of all those participating in the process of anamnesis, a collective narrative of the past begins to form ("Anamnesis and National Reconciliation," 53–54). This collective narrative is, Donadey argues, the prerequisite to reconciliation.

Memory Tags

For Sebbar's young protagonists, the act of remembering includes creating monuments to the courageous individuals who participated in Algeria's struggle for freedom. Hence, the young people not only encourage their parents to bear witness; they also edit French commemorative plaques that honor fallen World War II heroes, adding citations that proclaim the heroism of Algerian militants.

The first plaque they "edit" is on a wall of the Santé Prison. It reads, in bold letters:

> EN CETTE PRISON
> LE 11 NOVEMBRE 1940
> FURENT INCARCÉRÉS
> DES LYCÉENS ET DES ÉTUDIANTS
> QUI À L'APPEL DU GÉNÉRAL DE GAULLE
> SE DRESSÈRENT LES PREMIERS
> CONTRE L'OCCUPANT. (29)

> (ON NOVEMBER 11 1940
> IN THIS PRISON WERE HELD
> HIGH SCHOOL AND UNIVERSITY STUDENTS
> WHO, AT THE CALL OF GENERAL DE GAULLE,
> WERE THE FIRST TO RISE UP
> AGAINST THE OCCUPATION. [14])

Omer adds in bold letters in red paint:

> 1954–1962
> DANS CETTE PRISON FURENT GUILLOTINÉS
> DES RÉSISTANTS ALGÉRIENS

QUI SE DRESSÈRENT
CONTRE L'OCCUPANT FRANÇAIS. (30)

(1954–1962
IN THIS PRISON
WERE GUILLOTINED
ALGERIAN RESISTANTS
WHO ROSE UP
AGAINST THE FRENCH OCCUPATION. [15])

By remaining as faithful as possible to the vocabulary and syntax of the original commemorative language, he establishes a parallel between both texts and events. Superimposing their commemorative words in red paint, Amel and Omer pay homage to the martyrs drowned the day the Seine turned red with Algerian martyrs' blood.

Studying the two inscriptions, we note an important resemblance and a crucial difference between them. First, to emphasize the parallel between the two historical events, the altered plaque informs readers that both militant groups were protesting foreign occupation: the French high-school students rose up against one foreign occupier, the Germans; the Algerian nationalists rose up against another, the French colonizers. Second, to emphasize the difference between the two events commemorating heroic resistance to occupation, the altered plaque informs us that in contrast to the French students, who were *imprisoned,* the Algerian militants were *guillotined.*

The French historian Pierre Nora notes in the introduction to his extensive study of the relationship between history, memory, and memory sites that *lieux de mémoire,* or places of memory, share three qualities; they are material, symbolic, and functional ("Entre mémoire et histoire," xxxiv). For example, the war memorials erected in most French villages following World War I possess these characteristics. They are material, made of stone. They are symbolic, representing France's loss of almost an entire generation of young men conscripted to serve in the French army at the time. They are functional, listing the names of all the soldiers from that village who died in the war. By creating plaques to commemorate historical events—first the death sentence carried out against Algerian nationalists in the Santé Prison, then the homage to victims of the massacre of October 17, 1961—Sebbar's protagonists create their own *lieux de mémoire*. These memory sites are equally material, symbolic, and functional. They are durable, the red paint permeating the stone. They are symbolic, representing Algeria's loss of human life. They are functional, reminding all passersby of the historical event.

The altered plaque, which links one historical period with another, an example of multidirectional memory, encourages Donadey to draw the parallel between the *Vichy syndrome*, the French historian Henry Rousso's term designating France's inability to deal with its Vichy past, and the *Algerian syndrome*, a term Donadey uses for France's inability to deal with its Algerian past. In both cases, she notes, the shadowy French functionary Maurice Papon played an important role. A Nazi collaborator during World War II, Papon—who died in February 2007—was head of the Paris police at the time of the Algerian massacre on October 17, 1961. Having first ordered the deportation of French Jews to Nazi concentration camps in the Vichy era, then serving in Algeria to destroy the FLN, he subsequently ordered the violent repression of the Algerian demonstration as the Algerian War was drawing to a close ("Retour sur mémoire," 187–94). One of the handwritten notices Amel and Omar scrawl on a hotel façade explicitly condemns Papon for his brutality:

Ici des Algériens ont été matraqués
sauvagement par la police du Préfet Papon
le 17 octobre 1961. (88)

(On this spot Algerians were savagely beaten
by Prefect Papon's police
October 17, 1961. [67])

As the hidden history of repression is brought to light, the date confirmed, and participants such as Papon identified, anamnesis is confirmed.

By disclosing the hidden history of repression in this way, Amel and Omar contribute to the collective process of remembering, which extends beyond the pages of the novel. On October 17, 2001, the mayor of Paris, Bertrand Delanoë, placed a long-awaited commemorative plaque on the bridge at Saint-Michel dedicated

Á LA MÉMOIRE
DES NOMBREUX ALGÉRIENS
TUÉS LORS DE LA SANGLANTE
 RÉPRESSION
DE LA MANIFESTATION PACIFIQUE
 DU 17 OCTOBRE 1961

(IN MEMORY
OF THE MANY ALGERIANS
KILLED DURING THE BLOODY
 REPRESSION
OF THE PEACEFUL DEMONSTRATION
 ON OCTOBER 17, 1961)

Honoring those who died that day, the memorial confirms to the French and the Algerian public that *ce jour-là* is no longer a blank in history.

Almost two decades have passed since the publication of *La Seine était rouge,* and as Alec Hargreaves notes, several factors have emerged to end amnesia. First, France's ongoing relations with former colonies keep memories alive. Postcolonial nations, such as Algeria, have continued to base their claims to legitimacy on reminders of the dark days of colonialism and emphasize the independence struggle as a foundational event. Second, with the passage of time, participants in the Algerian War have sought to unburden themselves of guarded secrets. Generals Jacques Massu and Paul Aussaresses admitted, in their testimonies, the French army's use of torture on Algerian civilians during the war. Third, by testifying against Maurice Papon at the latter's much-publicized trial for crimes against humanity committed as a Vichy official from 1942 to 1944, the historian Jean-Luc Einaudi contributed to bringing the massacre that occurred on October 17, 1961, to a large public forum. Finally, Maghrebian immigrants, as well as their children and grandchildren, have used various forms of public discourse, including films and novels, since the 1980s to overcome the initial state of amnesia. Thus, Papon's trial, films, fiction, and memoirs all combine to break the silence surrounding the massacre.

Significantly, Stora, who first drew attention to the dangers of collective amnesia, later warned against the overabundance of memory produced by the increasing number of revelations: "Nous ne sommes donc plus du tout dans une phase d'occultation ou de déni mais, au contraire, nous sommes victimes d'une sorte d'instrumentalisation politique perpétuelle de l'histoire des mémoires" ("La guerre des mémoires," 13; We are no longer in a phase of concealment or denial; on the contrary, we are victims of a kind of perpetual political manipulation of the history of memories). Stora believes not only that societies need mechanisms for forgetting but that an overabundance of revelations risks creating new forms of political manipulation that replace the old. Sebbar shares his belief. She draws attention to the current competing memories, explaining that various factions—harkis, pieds-noirs, Algerians of different persuasions—want their historical accounts to prevail.[20]

Yet, two aspects of the novel merit further clarification. First, as the hidden history of repression is brought to light, the collective process of remembering has significant consequences for the individual and the community. In this regard, the quest embarked upon by Amel, Omer, and Louis at Amel's instigation not only involves public commemoration but also impacts their personal lives, influencing their relationships with one another and with their parents, members of the previous generation. Second, historians wedded to objectivity may question the veracity of the *témoignages*, the subjective eyewitness accounts. However, these critics must acknowledge that to repair the omissions and silences of accounts of French colonial history, historians may have to rely on the testimony of witnesses, particularly when French archives are closed to them, as they were to Einaudi and Amrane-Minne.

However, as Amrane-Minne noted when she incorporated oral testimony into her history of women's participation in the Algerian War, a *témoignage* remains a subjective account, one that complements but does not replace historical analysis (*La guerre d'Algérie*, 278). Similarly, Cole, who begins his study with a series of eyewitness accounts—one by an FLN demonstrator, a second by a French social worker, a third by a Paris policeman—cautions writers and historians of their limitations. He states:

> The problem of testimony can be reduced to this: proximity lends an unquestionable legitimacy to any account (who else are we going to ask?), but it also taints the narrative with the stain of the particular, a specific location—"there"—and a corresponding inability to see the whole. At best,

a witness possesses only an incomplete picture, and it is always possible to say that their specific location in a social world fraught with discordant ideologies gives their voice a partisan tone. This makes witnesses suspect in the eyes of a conventional history that values objectivity above all. ("Remembering the Battle of Paris," 23)

Thus, although the full picture may never emerge, the historian's task is to bring the testimony together with other documents in order to come closer to the facts. Moreover, in this era of greater accessibility to historical artifacts (archives, historical documents, films, interviews, literary texts), the quest for accuracy, truth, and reconciliation continues with greater facility and fewer obstacles. It is within this context—and in this spirit—that *La Seine était rouge* must be contextualized, reread, and most fully appreciated.

Before concluding the analysis of the novel, we may ask what part literary voices such as Sebbar's have played in the commemorative initiatives. By calling attention to the violence that extended to Algerians living in France during the Algerian War, she and other writers, historians, and journalists have worked to illuminate another chapter in the painful history of violence accompanying French colonialism in Algeria, and they have not been alone in this endeavor. In this regard, we should not forget that at the trial of Maurice Papon in Bordeaux in 1997 Einaudi linked the former prefect of Paris to the crimes committed during the Vichy period in France and on October 17, 1961. His testimony regarding the massacre in Paris was key to informing the public in France and beyond of the atrocities committed by the French police under Papon's jurisdiction, which the police had kept secret in the last few months of the Algerian War. Similarly, the film industry has also contributed to educating the public in France and beyond to the "obscured occurrence" (Rice, "Remembering 17 October 1961," 91). In 2005 the Austrian filmmaker Michael Haneke's film *Caché* brought the massacre to the screen as it revealed the tragic consequences to the life of an Algerian immigrant child whose parents had died in the massacre. Clearly, visual representations, oral testimony, and written accounts, both fact and fiction, have combined to break the silence.

To those readers who wonder why it took so long to expose the massacre, Cole offers the following response: "For the French it was the most public of their crimes; for the Algerians, it was the most distant and removed of their many traumas. In both countries, the anomaly of the event's location made its subsequent effacement all the more necessary, and all the more paradoxical for those who want to explain the event's curious afterlife in history and memory" ("Remembering the Battle of Paris," 25). Distance, however, is only one reason for the Algerians' silence. The historian goes on to explain that when, at the end of the war in 1962, Algeria's first president, Ahmed Ben Bella, came into conflict with the GPRA (Gouvernement provisoire de la République algérienne), Algeria's provisional government, the Fédération de France, by choosing the side of the GPRA, lost political power. In addition, to create a sense of national identity following the war, Ben Bella and then his successor, Houari Boumedienne, embraced a version of Algerian history that embellished the role of the rural Algerian combatant in the struggle for independence and minimized the contributions of the urban workers in France, as well as those of the Fédération de France, to the independence struggle (31). Thus, just as the French refused to recognize the Algerian immigrant workers as citizens and as victims, the Algerian government was reluctant to consider them active agents in the war of liberation.

If Sebbar is one of many voices to depict this collective trauma, she is an important one. As *La Seine était rouge* brings to light this tragic incident and its silencing by French authorities, it gives voice to the French citizens born in France to Algerian immigrant parents, young people struggling to come to terms with the past as they seek to find their place in the France of today, where cultural diversity remains a goal still to be achieved.

Childhood Memories of the War

Having noted that Maïssa Bey and Leïla Sebbar bring together three historical events—World War II, the Algerian War, and Algeria's undeclared civil war of the 1990s—I return to the critic Susan Suleiman's concept of the "1.5 generation," mentioned briefly in the previous chapter, to frame the discussion of Sebbar's collection of essays *Une enfance dans la guerre: Algérie, 1954–1962*. In her study of several writers of the Holocaust, *Crises of Memory and the Second World War,* Suleiman devotes a chapter to Georges Perec and Raymond Federman, two French writers of Jewish background who survived the Holocaust, escaping the fate of their parents and siblings, who were deported and perished in Nazi concentration camps. Admittedly, it would not be appropriate to compare the experiences of child survivors of the Holocaust with those of children living in Algeria during the independence struggle. However, among the Holocaust survivors and the children of Algeria, some share a common experience; they witnessed and in some cases endured traumatic incidents that as children they could only barely comprehend and as adults they brought into their writing.

Une enfance dans la guerre, Sebbar's collection of essays by forty-four writers—novelists, poets, storytellers, essayists, and historians, as well as philosophers and psychoanalysts—asks each contributor to delve into his or her personal recollections in search of one or more key memories that best convey the truth of that turbulent period, which they experienced as children and have found themselves revisiting, perhaps again and again, as adults. Sebbar calls upon members of the various ethnic and religious communities that made up Algeria during the colonial period—pieds-noirs, Jews, Arabs, Berbers, and those of mixed families—to explain how the experience of living through this period of violent conflict in childhood shaped their adult lives. Since the contributors to the collection are writers, one question at the heart of the project is the relationship between their war experience as children and their later written work. What impact did the Algerian War have upon the contributors' writing? How were they to write with an admittedly limited comprehension of the situation? Finally, how should the writer transmit the memory of the conflict to subsequent generations on both shores of the Mediterranean? By probing the complex relationship of the war experience to literary expression, Sebbar's literary project enters Suleiman's realm of inquiry.

What Suleiman calls the "1.5 generation" comprised child survivors of the Holocaust. Too young to have an adult understanding of what was happening to them, in some cases too young to have any memory of the events at all, they were nevertheless old enough to have *been there*. These individuals form three groups: 0–4 years, too young to remember; 4–10, old enough to remember but too young to understand; 11–14, old enough to understand but too young to determine their actions or those of their family in response to a crisis or catastrophe. In contrast, adults, as she explains, are not only aware of their predicament but capable of reacting to it. The division between childhood and adulthood tends to blur, however, when we consider that an eleven-year-old is capable of engaging in abstract thought and can describe his or her experience in ways that mirror adult perception, but a younger child cannot do this (*Crises of Memory*, 182).

In her analysis, Suleiman makes several additional points that are worth emphasizing. First, she privileges literary representation of the experience over "raw testimony" because, in her view, it conveys, through language, the child's helplessness at the time of the traumatic event and the adult's attempt to render that helplessness retrospectively (184). Second, she articulates the relationship between individual and collective testimony in terms of a delicate balance between the individual and the collective; she maintains that despite the collective nature of the historical event and its official commemorations, the experience remains an individual one, yet she acknowledges that the witness who recounts his or her own *individual* experience represents the *many* who either did not survive to testify or did survive but remain speechless (134). She writes:

> Testimony is always of necessity individual; but if it refers to a collective historical drama, it will, also of necessity, be about more than the experience of a single person. Even while it represents (in the sense of re-presenting, making visible) the unique perspective of the one who says "I," testimony in such a case also represents in the sense of being exemplary, of "standing for." The single witness, even while recounting his or her own experiences, represents all those who were in a similar position in the same time and place. Jean-Paul Sartre, in *What is Literature?* refers at one point to his and his generation's discovery of what he calls historicity—that is the realization that one's individual life was inexorably linked, down to its smallest details, to the lives of countless others. (134)

I suggest that this relationship between individual testimony and collective historical drama motivates Sebbar as well as Suleiman.

Turning to the collection of essays, we find a unity of form because Sebbar imposed specific rules. The narratives had to be *inédits*, texts not previously published; they had to be quite short, not more than seventy-five hundred characters, including spaces; and a childhood photo had to accompany each essay. A unity of content is evident as well because several common themes emerge: the silence on the part of parents and other adults with respect to the war, a silence designed to protect the children from fear and anxiety; the various signs of normalcy, such as school activities and family outings, that the war does not disturb; the escalating violence in the form of bombings and assassinations in public spaces; the forced exile and displacement as families fleeing danger move within the country or leave Algeria for France. Finally, and perhaps most importantly, the common trope of the lost Eden embodies the nostalgic memory of an Algeria where children were able to lead rather happy and emotionally satisfying lives until the war reached them. Indeed, just as feelings of anxiety unite the many disparate voices, so does the sense of nostalgia.

A study of the anthology reveals that the forty-four texts fall into two distinct groups: on the one hand, the voices of those who experienced the violence directly; on the other, the voices of those who were sheltered from it and felt the effects of the conflict indirectly. As the members of the various communities evoke their childhood in Algeria during the war, we learn that the Arab and Berber communities tend to form the first group; the pied-noir and Jewish families, the second. Particularly in large cities such as Algiers and Oran, pied-noir and Jewish families were able to shelter their children from most of the violence until the final months of the war, when members of the OAS (Organisation de l'armée secrète), pied-noir extremists, waged a fierce campaign of indiscriminate violence that led to widespread panic throughout the country and resulted in the hasty departure of most Europeans during the summer of 1962.

Anne-Marie Langlois, the daughter of pieds-noirs, describes an idyllic childhood on her father's farm in which "le bonheur semblait infini" (*Une enfance*, 159; happiness seemed infinite) until they were forced to leave, and Monique Ayoun, whose Jewish family lived in Algiers, defines her childhood in terms of "le bonheur, la lumière, la mer" (43; happiness, light, and the sea) until her uncle's assassination. Similarly, Jacqueline Brenot, whose family roots were urban pied-noir, views Algeria as "un pays d'azur et de miel" (79; a land of azur blue and honey) until, as the war draws to an end, her younger brother, playing in a neighborhood park in downtown Algiers, narrowly escapes being shot during a shootout between two warring factions (83). Thus, the war that France would euphemistically term *les événements* (the events) enters the world of these families, destroying the stability and serenity that had marked their lives for so long. As Ayoun writes: "Avant, ma famille était heureuse, elle se croyait protégée, intouchable, auréolée de grâce. Après, seulement après, nous sommes devenus humains et mortels" (43; Before, my family was happy; they believed they were protected, untouchable, crowned with grace. After, only afterwards, we became human and mortal). The emphasis she places on the break between before and after is an important characteristic of these narratives. Once the shots ring out and a victim falls, life for the individual and the community is never the same.

Yet, as the representatives of the Algerian Arab and Berber communities describe their childhood, they rarely evoke a before and after, instead thrusting the reader into a rude world in which there was always little protection and much brutality from the very beginning of the war.[21] At the age of seven or eight, Mehdi Charef, in the Kabyle countryside, views the corpse of his aunt Karima, hanged by French soldiers for having hidden a group of *moudjahidine* (97). No family photo accompanies his essay. It is possible that he was never photographed as a child. A pencil drawing of his mother, her dark, haunting eyes conveying the pathos of war, prefaces Charef's text. Similarly, Yahia Belaskri, growing up in M'dina J'dida, a poor Arab quarter of Oran, recalls the barbed wire encircling the quarter and the corpses of Europeans and Algerians in the streets (57). Noting that he never had toys in childhood and therefore always chose inappropriate ones for his children, he adds somberly that the sound of bullets replaced nursery rhymes in his war-ravaged universe. He recalls a day in 1961 when the OAS successfully set off a bomb in the school that caused grave injuries among the children (57). He concludes poignantly: "Comme d'autres ont donné leur vie, j'ai donné mon enfance" (58; As others gave their lives, I gave up my childhood).

In his preface to the collection of essays, Jean-Marie Borzeix remarks that children became exceptional witnesses to a drama that not only went beyond their understanding but threatened to upset their lives (6–7). Those who were children at the time now have grown children and grandchildren of their own. If by dipping a madeleine into a teacup Marcel Proust brought back his past involuntarily, the forty-four contributors to Sebbar's volume have done otherwise, delving deliberately into a past that holds nostalgia for some but disturbing, if not traumatic, memories for all. Yet, as with Proust, the journey back is sensory, evoking principally sight, sound, and smell. Grounded in childhood memories, the contributors' senses awaken as they recall the harsh reality of war. For example, the walk to school, a daily ritual of childhood that should reflect normalcy, is transformed to reference death as Jacqueline Brenot, recalling her school days in Algiers, remembers an odor. She writes: "Sur le chemin de l'école, une odeur putride a remplacé celle des roses" (83; On the path to school, a putrid odor replaced the smell of roses). Simone Molina remembers the sound of the muffled voice of the person who pulled her out from under the rubble of the bombed building, saving her life (207). Waciny Laredj recalls the warmth of his father's body when, as a five-year-old child, he sat for the last time in his father's lap. A combatant in the liberation struggle, his father died under torture in 1959 (167). Leïla Sebbar returns to the sound of military helicopters taking soldiers to or from some military operation against the Algerian combatants (241). As Maïssa Bey remarks, although the children call the helicopters *alouettes* (larks), they know them as instruments of war: "Les alouettes ne sont pas des oiseaux" (73; These larks are not birds).

Yet, visual images remain the most critical elements in the children's memories of the war. From his window, Alain Amato, at fourteen, sees a twelve-year old child, the victim of a grenade, die in the street below (35). Nourredine Saadi recalls the face of a man horribly disfigured (236). Tassadit Yacine recalls the visual image of her uncle being beaten by a group of soldiers and her intense physical reaction: "J'ai senti mes boyaux se tordre et j'ai détesté de toute mon âme les militaires qui se sont permis de battre à quatre mon gentil Dadda" (272–73; I felt my stomach cramp and hated with all my soul the four soldiers who took it upon themselves to beat up my sweet uncle). In this regard, Suleiman, in her theoretical approach to traumatic memory, chooses the term *revision* to denote the process whereby the memory of a traumatic past event is not merely repeated but continually reinterpreted in light of the subject's self-understanding (140). And Sebbar, by requiring each contributor to include a photo with his or her essay, emphasizes the visual element in the process of recovering memory. Significantly, the contributors' photos vary enormously, as class pictures, family snapshots, and individual photos create a visual panorama for the reader.

With barriers between communities forming as the war continues, children become increasingly aware of their families' social and economic standing in Algeria. They quickly develop their sense of identity: pied-noir, Jew, Arab, Berber. Yet, for a variety of reasons some find the question of identity problematic. For example, their families' political convictions may be different from those of the majority of families in their ethnic, social, or religious group. They may present characteristics, physical or otherwise, that obscure their ethnic identity. They may, by birth, be of mixed heritage. Christiane Chaulet-Achour, whose parents were pieds-noirs yet opted for Algerian independence, explains that they made her understand as a young child that she must never discuss in public what she hears at home: "On n'est pas du côté des copains et copines de l'école mais avec 'des fellaghas'" (*Une enfance*, 27; We are not on the side of our school friends but with the "rebels"). With a brother and sister in prison, she participates in the nationalist cause unwittingly, at the age of eight, by taking compromising documents away to school in her book bag during a police raid on the family apartment. José Lenzina, a thirteen-year-old pied-noir whose curly hair makes him look like an Arab, recalls the disparaging racist remark of a nurse at school who, mistaking him for an Arab, snarls: "Tourne un peu la tête Mohammed! Les odeurs de couscous, j'aime pas ça" (*Une enfance*, 174; Turn your head away Mohammed! I don't like the smell of couscous). He also recalls his parish priest's virulent sermon against Islam, his narrow escape during a drive-by shooting, and the sight of the body of a "rebel" in the village square.

Sebbar, the daughter of an Arab father and a French mother, describes her escape into library books to avoid the harassment by schoolmates who view her as a traitor to their cause. Withdrawing into silence, she listens attentively:

> Un colon assassiné, sa ferme incendiée, c'est le père de l'une de mes condisciples, un maquisard arrêté, incarcéré, torturé peut-être, c'est le père de l'une de mes condisciples. Des clans opposés se réunissent à l'une et l'autre bout de la cour du lycée. Je n'appartiens à aucun. (*Une enfance*, 243)

> (A colonizer assassinated, his farm burned down, he is the father of one of my classmates; a rebel arrested, jailed, maybe tortured, he's the father of another one of my classmates. Opposing clans meet at the opposite ends of the school courtyard. I belong to neither one.)

Similarly caught between two communities at war with each other, Nora Aceval, whose father was a pied-noir landowner, her mother an Arab, recalls her fear of "les justiciers arabes de l'ombre" (22; the Arab avengers in the shadows) seeking to punish her widowed mother, the woman whom they considered a traitor for having married a pied-noir, as well as her fear as French soldiers searched her family's home for evidence of complicity with the FLN, leaving furniture and clothing pell-mell in their wake. Thus, just as Sebbar seeks refuge in books, Aceval finds hers in the popular folktales her mother recounts to her children, offering them temporary shelter in the realm of the imaginary, a refuge where peace reigns for a while. With her interest in folktales sparked in childhood by her mother, Aceval has published several collections of Algerian folktales, translated from Algerian Arabic into French.[22]

In conclusion, as Sebbar probes the massacre of October 17, 1961, and the effects of the Algerian War upon the men and women who experienced the Franco-Algerian conflict as children, she not only widens the scope of inquiry geographically and temporally but supports Suleiman's thesis that collective historical trauma is rooted in an individual experience—every testimony is unique. Noting that Latin has two words for witness: *testis,* which means "spectator" or "bystander," and *superstes,* which also signifies "survivor," Suleiman argues that although the English word *testimony* is derived from the first, it is the survivor, not the uninvolved bystander, to whom we turn for testimony of a traumatic event (*Crises of Memory,* 133).[23] By bringing in the voices of Algerians in France during the war as well as those of Algeria's 1.5 generation through Sebbar's texts, I hope to have shown how both contribute important elements to the national narratives of France and Algeria. In addition, as a bridge between the preceding chapters, devoted to novels inspired by the Algerian War, and the following one, on testimonial literature, this chapter, by focusing on both fiction and written testimony, should confirm the relevance of both fiction and autobiographical narrative to the Algerian woman's war story.

6 TESTIMONIAL LITERATURE

Self-Reflection in the Works of Zohra Drif,
Louisette Ighilahriz, and Eveline Safir Lavalette

As various studies, including the earlier chapters of this work, confirm, the Algerian War was never an exclusively male endeavor. Women were involved in the anticolonial struggle from the beginning, contributing in both the political and military realms as well to the literature the war inspired. In this regard, the memoirs of former women combatants join historical studies and fiction to form the corpus of Algerian women's writings on the war. Testimonial literature, the focus of this chapter, not only engages memory in bringing past events of the war to light but compels us all—witnesses, narrators, listeners, and readers—to recognize the power of the word. As women tell their stories, they come to understand how the war in its multiple facets forced them to see themselves and their place in the world differently, opening the way to self-understanding and empowerment.

A first-person narrative reflecting lived experience, testimony in the form of a written memoir is a subgenre of autobiography. Yet unlike autobiography, which Philippe Lejeune defines as a "récit rétrospectif en prose qu'une personne réelle fait de sa propre existence, lorsqu'elle met l'accent sur sa vie individuelle, en particulier sur l'histoire de sa personnalité" (14; retrospective narrative in prose that a real person makes of his own existence, stressing his independent life and especially the history of his personality), the memoir does not necessarily relate an individual life story; it may focus on important periods, events, or experiences viewed through the eyes of the person who experienced them. The memoir (from the French *mémoire*, "memory") depends upon the ability to retrieve one's memories from a near or distant past, including those that are painful and traumatic. If it is difficult to portray intense traumatic experiences in fiction, as Djebar, Mechakra, and Bey have done, it is equally challenging to express traumatic experiences in the form of personal testimony, the task Zohra Drif, Louisette Ighilahriz, and Eveline Safir Lavalette set for themselves.

Self-reflection, critics remind us, occurs in postwar periods as the individual and community, in their search for meaning and understanding, ask, What have we achieved? What have we learned from the struggle? The three testimonial texts discussed in this chapter bring the reader into the immediacy of the war experience as their authors express their personal reflections upon past events. Each political activist's memoir charts her journey, revealing why and how she became involved in the independence struggle. In each instance, the process of revisiting the past has particular value because the subject, living well into her seventies or eighties, has had many decades to reflect upon the events that shaped her life. The three memoirists' individual narratives afford unique perspectives on the historical moments experienced, remembered, and now transmitted to younger generations. Although the three women share a historical moment in history, they reveal different objectives in offering the public their memoirs. Zohra Drif has a pedagogical mission, the desire to keep alive for posterity the story of the Battle of Algiers, a critical chapter in the history of the Algerian War in which she played a key role. Louisette Ighilahriz seeks to reopen the controversy in France and Algeria concerning torture by making public her personal experience as one of many victims. Eveline Safir Lavalette chooses to give her readers a personal memoir comprising prison diaries, contemporary chronicles, and photos that chart a life shaped by political engagement. Hence, the memoirists' intentions in putting pen to paper are personal, political, pedagogical, and also literary; the story must be told, and it must be told well.

Zohra Drif

A practicing lawyer and member of the Algerian Senate following independence, Zohra Drif was a law student at the University of Algiers at the beginning of the Algerian War. By 1956 she had joined the ZAA (Zone Autonome d'Alger), the urban network of the FLN, led by Yacef Saadi, interrupting her studies to heed the call of political engagement. First a courier transmitting messages and parcels, Drif assumed a far more active role in the organization when, on September 30, 1956, she, Samia Lakhdari, and Djamila Bouhired placed bombs in three strategic sites in downtown Algiers frequented primarily by Europeans: two bustling cafés, the Cafétéria and the Milk Bar, and the Air France office in the Mauretania Building. The latter bomb failed to explode; the first two caused considerable damage, injury, and loss of life. By carrying out her mission successfully, Drif confirmed her vital role in the historic Battle of Algiers and entered the annals of Algerian history. In the months that followed, she lived clandestinely in the Casbah with other members of the ZAA.

Arrested on September 25, 1957, Drif spent the rest of the war years in prison. Upon her release from prison at independence, she completed her law degree, married Rabah Bitat, one of the leaders of the independence movement, and embarked upon a career in law and politics. Now retired from active public life, she remains a prominent historical and political figure in Algeria today. Her *Mémoires d'une combattante de l'ALN: Zone Autonome d'Alger* (2013), translated as *Inside the Battle of Algiers: Memoir of a Freedom Fighter* (2017), provides us with a crucial reexamination of events of the Algerian War. It complements *La mort de mes frères* (The death of my brothers), a short essay she published in 1960, while still a political prisoner in France and before the war had come to an end. Revisiting the same historical moment, the Battle of Algiers, the recent memoir reveals in depth and detail the thoughts and actions of a key member of the FLN unit that waged guerrilla warfare in the capital.

Why did the former combatant choose to publish a memoir after so many years had passed? Drif explains that she felt compelled to return to the events and write her reflections following the death in 2012 of Samia Lakhdari, the close friend with whom she shared much of her political trajectory. In addition, an incident that occurred the same year reinforced her commitment to the writing project. Participating in a debate in Marseille fifty years after the end of the war, she encountered a public that expected her to condemn her role in the independence struggle, a position she could not accept. She resolved at that time to summon her memories of her experience and commit them to print (*Mémoires*, 14–15).[1]

Guided by the firm conviction that one must know the past to create a sustainable future, Drif informs her readers that she intends to transmit to the youth of her country a dual legacy, an awareness of the oppression that weighed upon the colonized during the colonial era and an understanding of the difficult struggle that led to independence. Proposing to relate historical events through her interpretive lens, she insists upon the collective dimension of the war experience and women's role in it. Stressing the importance of acknowledging women's participation in the independence struggle, she pays tribute to her sisters in combat, many of whom have since passed away. Identifying some by name—Djamila Bouhired, Hassiba Ben Bouali, Oukhiti (Fatiha Bouhired-Hattari), and Samia Lakhdari—she also pays homage to the anonymous women of the Casbah. Praising their courage, faith, and mobilization, she expresses her personal gratitude to all who fed, sheltered, and protected the members of her network (16). She claims to propose neither a history of the Algerian War nor an autobiography, but rather to put forth the key factors that led to her political engagement and chart her experience as an urban guerrilla during the Battle of Algiers. Following the path of memoirists before her, she promises to tell only what she lived, saw, and heard, aware that her memory may betray her at times (17).

Although students of history may welcome the publication, a thick volume of more than five hundred pages, for its historical details, I propose to focus on the psychological dimension of the work, analyzing the text as a journey from alienation to integration, the former rooted in the colonial experience, the latter achieved through participation in the anticolonial struggle. In this regard, I suggest that the text recalls the bildungsroman, a fictional narrative of a young person's journey to maturity. Anchored in reality rather than in fiction, Drif's memoir describes her coming of age in war-torn Algeria, first her formal education within the colonial school system; then her political formation in the FLN. Her formal education requires mastery of the colonizer's language and imposed curriculum, while her political education involves a different set of skills—although her French language skills remain crucial—as she commits to the life of the urban guerrilla with its risks and perils. The one brings her into French colonial space, opening her world to French language, culture, and knowledge and yet creating a profound sense of alienation. The other takes her to the heart of anticolonial resistance, where, among members of the urban resistance network in the Casbah, she finds a place of shared values; she finds her home.

Sketching the sociohistorical context in which she grew up, colonial Algeria from the 1930s to the early 1950s, Drif acknowledges the key role played by both parents in equipping her with a dual education, in Arabic and French language and culture, that will launch her on her path and determine her future. Her father teaches her that a Western education provides the tools, techniques, and weapons to fight against French assimilationist policies. Her mother insists that her education in the French colonial school system will pave the way for future generations of young Algerian women. Yet, neither her father, who tacitly supports his daughter's militancy, nor her mother, who opposes it, imagines that their daughter's experience in the French colonial school system, followed by the outbreak of the Algerian War, will lead to her radical political engagement.

In the chapters that retrace her educational journey in the colonial schools, Drif emphasizes that her early years were marked by a sense of alienation and injustice. The only native child in her class in her elementary school, she was made to feel acutely aware of the cultural divide between the native Arab and Berber population and the "Algerians," the name the European settler population called themselves. On one level the differences she discerned were superficial: the girls in her class had short hair and wore short skirts; she, in contrast, kept her hair in long braids and wore long skirts. At recreation time, her classmates munched on croissants and brioches, as she savored Oriental pastries, the *maqrouta* and *mbardja* her mother prepared for her. On a deeper level, however, cultural markers reflected the sharp division between the colonizer and the colonized, the powerful and the oppressed. To meet the challenge of navigating alone in this foreign world, she excelled at school. However, the day that a classmate whom she had considered her closest friend reproached her for her academic success, young Zohra came to understand that she would always remain the inferior other in the eyes of her pied-noir classmates.

Admittedly an outsider in primary school, Drif remains one in high school as well until Samia Lakhdari enrolls in her school and they become fast friends. After obtaining their baccalaureate degrees in 1954 and 1955, respectively, Zohra and Samia begin their study of law at the university. Committed to the anticolonial struggle, they decide to contact the FLN, are accepted into its ranks, and become couriers, distributing subsidies to the families whose men have been killed or imprisoned, as well as messages and arms.

These responsibilities change dramatically, however, following an attack in Algiers by European ultras.

On August 10, 1956, a hidden bomb set off in the Casbah on the Rue de Thèbes kills a large number of Algerian civilians; the FLN decides to respond in kind, to use concealed bombs to wage guerrilla warfare in the cities. To implement the plan, the organization turns to its young female members, believing that young, Western-educated women such as Drif and Lakhdari will most easily pass undetected in a city heavily patrolled by French paratroopers. According to Drif, not only did the head of the network, Yacef Saadi, accept them but he allowed the three to select the sites they would attack in the early evening of September 30, 1956. She explains that she chose the Milk Bar because of its symbolic value: the café catered to a clientele she considered impervious to the injustices of the colonial situation (176). Moreover, it bordered Place Bugeaud, named for a "sinistre général exterminateur de notre peuple" (176; a sinister exterminator of our people [110]).

Reconstructing the events of the fateful bombing of the Milk Bar, which claimed three lives and injured more than a dozen others, Drif meticulously recounts in detail the preparation for the attack, its execution, and its aftermath. She explains, for example, that in preparation for their mission the three *bombistes* disguise themselves as chic Europeans who would not appear out of place in the venues they had chosen.[2] She then draws the reader into the immediacy of the situation by recalling each moment and describing each gesture with precision: she walks nonchalantly into the café, calmly chooses her seat at the counter, orders a Peach Melba, and carefully slides the bomb hidden in a beach bag between her stool and the counter, all the while aware that she has barely fifteen minutes in which to place her order, eat her dessert, pay the bill, and leave. Although meticulous in her gestures, she pays scant attention to the people seated at a nearby table and the noisy crowd of men and women behind her. She does not seem aware that several children are in the café that afternoon.

Reliving the physical sensations she experienced both immediately before the explosion and afterwards—headache, numbness—and her subsequent loss of control as she sobs uncontrollably upon returning to the Lakhdari home, Drif reveals how difficult this mission was; her mind and body attest to the trauma. When she revisits the events more than fifty years later, she admits to the emotional toll of recalling the events of that day: "Ces moments, je les ai vécus mais je n'ai jamais su les dire" (185; I have lived these moments, but have never known how to describe them [116]).

Perhaps most significant is her reflection on how she saw her mission: "Ce qui me guidait, c'était l'exigence absolue, le devoir sacré de réussir ma mission pour que mon peuple ne désespère pas" (185; What guided me that day was absolute necessity, the sacred duty to succeed in my mission, so that my people would not despair [116]). With these words, she draws the reader into the mind of a combatant prepared to take the lives of others and sacrifice her own in the struggle to liberate Algeria. Viewing her world as one divided between the colonized—her people—and the European settlers who had robbed the indigenous population of their lands—her enemy—she commits herself to violence, embracing the view that the end justifies the means. She adopts the position that Frantz Fanon affirms in the very first chapter of *Les damnés de la terre* (*The Wretched of the Earth*), his seminal theoretical text on colonialism: "La décolonisation est toujours un phénomène violent" (29; Decolonization is always a violent phenomenon [35]).

In the introductory chapter to this study, I noted that the West is heir to a tradition that assumes that in time of war men occupy the dangerous battlefields, while women remain safe and secure at home. The political theorist Jean Bethke Elshtain explains that we embrace the assumption that men are the "life takers" and women, the "life givers" (*Women and War*, 195), aware that legendary women warriors such as Joan of Arc are quite rare in history. A scholar of Western history and politics, Elshtain does not reference Muslim culture and societies, yet they also delineate space in terms of gender—men in public space, women in private space—situating men on the battlefield and women at home in time of war. Thus, when young Algerian women begin placing bombs in strategic locations in cities, they break stereotypes and alter expectations common to the colonized and the colonizer.

Examining Drif's radical departure from conventional expectations concerning women and war, the critic Brigitte Weltman-Aron concludes that Drif saw herself as a soldier in combat. Committed to her cause, she was convinced that the means with which to fight for Algerian independence were justified, given the revolutionaries' limited access to weapons and military power. In her role as clandestine combatant, she questions neither the act nor its consequences at the time. Significantly, when Drif looks back on the events, she confirms her initial position. Speaking for herself and

Lakhdari, she expresses no regrets, stating: "Ni aujourd'hui ni jamais, nous n'avons regretté nos actes" (169; Samia and I did not regret our actions in 1956 or 1957, nor do we today, nor will we ever [106]).[3]

However, one of the bomb's victims, the French journalist Danielle Michel-Chich, who as a small child lost her grandmother and a leg in the attack at the Milk Bar, disputes Drif's position. For Michel-Chich, Drif engaged in an unjust act of war by undertaking an action that could not distinguish between the guilty and the innocent (93). In her view, Drif accepts the sacrifice of the innocent, an act she deems unjust.[4] Yet we may argue, as Weltman-Aron does, that the conflict being waged in Algeria at the time must be understood in terms of its complexity. The bomb set off at the Milk Bar was a retaliatory response by the FLN to the attack by pied-noir radical extremists; it was not an attempt to escalate the war. Hence, the FLN decision to respond to violence with violence—an eye for an eye—reveals the complexity of the armed struggle between the settler and the colonized that transformed Algeria into a "traumascape"—"a distinctive category of place, transformed physically and psychically by suffering" (Tumarkin, *Traumascapes*, 13)—in a war that will last almost eight years and result in many civilian casualties on both sides.

By carrying out her mission successfully, Drif not only confirms her commitment to the anticolonial war but also contributes to the idealized image that emerges of the female bomb carrier: a woman who, through her action, assumes agency for herself and her sisters as she actively engages in the struggle to free her country from the yoke of colonialism.[5] Following the September bombings, the FLN sequesters the young bomb carriers, now integral members of the ZAA, in the Casbah. For Drif, whose family lives in western Algeria, this relocation marks the first time she enters a home in the famous old neighborhood of Algiers.

A site of both Algerian resistance and French military oppression during the war years, the Casbah (in Arabic, *al-qasaba*, meaning "fort" or "citadel") was inhabited first by Phoenicians traders in the sixth century BC and grew over the centuries into a densely populated area within the city of Algiers. Its winding streets, steep staircases, and traditional Moorish houses characterized by their tiled patios, horseshoe-shaped arches, and rooftop terraces became widely known in nineteenth-century Europe and the United States through the paintings of Delacroix, Gérôme, and their fellow Orientalist painters, who began visiting Algeria in the years following the French conquest of 1830.⁶

As the West came to view the Casbah through a distinctly Orientalist lens in the nineteenth century, the twentieth century saw cinema developing a colonialist fantasy, with films such as Julien Duvivier's *Pépé le Moko* (1937), in which Jean Gabin plays a Parisian jewel thief who has taken refuge in the Casbah, a space inhabited by thieves, pimps, and prostitutes of all nationalities.⁷ Following the success of Duvivier's film, the Hollywood remake, *Algiers,* starring Charles Boyer and Hedy Lamar, brought the fantasy of the Casbah as an exotic space of debauchery to American audiences the following year. Thus, nineteenth-century painting and twentieth-century cinema combined to project the image of the quarter as a mysterious labyrinth, a refuge and a prison for its exotic inhabitants, odalisques in the master's harem and members of the underworld in obscure hideouts. When Drif went to the Casbah in 1956, Algerian insurgents had redefined the quarter as a space of political rebellion. Yet, as Pontecorvo reveals in *The Battle of Algiers,* a film based on Saadi's memoir, the derelict element was still present. An early sequence in the film depicts the FLN cleansing the Casbah of its pimps and thieves as the anticolonial war against the French begins.

Geographers, architects, and sociologists remind us that places are always complex constructions of personal and interpersonal experiences. The humanist geographer Yi-Fu Tuan defines place as a center of shared values.⁸ The sociologist Eugene Victor Walter uses the term *places of experience* to describe meaningful places that capture experience and store it symbolically (*Placeways,* 117). As Walter explains, meaningful places grant a sense of continuity and energy.⁹ The Casbah becomes an important spatial referent for Drif, a "place of experience" that gives her a sense of meaning, continuity, and energy, a place of shared values for Algerian nationalists like herself.

Drawing her readers into this legendary space, Drif depicts her time there—September 1956 to September 1957—as an important educational experience, crucial to the formation of her national identity both culturally and politically. On the one hand, she comes to value the quarter as a bastion of traditional culture and values. On the other hand, political engagement brings her into contact with FLN leaders, militants from various regions of Algeria, as well as inhabitants of the Casbah who support the nationalist struggle. Through the experience of living in the quarter, she comes to a better understanding of her nation's past, lives intensely in the present, and through political engagement acquires a roadmap for the future.

Drif's contact with the women of the Casbah provides both a cultural and a political education. First, she moves into a cultural space barely touched by French colonialism, one that she values as authentically Algerian. Adapting to the role of *Casbadjiya*, woman of the Casbah, by donning the traditional garb and living with artifacts and architecture from precolonial Algeria, she becomes increasingly aware of numerous ethnographic details of her new life and surroundings. Assuming the role of ethnographer, she provides her readers with the Arabic names and descriptions of traditional dishes, articles of clothing, objects, and architectural designs (*Mémoires*, 245–46; *Inside the Battle of Algiers*, 151–52). Thus, she becomes a custodian of memory, transmitting age-old traditions textually, as the *Casbadjiyate* do orally. Moreover, by providing readers with cultural references, she makes the text more accessible to a reading public beyond Algeria's borders.

Most importantly, Drif's respect for the women of the Casbah extends beyond an appreciation of their role as guardians of tradition; she recognizes and values their commitment to the anticolonial struggle. Expressing her gratitude to them, she acknowledges that without their help she would never be able to navigate the maze of winding streets and adjoining rooftop terraces, successfully eluding French military patrols. Finally, her love and respect for Oukhiti (Fatiha Bouhired-Hattari), the young widow who opens her home to the militants at great risk to herself and her family, reflects her profound esteem for individuals and the community.

As the *Casbadjiyate* educate Drif culturally, Algerian revolutionaries grant her new political awareness. Living among the members of the ZAA, including Yacef Saadi, Ali La Pointe, Hassiba Ben Bouali, and Djamila Bouhired, she also meets the historic leader Larbi Ben M'Hidi, who with Abane Ramdane organized the eight-day strike in 1957 that brought international attention to the Algerian struggle at the same time that it intensified French military repression in the Casbah.[10] Assuming greater responsibilities within the ZAA, she writes tracts, articles, and official correspondence, helps prepare legal briefs, and attends important meetings. For example, following Djamila Bouhired's arrest, she meets with the lawyer Jacques Vergès and helps him draw up the documents that aid in Bouhired's defense and expose the French military's use of torture. Similarly, when Saadi meets with the French anthropologist and former member of the French Resistance Germaine Tillion in the hope that she will agree to bring to the French government the proposal that France end the policy of executing Algerian political prisoners in exchange for an FLN moratorium on concealed bombs, Drif is present at both of their meetings.[11]

Although the Casbah represents an important spatial referent for Drif, a "place of experience" where she acquires a sense of meaning, continuity, and energy, it proves increasingly dangerous. Offering refuge and protection to the militants when Drif first arrives, the quarter proves highly vulnerable to French military operations in the months that follow. Once the eight-day strike ordered by the FLN begins in late January 1957, the neighborhood is systematically searched and suspected FLN members and sympathizers are brutalized as the French military carry out a rigorous campaign of repression against the civilian population. At first, Drif and her companions elude the military patrols and even manage to keep a military search party from discovering the bomb-making materials stored on the roof. However, on the night of February 2 the soldiers break into to their refuge and terrorize and torture the occupants, including a fourteen-year-old boy. From their hidden crawl space in the house, Drif, Saadi, Ali la Pointe, and Hassiba Ben Bouali escape arrest but not trauma; they hear the victims' screams but are powerless to intervene. Drif writes that more than fifty years later she is still awakened by the screams of those tortured that fateful night (356; 230). Although torture is not the main focus in Drif's memoir, as it is in Ighilahriz's, it figures in her text. Indeed, even before the fateful night of February 2, Drif expresses her fear that "pire que la peur de la mort, était la torture" (381; even worse than the fear of death was the fear of torture [242]). In that same passage, she states that she would chose death rather than surrender and face torture.

Following the raid of February 2 the group becomes increasingly nomadic, moving from one refuge to another. In the attempt to protect the families that shelter them, they sleep huddled in hidden spaces in their homes. Barely able to move and breathing with difficulty in cramped dark spaces, Drif describes the panic she experiences each time the cover is placed over the crawl space: "J'essayais de réguler les battements de mon cœur, que je ressentais, que j'entendais, au niveau de ma gorge. Je me sentais hors du monde des vivants" (516; I tried to control the beating of my heart which I felt and heard up in my throat. I felt apart from the world of the living [308]). It is with a sense of foreboding that she calls the hidden refuge an *abri-tombeau*, a shelter that resembles—and foreshadows—a tomb.

Drif is arrested with Saadi on September 25, 1957, almost a year to the day after she first arrived. As the police drive her away to face interrogation and an unknown future, she reflects upon her relationship to the "place of experience" she has come to know as home. The Casbah, she notes, has educated her, teaching her the meaning of hospitality, fraternity, and solidarity. She writes:

> Je regardais, les yeux embués, la Casbah devenue ma cité bien aimée. Elle qui m'accueillit les bras ouverts, m'offrit sans compter son patrimoine et ses splendeurs, sa beauté et celle de ses enfants, son hospitalité et celle de ses habitants, elle qui me fit découvrir ce que la fraternité veut dire et la solidarité peut bâtir. (536)
>
> (I stared with moist eyes at the Casbah, my beloved adoptive city. She who had welcomed me with open arms, offered me not just her heritage and marvels, but also her beauty and that of her children, her hospitality and that of her inhabitants, she showed me what fraternity means and what solidarity can build. [321])[12]

Rather than dwelling on the ominous future that awaits her—incarceration, interrogation, and a trial—she turns to the past at this moment, seeking strength in the collective, hoping, perhaps naïvely, that memory will sustain her in the next difficult phase of her life. Neither she nor Saadi knows at this point that Germaine Tillion, upon learning of their arrest, will immediately contact the French minister for Algeria, Robert Lacoste, to demand that they be treated as political prisoners, with all legal procedures strictly followed. If Tillion's intervention spares them from torture, it may also save their lives.[13] Following their arrest, Saadi and Drif spend the rest of the war years in prison, whereas Ali La Pointe, Hassiba Ben Bouali, the young Omar, and Mahmoud Bouhamidi are killed the following month after Colonel Godard orders their refuge bombed upon their refusal to surrender.

Having fulfilled her promise to tell only what she lived, saw, and heard with respect to the Battle of Algiers, Drif leaves her readers with the prospect that she will continue her work as a memoirist, adding chapters on her life in prison, independence, and the work of constructing the new nation. For those of us who examine the history of the Algerian War through multiple interpretive lenses, Drif's memoir remains an important legacy to her nation.

Louisette Ighilahriz

If Drif reveals one objective in writing her memoirs, her desire to keep alive for posterity the story of the battle of Algiers, Louisette Ighilahriz expresses another, her commitment to reopening the debate concerning torture by divulging her personal experience as a victim. As noted in the introduction to this study, torture during the Algerian War first became a public issue in 1957, when Georges Arnaud and Jacques Vergès published *Pour Djamila Bouhired*, a polemical text that details the torture suffered by Drif's companion in arms at the hands of her captors. The following year, Henri Alleg published *La question*, his account of being tortured by the French military in Algeria. In 1962, as the war drew to a close, Simone de Beauvoir and Gisèle Halimi published *Pour Djamila Boupacha*, a text that specifically denounces the use of sexual torture upon Algerian women combatants by their French military interrogators.[14]

Over time, other testimonies concerning torture have come to light, including those by high-ranking French military officers who, having participated in these violent actions during the Algerian War, began to unburden themselves of guarded secrets. Generals Jacques Massu and Paul Aussaresses both exposed the French army's use of torture. Louise Ighilahriz is the first Algerian woman to bring the issue before the French and Algerian public in testimony that reveals her own traumatic experience of rape and torture at the hands of the French military.

In the previous chapters, I have noted that trauma specialists insist that bearing witness is crucial to the individual and collective healing process. Examining the effect of trauma upon the community and the individual, the historian Benjamin Stora notes the damaging effect of repressed memories upon both the collective and the individual. Stating that the amnesia surrounding various events of the Algerian War has been harmful to both France and Algeria, he describes the repressed memories of the war as a form of gangrene (*La gangrène et l'oubli*). In this same vein, psychotherapist

Dori Laub warns that survivors of traumatic events who do not tell their stories become victims of a distorted memory, and concludes: "None find peace in silence, even when it is their choice to remain silent" ("Truth and Testimony," 64). In this regard, as I examined Maïssa Bey's novella *Entendez-vous dans les montagnes...*, I paid particular attention to the analyses of Cathy Caruth, a trauma theorist who, working with Freudian concepts, emphasizes the time gap between the traumatic event and the memory it evokes, making it difficult for the truth surrounding the event to emerge. She writes: "This truth, in its delayed appearance and its belated address, cannot be linked only to what is known, but also to what remains unknown in our very actions and our language" (*Unclaimed Experience*, 4).

Truth in its "delayed appearance and its belated address" is at the heart of Louisette Ighilahriz's memoir. Surviving the war, Ighilariz remained silent, living with her wound, the trauma of rape and torture, until she found the courage to tell her story four decades later. As she explains, she had not only to find the words to describe the abuse she had suffered but also to go against her family's wishes, as well as those of former comrades, and government officials who opposed her decision (*Algérienne*, 111). Thus, a crucial element in the memoir is her struggle to end her silence by articulating her repressed memories. We may assume that in making her private trauma public, she, like Drif, became aware of the ticking clock. As members of their generation disappear, former combatants worry that Algeria and France risk losing precious testimony if it is not made public now or in the immediate future.

An FLN operative like Amrane-Minne and Drif, Ighilahriz, who did not plant bombs but did transport weapons, was also captured, tried, and jailed in 1957. Like her fellow memoirists Drif and Lavalette, she wrote her text in French. Yet in contrast to them, she engaged a professional journalist to help her collect and record the testimony she would bring before the French and Algerian public. And while Drif and Lavalette published their memoirs in Algeria, Ighilahriz chose a French publisher, making her work available first and foremost to French readers, a choice that reflects her objective of addressing the citizens of the nation whose military abused her.

Given the collaboration between two women—Nivat, the journalist, and Ighilahriz, the informant—readers may consider this work an autobiographical project with two authors, a narrator/protagonist and a listener/scribe (Jaccomard, "L'autobiographie de Louisette Ighilahriz," 136). Yet, another participant was also crucial to bringing the text to the public: Ighilahriz's sister Ourdïa. Ighilahriz shares a key part of her journey to the past with Ourdïa, who accompanies her on the crucial mission, a visit to the grave of Commandant Richaud, the French military doctor she credits with saving her life. If Ighilahriz's testimony can be read as a highly personal account that puts her battered body and intimate thoughts before the public, it can also be considered a collective endeavor, since she calls upon two other women, her sister and her scribe, for support in completing her mission and releasing her story to the public. Schooled in French, Ighilahriz was capable of crafting her own memoir. A rather independent woman, she could have made the journey to Richaud's gravesite alone. Thus, her choice to seek support from two other women confirms that the project was difficult in emotional terms, yet one she felt called upon to carry to its conclusion.

Participating in this project, Nivat is more than an attentive listener; she organizes the text and adds her own comments to it. As the historian Alessandro Portelli reminds his readers, the individual who deals with oral history is obliged to work on both the factual and narrative planes while forging a critical bond with the person entrusting his or her story to the journalist or historian (*The Order Has Been Carried Out,* 15). In this regard, Nivat's words, in a passage that precedes Louisette's autobiographical narrative (*Algérienne,* 17–20, set off in italics in her book), express her reaction following her first encounter with Ighilahriz, a meeting that establishes trust between the narrator and the narratee: "Dès la première seconde où j'ai croisé son regard, j'ai cru en cette femme. [. . .] Je savais qu'elle parlerait, parce qu'elle avait beaucoup à raconter et souhaitait le raconter. Je n'ai pas été déçue" (18; From the moment our eyes met, I believed in this woman. [. . .] I knew that she would speak, because she had a lot to say and wanted to speak out. I was not disappointed). Confirming her competence as an attentive listener, Nivat then assumes her role as scribe by meticulously noting the chronology of events. On September 21, 2000, Louisette and Ourdïa visit Richaud's grave in Cassis, France. On October 31 of the same year, Nivat meets Louisette in Algiers. On December 31, after Louisette has gone back to Algiers, Ourdïa returns alone to the cemetery to place the plaque with her sister's inscription on Richaud's grave: "Où que tu sois, tu seras toujours parmi nous. Louisette" (16; Wherever you are, you will always be among us. Louisette). To this plaque, decorated with a dove carrying an olive branch, Louisette has added in black ink, "Avec toute ma gratitude.—Louisette" (15; With all my gratitude.—Louisette).

Although Richaud is part of the oppressive French colonial regime that almost takes her life, he places his duty as a doctor, a healer, above his role as a military officer; by transferring her from the hospital in which she is systematically tortured to a prison where she is safe from abuse, he saves her life. Readers learn that Ighilahriz tried unsuccessfully to meet her protector before his death in 1997. However, with her visit to his grave and meeting his daughter, albeit after his death, her personal quest ends; the wound may heal. As the critic Sylvie Durmelat explains, Ighilahriz's delayed response to Richaud's benevolent action allows her to embark upon a search forward, a quest for a healing presence, rather than a journey back to "an agonizing and horrific past" ("Revisiting Ghosts," 151).

Why did Richaud intervene to save the young militant? It appears from her recollections that his motive was personal: the young prisoner reminded him of his own daughter, to whom he was quite close. Ighilahriz, in turn, was very strongly attached to her family; her father's militancy sparked her own political commitment. Hence, the close father-daughter relationship in one family becomes the catalyst for another action, suggesting that both families had more in common than they acknowledged in wartime. One paternal presence, a French doctor, would indeed replace the other, a jailed Algerian militant, by protecting the latter's daughter. Indeed, Richaud plays the role of the admonishing parent when he states: "Mon petit, vous êtes bien jeune pour le maquis. Je vous en prie, laissez ça aux autres. Aux hommes, par exemple!" (123; My child, you are too young for the resistance. I beg of you, leave that to others, to men, for example!). Here Richaud reveals his own male-gendered perception, shared, in fact, by many Algerian men of the times but opposed by Louisette's father, an ardent militant whose entire family was mobilized in the anticolonial struggle.[15] Yet, rather than objecting to his biased attitude toward female combatants, she values his action in saving her life, dedicating her memoir to her parents, her grandchildren, and him.

At the gravesite, Ourdïa, in a commemorative gesture to the French officer, symbolically offers him a cup of coffee from the thermos she had brought: "Ourdïa tient à prendre un café 'avec le docteur Richaud,' et extirpe le Thermos de son cabas" (15; Ourdïa wants to have a cup of coffee "with Doctor Richaud" and takes the thermos out of her shopping bag). Like

Mexican families who picnic in cemeteries on the Day of the Dead to honor their beloved departed family members, the two Algerian women symbolically bring the deceased briefly into their world.[16] Imitating a ritual rooted in Christian tradition, a visit to the graves of the departed on November 1, these Muslim women engage in an ecumenical gesture as they celebrate one man's humanitarian act that saved a young girl's life. Depicted in the pages of the memoir, the commemorative act provides a crucial frame for the narrative that follows. The memoirist does not intend to present a world divided between torturers and victims, but rather to show the complexity of war, in which charitable actions occur and must be recognized.

The ritual the two women initiate, almost joyous in its unfolding, contrasts sharply with the text that follows, Ighilahriz's autobiographical narrative of war. The healing that occurs as a result of the cemetery visit initiates a flashback to the events of 1957. That year, Ighilahriz was caught in an ambush, gravely wounded by gunfire, and transported to the 10th Paratroopers Division, where she was tortured before she was transferred to prison at Richaud's command. As she recalls her battered body, she finds the words to describe the brutal interrogation: "Mais l'essentiel de ses tortures ne s'exerçaient pas à mains nues. Il était toujours armé d'ustensiles pour s'acharner contre mon plâtre" (113; But he did not carry out most of his torture with his bare hands. He was always armed with implements to attack my plaster cast).

In addition to describing her tortured body, she evokes the degrading state in which she, as a prisoner, was placed: "Mon urine s'infiltrait sous la bâche du lit de camp, mes excréments se mélangeaient à mes menstrues jusqu'à former une croûte puante" (117; My urine passed through the sheet covering the camp bed, my excrement mixed with my menstrual blood, forming a stinking crust). Throughout the physical ordeal, however, she never denounces the members of her FLN cell, attributing her psychological strength to the knowledge that her FLN section leader had been killed (thus she could never be confronted with his testimony) and to her ability to overcome the effects of truth serum by focusing her mind on trivia when it was administered. Nevertheless, at the time of the fortuitous meeting with Richaud, she feared that she was losing the ability to resist: "J'étais en train de devenir folle" (117; I was losing my mind).

In her written testimony, Ighilahriz describes the brutality of Graziani, her interrogator, who poked her wounds and beat her with his fists. Yet she dismisses the possibility of rape: "Il ne pouvait pas non plus me violer, j'étais trop dégueulasse!" (113; He couldn't think of raping me. I was too disgusting!). Later, in oral testimony at the trial of a former French officer, General Schmitt, she testified that Graziani raped her (Durmelat, "Revisiting Ghosts," 154). The discrepancy between what she first allows in print and what she finally states in oral testimony reveals the difficulty she experienced in speaking the truth. Torture implies physical pain; rape, sex, albeit nonconsensual. In Muslim Algeria, where the loss of female virginity before marriage is taboo, it is understandable that the victim experienced great difficulty in speaking openly about her rape, even though it had occurred many years earlier. By coming forth to tell her story publicly, Ighilahriz encourages other Algerian women and men to discuss their experiences publicly as well.

Once the process of anamnesis begins, both individually and collectively, then healing, as Stora and Laub affirm, can occur. Yet Ighilahriz, like Amrane-Minne, Mechakra, Bey, and Drif, reveals the difficulties experienced by individuals engaged in the process of recovering traumatic memory. Although she walks through the door that Amrane-Minne opened, she does so by revealing the truth in stages: torture in her written text, rape in her oral testimony. Significantly, she finds support in the companionship of women, of the sister who accompanies her to Richaud's grave and the journalist to whom she confides her story. Hence, the female bonding that Amrane-Minne emphasizes in her historical text and interviews with former combatants occurs here as well. Nevertheless, we cannot conclude that following Ighilahriz's testimony Algerian women in general were resolved to oppose social pressure and come forth with their testimony of torture and rape.[17]

Probing the relationship of trauma to self-representation, the critic Leigh Gilmore concludes that trauma always involves "complicated stories" (*Limits of Autobiography*, 31), is never exclusively personal, and requires historical contextualization in order to be fully understood. Gilmore adds that when we place a personal history of trauma within a collective history, we must recognize that both collective and personal memory possess repressed memories, including traumatic memories of racial and sexual violence. Moreover, as difficult as it may be to acknowledge "my" trauma, yet another burden of trauma, she explains, lies in the difficulty of speaking in the plural, of acknowledging that "my" trauma is "our" trauma. By owning the experience collectively, the individual is called upon to situate his or her personal agony "within a spreading network of connections" (31). In this regard, the relationship of the individual to the collective in *Algérienne* leads the critic Hélène Jaccomard to entitle her study of the memoir "L'autobiographie de Louisette Ighilahriz ou la biographie d'une nation torturée" (131; The autobiography of Louisette Ighilahriz or the biography of a tortured nation). In Jaccomard's view, Ighilahriz has us read her autobiographical text as a synecdoche, a work in which her individual experience stands for her nation's, an analogy borne out by the oscillation between silence and disclosure—the locking and unlocking of the past—and the movement back and forth between the singular and the plural, as confirmed in the concluding pages of *Algérienne* when Ighilahriz states:

> J'écris pour rappeler qu'il y a eu une guerre atroce en Algérie, et qu'il n'a pas été facile pour nous d'accéder à l'indépendance. Notre liberté a été acquise au prix de plus d'un million de morts, de sacrifices inouïs, d'une terrible entreprise de démolition psychologique de la personne humaine. Je le dis sans haine. [. . .] Le souvenir est lourd à porter. (258)

> (I write to recall that there had been a terrible war in Algeria and that it has not been easy for us to achieve our independence. Our liberty was won at the price of more than one million lives lost, unimaginable sacrifices, a terrible campaign of psychological destruction of the human being. I say this without hatred. [. . .] The memory is difficult to bear.)

Breaking her silence, Ighilahriz reveals the tensions between keeping silent and disclosing the facts. Speaking, she articulates the risks and sacrifices demanded of women, who, when caught by the French colonial authorities, faced torture, rape, prison, and death. At the same time, she exposes the pressure placed upon the victims of abuse by both Algerian and French societies to remain silent. Significantly, she tells her readers that her mother made her promise never to speak to anyone of the violence she had suffered; hence, she waited decades before breaking that promise (129).

Returning to the historical event decades later to tell her story as she remembers it, the memoirist puts into practice the historian Paul Ricoeur's reflection concerning trauma: "qui dit intransmissible ne dit pas indicible"

(*La mémoire, l'histoire, l'oubli*, 584; what cannot be fully communicated can nevertheless be expressed). By entrusting other women with her testimony and with the task of inscribing it, Ighilahriz spares herself the pain of reliving traumatic events alone (Durmelat, "Revisiting Ghosts," 152–53). When her personal narrative reaches the public, her individual voice becomes part of the collective; as she reclaims agency, she opens the way for her former sisters in combat to do the same.

Eveline Safir Lavalette

Eveline Safir Lavalette's memoir, *Juste Algérienne: Comme une tissure* [Just Algerian: Like intersecting threads], published in 2013, the same year as Drif's, adds additional perspectives to women's experience of war.[18] Presented as a journal composed of entries written over several decades, it widens the temporal range of the previous testimonials to include the dark decade of the 1990s and concludes in 2013, a year before Lavalette's death at the age of eighty-six. As the writer looks outward, describing political events, and inward, probing her personal thoughts and concerns at the various stages of her life, she creates a work that is stylistically complex, interweaving poetry with prose and alternating first- and third-person narration; she writes in the first-person singular—*je*—to recall her childhood and in the third-person singular—*elle*—to recount her prison experiences and to evoke the dark years of the 1990s. Yet, what distinguishes Lavalette clearly from Drif and Ighilariz is her path to political engagement. Of pied-noir origin—her ancestors had come to Algeria in the 1870s to participate in France's colonial venture—she distanced herself from her privileged colonial background to embrace the struggle for Algerian independence.[19]

Born in Algiers in 1927, Lavalette grew up in Rouiba, a suburb east of Algiers; her father was a wine merchant by profession, her mother a pious and conservative homemaker. As she explains in the early pages of the memoir, her awareness of the injustices of colonialism began in childhood. The two windows of her bedroom opened onto two distinct views, one a vast expanse of fields, the other a lovely flower and vegetable garden and the railroad. From the first, she would glimpse a group of Algerian laborers toiling in the fields of a colonial landowner; from the second, a group of Algerian workers widening the railroad tracks. Both formed "tout un univers autre"

(*Juste Algérienne*, 38; a completely different universe) of the oppressed, one that remained largely invisible to the European population. Although as a child she could not grasp the reasons behind the political and economic barriers, she was aware of their existence, and, as she notes, these barriers made her uneasy. Surprisingly, her early political sensitivity was strengthened in adolescence through her participation in the Guides de France, the French scouts. This Catholic youth movement was socially conservative in its orientation, encouraging young women to embrace traditional roles as wives and mothers, yet it urged them to participate in civic and political life, a directive that led Lavalette to form close ties to a small group of liberal Catholics within the pied-noir community who, in contrast to the majority of Catholics (which included her parents), embraced the nationalist cause.[20]

In the years leading up to the outbreak of the war, Lavalette's social activism took various forms. In 1948, at the age of twenty-one, she began teaching Algerian children in the Casbah in a school run by the Soeurs Blanches (White Sisters) while assuming a leadership role in the Guides de France. She left teaching for the CFTC, the Confédération française de travailleurs chrétiens (French Confederation of Christian Workers), a progressive Catholic workers' union, in which she held a staff position from 1950 to 1956.[21] During those years she also frequented the AJAAS, the Association de la jeunesse algérienne pour l'action sociale (Association of Algerian Youth for Social Action), an association of leaders of various youth movements—Muslim, Catholic, Protestant, Jewish, and secular. In 1954 the AJAAS launched the anticolonial journal *Consciences maghrébines*, and Lavalette joined its production and distribution staff.[22]

When the Algerian War began on November 1, 1954, Lavalette confirmed her commitment to it, writing in her journal: "Je lis la proclamation du 1er Novembre, je la fais mienne" (*Juste Algérienne*, 41; I read the proclamation of the first of November and make it mine). Within a year, she had become a courier for the FLN, transmitting messages and supplies from Benyoucef Ben Khedda, a leader of the ZAA in Algiers, to Hadj Ben Alla, the head of Wilaya V, in Oran. She was also on the staff of the clandestine FLN journal *El Moudjahid* and sheltered FLN leaders in her apartment in Algiers (43). Arrested in 1957 while on a mission to Oran, she soon joined fellow FLN operatives Drif, Ighilahriz, and Amrane-Minne in prison in Algiers. In her memoir, she, like Drif, pays tribute to her fellow *moudjahidate*.

The title of Lavalette's memoir, *Juste Algérienne: Comme une tissure*, is significant. First, by omitting the indefinite article in the first phrase, she proposes two readings: *Juste une Algérienne* (Just an Algerian woman) and *Une juste Algérienne* (A just Algerian woman), suggesting that she defines herself as a citizen of Algeria, with no reference to religious affiliation or specific origin, and as an individual committed to the values of truth and justice. Second, with the accompanying phrase *Comme une tissure*, a figurative reference to the intersection of the warp and woof of woven fabric, the memoirist conceptualizes her role as that of a weaver; her memoir, a woven carpet or tapestry:

> J'ai essayé de retisser, sans apprêt, seulement
> avec le fuseau de ma mémoire
> avec la navette de mes années
> > ce qui fut
> > et ce qui est. (31)

> (I tried to weave, simply, only
> with the spindle of my memory
> with the shuttle of my years
> > what was
> > and what is.)

Extending the metaphor, we can say that the memoirist, in the text that follows, weaves the strands of her life of political engagement into the "fabric" of the new nation.[23] Significantly, Lavalette returns to this trope during her period of exile in Avignon in 1995. In "Un tapis pour Amar" (175–77; A carpet for Amar), a short piece in her memoir that combines poetry and prose, she assumes the voice of a carpet to speak out against the violence that had overtaken Algeria and forced her into exile. If we recall that in Yamina Mechakra's novel *La grotte éclatée* the art of weaving, Algerian women's traditional art form, becomes the metaphor for the weaving together of multiple women's voices, we find Lavalette evoking the same relationship between her writing and this form of expression perfected by Algerian women; largely illiterate, they expressed their creativity through their weaving.[24]

Choosing the form of a personal journal made up of entries of various lengths written over a period of several decades, Lavalette offers her readers a fragmented text whose chronological order is at times disrupted through the process of rewriting. For example, Lavalette tells us that a poem composed in prison in 1957, at the time of the eight-day strike in Algiers, was rewritten in 2010, although she neglects to say how the original was transformed (61–63). She does explain that some poems were memorized during the prison years and transcribed later.

Examining the prison poems, we find the writer emphasizing the personal significance of her poetry in a distinctive way; she brings to the published text a photo of the notebook in which she wrote her poems while in prison in Algiers, as well as a photo of a two-page excerpt from "La prison centrale." The handwritten excerpt, with some words crossed out and others written in tiny cramped script, is a poignant personal artifact that Lavalette kept throughout her life, sharing it with her readers almost six decades after it was written. It is a reminder that all her poems—some committed to memory, others recorded in notebooks—were of great comfort to her during very dark days.

Adopting the terse minimalist style that characterizes Amrane-Minne's verse, "La prison centrale" brings the reader into the world of the incarcerated as the poet charts her own experience within the prison walls. Set in the detention center in Oran, where she was held following her arrest, the poem begins in prose, then moves into free verse, revealing that the process of dehumanization occurs immediately; the prisoner, now designated by a number—3590—must struggle to maintain her identity. She will call herself Princess 3590, and through memory she will hold on to the world beyond the prison walls: "Et pourtant, tout est là, loin—mais présent" (71; Nevertheless, everything is still there, distant—but present).

Drawing attention to the harsh and unjust penal system implemented by "Les hommes qui jugent, les hommes qui condamnent, et les hommes qui gardent" (70; The men who judge, the men who convict, the men who guard), she exposes the psychological and physical abuse to which she is subjected:

Elle a rencontré la haine des questions
qui se posent dix-huit heures d'affilée
. . . .

Elle a su la souffrance extrême
—il n'y a pas de mot vivant
pour dire, Faraday,
ce qu'on fait de tes lois apprises au lycée. (71–72)

(She felt the hatred of the questions
posed eighteen hours straight
. . . .
She has known extreme suffering
There are no words,
Faraday, to express
what they have done to your laws we learned in high school.)

Following the explicit reference to the interrogation session, she refers indirectly to the physical torture administered through *la gégène,* the electric generator invented by Michael Faraday, the nineteenth-century British inventor who never anticipated that his electric motor would be used as a torture device. Hence, in terms that are explicit and implicit, and in language that is terse and concise, she conveys her suffering; it is emotional as well as physical. Articulating her fears, she admits to the fear of acquiescing to her interrogators, on the one hand, and losing her grasp of the presence of life beyond the prison walls, on the other:

Elle a été pétrie du doute de soi
De la peur de dire oui
De l'oubli du jaune intense
Du violet dur
De la chaleur de midi, des plaines immenses
Et d'un rideau tiré près d'une cheminée. (72)

(She had been filled with self-doubt
with the fear of saying yes
of forgetting the intense yellow
the harsh violet
of the noonday heat, of the vast plains
and of a curtain drawn near a fireplace.)

Having expressed her fears, she can then overcome them, finding strength and the power to resist through the genuine affection expressed by her fellow comrades. Concluding the poem on an inspiring note, she recalls being cheered and celebrated in song by her fellow male prisoners as she was led back to her cell following a grueling session of harsh interrogation:

> Sale, épuisée d'interrogatoires, de sévices, de supplices,
> elle était passée devant les grilles
> qui enfermaient des hommes enchaînés
> et qui pour elle
> s'étaient levés
> et avait chanté.
> Elle croit bien qu'elle avait un peu pleuré. (75)

> (Dirty, exhausted by interrogations, abuse, torture
> she passed in front of the bars
> that enclosed chained men
> who had risen for her
> and sung.
> She believes that she had cried a little.)

Comparing the final verse of the handwritten original with the printed version, we find that they conclude somewhat differently. In the prison notebook she had written:

> Elle croit bien qu'elle avait un peu pleuré
> Peut-être parce qu'elle n'avait jamais été
> > Autant aimé. (25)

> (She believes that she had cried a little
> Perhaps because she had never been
> > So loved.)

Hence, we discover that the final verse of the handwritten original has been omitted from the later printed version, which ends: "Elle croit bien, qu'elle avait un peu pleuré" (75; She believes that she had cried a little). Why this particular revision? We may hypothesize that upon later reflection the poet chose to conclude with the verb *pleurer*, "to cry," rather than *aimer*, "to love," in order to couple the sentiment of solidarity, her sense of belonging to the community of the colonized, with the profound sadness at having been tortured by the French military, who judged her a traitor to be punished. Yet it is also possible that in the period following Algeria's undeclared civil war of the 1990s, an era during which Francophone intellectuals became targets of Islamist terrorists and many, including Lavalette, were forced into exile, she could not express the same sense of solidarity experienced in the earlier period. In either case, the revised ending attests to the poet's approach to her poetry: her poems are organic works to be reworked and modified.

For Lavalette, the dark decade of the 1990s, a difficult period for most Algerians, marked a period of intense personal grief. On January 13, 1993, her husband, the Algerian journalist Abdelkader Safir, died, following a long illness. On December 28, 1993, the heightened violence of the civil war forced her to leave her home in Benchicao, a village east of Medea, and begin a period of exile that took her to Avignon from 1995 to 1997 before returning to Algeria, first to Algiers in 1997 and then in 2000 to Medea, where she spent the last years of her life. During these years, she wrote of the fear that gripped Algeria, caught up in fratricidal warfare:

> Le bruit silencieux de la peur
> Peur des brouillards.
> Peur du moindre son. (195)

> (The silent sound of fear
> Fear of the fog
> Fear of the slightest sound.)

Forced into exile, she expresses a sense of injustice and pain:

> Elle a fait partie de ceux qui ont travaillé de toutes leurs forces pour un pays vrai, fraternel, un pays juste.
> Et l'exil est brûlant, intolérable, injuste. (182)

(She was one of those who worked with all their strength to build a country that was true, fraternal, and just.

And exile is burning, intolerable, unjust.)

Significantly, in these final years of personal and collective trauma, Lavalette once again refers to herself in the third-person singular: *elle* replaces *je* in the text. She explains in the memoir that before 1962 she used *elle* as a "sujet commun dans le sens grammatical du terme" (139; common subject in the grammatical sense of the term), considering it an expression of unity and common direction as individuals struggled for the same goal, independence. At the end of the war, however, *elle* becomes *je* as common paths diverge. Then, as Algeria enters the dark years of civil strife and terrorism, she returns to *elle*, the common subject, as a new political struggle begins, this one against Islamic radicalism (139).

Although Lavalette's explanation appears logical and coherent, the psychiatrist and essayist Alice Cherki, while admitting that it is difficult to choose between the first-, second-, and third-person singular in this literary form, nevertheless questions whether Lavalette's stylistic choice reflects timidity: "L'écriture sensible d'une femme qui n'ose pas dire 'je' pour parler d'un engagement, de prison, de torture, d'exils renouvelés?" (*Mémoire anachronique*, 245; Is it the sensitive writing of a woman who dares not say "I" when speaking of commitment, prison, torture, recurring exile?).

Contrary to Lavalette and her critic, I consider the use of the third-person singular an expression of neither unity nor timidity but rather her way of distancing herself from traumatic events—torture, death, exile—first during the Algerian War and then again during the civil war of the 1990s. By creating distance between herself and the self she projects on paper, she is able to articulate previously occulted traumatic events. I suggest that just as Ighilahriz uses interlocutors to help her tell her story (her sister, Ourdïa, and the journalist Anne Nivat), Lavalette adopts a psychological aid(e); she distances one self, the writer, from traumatic events by using another self, the protagonist, as her alter ego.

Clearly, both Ighilahriz and Lavalette express the will to disclose hidden history and yet the difficulty of breaking the silence. And if truth, in its "delayed appearance and its belated address," is at the heart of Ighilahriz's memoir, it is present in Lavalette's as well. Ighilahriz could not speak of the rape she endured while in prison for several decades; nor was Lavalette able to exteriorize her trauma. Tortured in prison, she was then transferred to the psychiatric ward of Mustapha Hospital in Algiers, where the consulting psychiatrist judged the pied-noir who embraced the anticolonial struggle to be insane and prescribed twenty-one sessions of electroshock therapy. Thus, her torture continued, but under the guise of psychiatric treatment. She did not disclose this personal trauma publicly for many years, explaining in her journal that she remained convinced that no one would believe her. Indeed, in 2006, when she writes about it, she wonders if times have changed: "Et aujourd'hui sera-t-elle entendue?" (100; Will she be heard today?).

As Lavalette and Ighilahriz struggle to articulate their trauma, each retraces her attempt to find the individual who showed her support during her dark days in prison. Ighilahriz attempts to find the French military doctor who saved her life in prison. Lavalette seeks out the one French deputy who refused to participate in a cover-up of the torture of prisoners in Algerian jails. Although she was aware that the French parliamentary commission of 1956, charged with investigating allegations of torture by the French military in Algeria, had disregarded all evidence to the contrary, it was not until 1995 that she learned that it had not reached a unanimous decision. One deputy, Dr. Hovnanian, had refused to accept the false conclusion. Expressing her gratitude to the lone voice of truth and justice, Lavalette concludes: "Les Justes sont des justes jusqu'au bout" (180; The Just are just until the end).

Acknowledging Dr. Hovnanian as one of the just, Lavalette applies the same term to him that she grants herself in the title of the memoir, recognizing him as an individual who shares her sense of justice and paying tribute in this way to all individuals who, in turbulent times and despite the consequences, remain committed to the values of truth, reason, justice, and fairness. Should we read her profound gratitude to this *juste* as also a reference to "Les Justes parmi les nations" (The righteous among the nations), a reference to Israel's recognition of the non-Jews of various nations who, in the name of justice, risked their lives to aid Jews persecuted by the Nazis? In other words, does she, like Maïssa Bey and Leïla Sebbar, call upon multidirectional memory to situate Algeria's struggle within a larger historical context, that of the collective struggle for truth and justice in the twentieth century?

Why had Lavalette not learned earlier of the lone dissenting voice? She explains in her letter to the former deputy that upon her release from prison she tried to put the trauma behind her: "Il faut tourner la page, voire la déchirer pour continuer à respirer, à sentir, à comprendre, à aimer" (179; You have to turn the page, indeed destroy it in order to continue to breathe, feel, understand, and love). Her conviction that victims of hatred and violence must break with the painful past in order to "breathe, feel, understand, and love" helps explain why truth tends to reach us in its "delayed appearance and its belated address" and why Lavalette, like Ighilahriz, vacillates between silence and disclosure.

Indeed, Lavalette's reticence in opening her private world to public scrutiny takes several forms in the text. She designates fellow prisoners by their first names or initials, keeping their identity hidden. Similarly, the personal photos that serve to contextualize her world are often enigmatic; some captions name individuals not cited in the text, others identify some but not all the persons in a group photo, and in some snapshots faces remain indistinct. Most significantly, Lavalette guards her family's privacy; we readers never learn how her relationship with her parents evolved in the postindependence period. Indeed, as her editors note in their introductory comments on the book jacket, "Le lecteur devra se 'contenter' de bribes, de fragments, de sensations" (The reader must be "content" with snatches, fragments, sensations).

As these "snatches, fragments, sensations" convey Lavalette's reluctance to open her private world to public scrutiny, they also reflect the circumstances in which the memoir came into the public domain. Lavalette eventually shares with her public a work originally destined for no reader but herself. The text reaches the public only after she has shown it to the Algerian journalist Ghania Mouffok, who urges publication. Yet, Lavalette remains hesitant, not fully convinced that her writings would interest the public today and not sure whether she was an important enough historical figure to merit publication; her text would not appear for another thirteen years.

In conclusion, the three memoirists whose work forms this chapter contribute, each in her own way, to shedding light on the anticolonial war in which they participated and in a larger sense to the growing body of literature we may term women's reflections on war. Drif, who played a key role in the Battle of Algiers, bequeaths a narrative of that crucial historical moment to posterity. Ighilahriz, by disclosing the trauma of her rape in prison, publicly denounces silence and secrecy and encourages her compatriots to follow her lead in unearthing occulted history. Lavalette offers her readers personal writings in the form of prison diaries, poems, and contemporary chronicles, as well as photos, that chart a life of political engagement shaped by a keen sense of social justice. All three emphasize two important points, one concerning the memoirist, the other, the memoir. First, although the period of engagement in the violent anticolonial war was relatively brief in each memoirist's long life, her commitment to the struggle and events that followed clearly shaped the way in which she came to view the world and live the rest of her life. Second, by linking the intimate to the political, the memoir gives voice to the individual, thereby introducing a much-needed corrective to the epic narratives and romantic fictions that war tends to inspire.

7 REMEMBERING ZOULIKHA IN ASSIA DJEBAR'S FILM AND FICTION

We have seen that writers, in their attempt to restore Algerian women to their proper place in the history of their nation, bring in voices from the margins, recover hidden histories, and put a human face on historical events. Moreover, as they depict the collective history of the anticolonial struggle, they do not neglect individual experience. Assia Djebar has played a leading role in this endeavor. As this study draws to an end, I turn back to Djebar (whose early works are examined in chapter 2) to examine her penultimate novel, *La femme sans sépulture* (Woman without a tomb), published in 2002, as well as her 1977 film, *La nouba des femmes du Mont Chenoua*, both of which introduce a relatively unknown historical figure whose nationalist activity had not been recorded in the annals of history: Yamina Echaïb Oudaï, known as Zoulikha, the heroic resistant who came to be called the martyr of Cherchell.

Born in 1911, Zoulikha joined the Algerian resistance in her native city of Cherchell in 1956. Captured, she was tortured and then killed by the French military on October 25, 1957. Although her family received official notice of her death at the time, her body was never returned to them for burial; Zoulikha became a "femme sans sépulture," a woman without a tomb. Although revered by the men and women of Cherchell for her courage and commitment to the independence struggle, Zoulikha was largely unknown to Algerians beyond her native region until the publication of Djebar's novel. Significantly, Amrane-Minne, whose own resistance network had been in Algiers, admitted that she did not know of her, adding that so many militants lived and died in anonymity.[1]

Given Djebar's family roots in Cherchell and the surrounding villages of Mount Chenoua, it is not surprising that she would evoke the life of this *moudjahida* in her work. As she explains in the prelude to the novel, only a wall separated her father's family home in Cherchell from the Oudaï family's patio (13). More surprising, however, is her use of film and text—*La nouba des femmes du Mont Chenoua* (1978) and *La femme sans sépulture* (2002), the two separated by more than two decades—to bring Zoulikha into history. Yet, repetition, the revisiting of historical or personal events that mark the individual and the community, is, as the critic Anne Donadey has aptly noted, a characteristic of Djebar's work (*Recasting Colonialism*, 79–87).

In this chapter, I posit that Djebar's intent is neither to unearth occulted history—Zoulikha's commitment to the independence struggle was well known in her region—nor to provide additional historical elements to her biography, but to transform the militant into a powerful legendary figure whose courage and political commitment would serve to empower Algerian women via the transmission of her life story. This hypothesis is supported, in my view, by the fact that Djebar made the film during Houari Boumediene's presidency, when conservative forces were able to relegate women to secondary status, and published the novel two decades later, when Islamic fundamentalism threatened Algerian women's rights, if not their lives. Thus, she calls attention to the precarious sociopolitical position of women in two distinct historical periods, the 1970s and the 1990s. In each era, Zoulikha's life story becomes a cautionary tale against violence, injustice, and amnesia, as well as a reminder to Algerians that they must never forget women combatants who gave their lives in pursuit of freedom.

As postcolonial writers explore the legacy of colonialism, not only hidden history but also little-known facts come to light. When Djebar delved into French colonial archives in preparation for her novel *L'amour, la fantasia* (*Fantasia: An Algerian Cavalcade*), Baron Barchou de Ponhoën's description of the battle of Staouéli, with its portrayal of Algerian women on the battlefield, drew her immediate attention (*L'amour, la fantasia*, 28–29; *Fantasia*, 18). As previously noted, Barchou's report is clearly biased, depicting these women as part of a savage horde (see chapter 2). Djebar cites his passage in her novel but then rewrites it, reinterpreting the Algerian women's actions on the battlefield as heroic. In her view, the women of Staouéli, who actively resisted the French military invasion in 1830, foreshadowed Algerian women's more recent *moudjahidate,* the women combatants of the Algerian War.

Calling her readers' attention to the actions of these and other forgotten women of Algerian history, Djebar offers a counternarrative to those who have ignored women's militancy in Algeria's anticolonial struggles. Hence, she, like Amrane-Minne, uses archives and oral testimony to bring women's hidden histories to light, yet Djebar begins her speleological endeavor in an earlier era. After first resuscitating the women combatants of Staoueli, she turns her attention to the *soeurs disparues,* the vanished sisters, of the more recent past, the Algerian War. Here, she uncovers the life story of Zoulikha Oudaï.

As we follow Djebar, who uses her triple role as historian, writer, and filmmaker to retrace Zoulikha's life, we find her developing the themes of memory and mourning in both *La nouba* and *La femme sans sépulture.* In this regard, these creative works may be considered meditations on collective and individual memory of the Algerian War, as both propose a dual narrative: a search for Algeria's vanished sisters and a quest for a vanished self.

As a historian in search of Algerian women's war story, Djebar uses oral interviews to bring the testimony of former women combatants to the public at large, aware of the importance of oral transmission—women speaking to women—in circulating empowering narratives such as Zoulikha's. As a filmmaker and novelist, she depicts a fictional protagonist on a spiritual quest, an inner journey that leads Lila (*La nouba*) and the unnamed narrator (*La femme sans sépulture*) to renew their bonds with the women of Cherchell and the neighboring villages of Mount Chenoua, the region of their childhood home and Djebar's as well. This return to one's origins, as well as numerous autobiographical traces, leads the critic Ana Medeiros to term the novel "a fiction with an autobiographical/documentary basis" ("Fantastic Elements," 3), a definition that easily extends to *La nouba.*

In *La nouba* Djebar introduces her heroine via a dedication followed by a praise song, and then returns to her briefly as the women who knew her best—close friends and family—retrace Zoulikha's past, focusing on her political activities during the Algerian War. In *La femme sans sépulture,* as she traces the militant's life Djebar anchors her in reality but then transforms her progressively from historical to mythic figure. If the cinematographic depiction of the *moudjahida* is an unexpectedly fleeting one, the textual representation is equally surprising. Rejecting the model of the classic historical novel, which would faithfully re-create the key elements of a historical figure's life, it offers readers instead a hybrid work that combines fictional and factual components. In both the film and the novel, she offers us a fragmented narrative that in its innovative approach to plot and character define so much of her work and, in its complexity, often poses significant challenges to viewers and readers alike. Yet, this fragmentation accords with Djebar's view of narrative: "La narration ne doit pas raconter l'histoire mais l'interrompre: c'est-à-dire, la suspendre, la surprendre à tout prix" (Zimra, "Sounding Off the Absent Body," 108; Narration must not tell the story but interrupt it, which is to say, suspend it, surprise it at all costs).[2]

Picking up on the filmmaker-novelist's commitment to the interrupted, suspended narrative, I propose that we view her stylistic experimentation, the fragmentation that gives rise to a disjointed, nonlinear construction, as her way of calling attention to her nation's inability to remember the past adequately and mourn the dead appropriately, particularly with respect to Algeria's *moudjahidate*, the nation's women combatants. I am suggesting that form and content converge as Zoulikha, "the woman without a tomb," becomes emblematic of Algeria's inability to reconcile the past and the present. Thus, Djebar's interest in Zoulikha's life story, which she depicts in both film and fiction, fits it into the broader scope of inquiry, her nation's relationship to its history, memory, and mourning. In this regard, she joins the postcolonial historian Benjamin Stora, who, in *La gangrène et l'oubli: La mémoire de la guerre d'Algérie*, contends that a state of amnesia surrounds many events of the Algerian War and has been harmful to both France and Algeria. It is within this framework of national amnesia that we find Djebar embarking upon the project of recounting Zoulikha's life story, seeking through film and text to grant the martyr of Cherchell a proper burial—metaphorically, if not physically.

La nouba des femmes du Mont Chenoua

Djebar turned to cinema in the late 1970s, after several years of reflection and silence following the publication of *Les alouettes naïves* in 1967. She explains:

J'ai pensé sincèrement que je pouvais devenir écrivain arabophone. Mais pendant ces années de silence, j'ai compris qu'il y avait des problèmes de la langue arabe écrite qui ne relèvent pas actuellement de ma compétence. C'est différent au niveau de la langue de tous les jours. C'est pourquoi, faire du cinéma pour moi ce n'est pas abandonner le mot pour l'image. C'est faire de l'image-son. C'est effectuer un retour aux sources au niveau du langage. (Qtd. in Fanon, "Une femme, un film," 3)

(I sincerely thought that I could become an Arabic writer. But during these years of silence, I learned that there were problems with written Arabic that go beyond my competency. It is different at the level of the spoken language. That is why, for me, filmmaking does not involve abandoning the word for the image. It means creating the *image-son,* the image with the sound. It is a return to one's linguistic roots.)

Choosing to work in dialectal Arabic, her mother tongue, and in film, a new medium for her, signaled a return to her community of origin. Shooting her first film in her native region, she introduces autobiographical elements connected to both her maternal and paternal lineages: the city of Cherchell, her birthplace, is home to her father's family; the rural villages of Mount Chenoua are home to her mother's family. Thus, the title *La nouba des femmes du Mont Chenoua* (The nouba of the women of Mount Chenoua) not only situates the film geographically, in the Berber villages near the coastal city approximately sixty miles from Algiers, it conveys significant autobiographical references, specifically an emphasis on her maternal roots.[3]

The title of the film also plays upon the various meanings of the Arabic word *nouba.* On the one hand, it signifies "taking turns" and designates a type of music that in the past had been performed by a group of musicians playing in turn in front of dignitaries' homes. On the other hand, it refers to individuals taking turns speaking, hence to women's conversations. In addition, the expression *faire la nouba* occurs in colloquial French and means to have a good time, to throw a party. Thus, it too makes an indirect reference to lively music and animated conversation.

Djebar emphasizes the musical references by dedicating the film to the Hungarian composer Bela Bartok as well as to Zoulikha. As she honors all Algerian women who fought for independence by paying homage to a martyr of Cherchell, she also shows her gratitude to the Hungarian composer, who in 1913 traveled to Algeria to study its folk music. With the dedication to Bartok and the inclusion of his music in her first film, Djebar pays tribute to one of the rare renowned European musicians to recognize Algeria's vibrant musical tradition and draw inspiration from it. As a bilingual artist—an Arabic-language filmmaker and a Francophone writer—she affirms her commitment to Algeria's oral tradition.

La nouba offers a praise song to Zoulikha that ends optimistically, with an expressed hope in Algeria's future:[4]

> Mon chant parle toujours de liberté
>
> . . . .
>
> Zoulikha tout ce qui était difficile pour toi sera facile
> Le pays de la séparation, derrière toi tu le laisseras
> Nous vivrons un rêve d'aisance et de bien-être
> Nous régnerons librement, dans une joie merveilleuse!
>
> (My song always speaks of liberty
>
> . . . .
>
> Zoulikha, all that was difficult
> All that was difficult for you will be easy
> The country of separation, you will leave it behind
> We will live a dream of ease and well-being
> We will reign freely, in marvelous joy!)

Presenting a utopian vision of postcolonial Algeria that Zoulikha unfortunately did not live to see, Djebar nonetheless introduces a disquieting element, "the country of separation." For Djebar, the phrase signifies both the separation between colonizer and colonized and the gap in understanding between Algerian men and women. The anticolonial struggle ended with the victory of the colonized, but the postcolonial period did not result in the triumph of women's rights. Making the film in the late 1970s, she saw that Algerian women's historical contributions to the independence struggle were increasingly overlooked and that women were bypassed in the construction of the postcolonial nation.

This film lauding Zoulikha depicts her as a shadowy presence whose political commitment and courageous actions inspire the praise song that frames it, but she is not its main focus. Set in postcolonial Algeria, the film centers on a fictional protagonist who revisits the rural village of her childhood. Lila, a young woman living in an Algerian city, presumably Algiers, returns to Chenoua after a fifteen-year absence, haunted by traumatic memories of the Algerian War—not only her time in prison but particularly the loss of her brother, an FLN combatant—and troubled by a dysfunctional marriage. By reconnecting with the world of her past, Lila eventually finds the peace that has eluded her. Most important to her psychological recovery is her connection to the rural women who share with her their recollections of life in the maquis during the anticolonial war. As they articulate their war memories, she is able to overcome her own war trauma.

As the camera follows Lila, the city dweller, rediscovering the landscape of her youth, the viewer also comes to appreciate the natural beauty of this rugged mountain landscape, which contrasts sharply with the dark interior of the country house where she is living while vacationing with her husband and child. Thus, visual elements—dark interior rooms in contrast to the bright outdoor landscapes—convey her solitude. We see the isolation Lila experiences within her marriage reflected in the phrase "the country of separation"; it acknowledges the divide between men and women expressed in the praise song to Zoulikha.

This camera sequence lays the groundwork for *La femme sans sépulture*, for Djebar will use the same format, the French-educated Algerian woman coming from the capital city to speak with women in towns and villages about their war experiences, and the same narrative technique, the translation and adaptation of Arabic-language testimony into a French written text. This link is particularly apparent to viewers of the film, who watch Lila leave her jeep with her tape recorder to conduct her interviews and find the anonymous narrator of the novel coming to Cherchell in a similar vehicle and with the same recording material. We should add that the protagonist, Lila, played by the Algerian actress Sawan Noweir, bears a striking resemblance to Assia Djebar, a casting decision that reinforces the autobiographical connection between the filmmaker and her fictional character.

As Lila listens attentively to the women and records their war narratives, the film's sound track presents various styles of music. To ensure that music is an essential part of the film, Djebar uses the form of the Andalusian symphony, a composition in seven parts, to structure it: the *touchyia*, or overture; the *istikhbar*, or prelude; the *meceder*, adagio; the *btaihi*, allegro; the *derj*, lento; the *nesraf*, moderato; and the *khlass*, or finale. She writes that the sound created by the blending of various traditional instruments completes the structure of the symphony.[5] And to further personalize the film, Djebar, who is quite well versed in Andalusian music, adds her own composition to the soundtrack.[6]

Djebar's camera, as I have noted, takes her viewers on a journey from a rather dark enclosure to the bright and expansive outdoors. The film begins with Lila, her husband, and their daughter indoors, in the small house where they are living while on vacation, and ends with Lila outside, first, on a fishing boat at sea and then climbing up a hillside, passing a group of seated women, and entering the village cemetery. This brief outline suggests that the film is structured as a journey to empowerment, charting a woman's psychological evolution, which ends with her new sense of independence and freedom. This structure is quickly undercut, however, by sequences that are consistently fragmented, interrupted, and nonlinear. The lack of a formal stable structure leads the critic Réda Bensmaïa to describe *La nouba* as a composition comprising five series in which the movement between fiction and documentary replaces the logical and chronological order that viewers anticipate ("La nouba," 880). The five series are (1) a fictional series involving Lila, her husband, and their child; (2) a documentary series involving the women and children of Mount Chenoua; (3) a series that is both documentary and fictional involving dreamlike or poetic "illustrations" inspired by the women of Mount Chenoua; (4) a documentary and fictional series involving natural landscapes and seascapes; and (5) a documentary series comprising archival film footage of scenes of violent repression during the war of national liberation. Clearly, Djebar's film challenged the expectations of many viewers of the period accustomed to a linear narrative with a predictable evolution of events and psychological development.

Turning to Zoulikha's life story in the fourth section, the *btaihi*, we see this fragmented sequencing quite clearly. First, we hear several women's voices, including those of Zoulikha's daughters, present aspects of her life story. They explain, for example, that following the death of her husband, Zoulikha left her children with relatives in Cherchell to join the rebels in the mountains, a chapter in the militant's life that is explored in greater detail in the subsequent novel. The women's oral narratives compose the sound track that accompanies the camera's multiple, varied shots of the city of Cherchell. Following this documentary sequence, the camera follows Lila to a well-known historical site in the region: Kub-er-Rumia (Arabic) / Le Tombeau de la Chrétienne (French). The impressive circular stone pyramid erroneously called the Christian woman's tomb was built in 3 BC by the Berber king Juba II as a mausoleum for him and his wife, Queen Cleopatra Selene II, daughter of Cleopatra VII and Mark Antony. Archaeological excavations reveal that the two probably were not buried within its chambers, since no bodies or signs of funeral rites were ever discovered.[7]

Lila's visit to the site following her interviews with Zoulikha's family and friends introduces the theme of commemoration and poses the question of how Zoulikha, the woman with neither tomb nor memorial, should be honored. What tribute would be appropriate? Given its materiality—an imposing pyramid measuring 33 meters high and 128 meters wide—the mausoleum erected by Juba II for his remains and those of the queen contrasts dramatically with the immateriality that defines Zoulikha in the film.

As previously noted in chapter 5, the French historian Pierre Nora explains in the introduction to his extensive study of the relationship between history, memory, and memory sites that *lieux de mémoire,* or places of memory, share three qualities: they are material, symbolic, and functional ("Entre mémoire et histoire," xxxiv). He goes on to explain that war memorials erected in most French villages following World War I reflect these characteristics: they are material, made of stone; they are symbolic, representing France's loss of almost an entire generation of young men; they are functional, listing the names of each soldier from that village who died in the war. The memory of Zoulikha, her life and her deeds, had no such material trace; she remained a haunting presence.

Djebar emphasizes Zoulikha's spectral presence with the seven-minute sequence that directly precedes Lila's visit to the mausoleum. In that sequence the voices of three women, the martyr's two daughters and her sister, speak of her offscreen as the camera zooms in on the city of Cherchell and out again. As the critic Florence Martin remarks, Zoulikha has become a "visible blank" (*Screens and Veils,* 60), existing only through the voices of those who knew her. We know, however, that vestiges of Zoulikha do indeed remain; these include photos and objects belonging to her. Thus,

Djebar could have shown any one of numerous photos of Zoulikha or her family or filmed her home in Cherchell, her mountain hideout, and even the clearing on the outskirts of town where she was captured and then led away by French soldiers to the military camp where she died. Yet, the filmmaker chooses to represent her as a shadowy figure whose portrait the viewer never sees, a legendary spirit belonging to the world of the vanished. And to further emphasize Zoulikha's ethereal presence, the camera projects views of the city, with its streets, courtyards, and patios, as the women remember her, thereby connecting her to Cherchell in a way that suggests that she has become a haunting presence for the entire community, not only for her family and friends.

Djebar has stated that her first intention when turning to film was to make a documentary about the women of her native region. She began her project with conversations recorded with six former combatants: Zohra Sahraoui, Aïcha Medeljar, Fatma Serhane, Kheira Amrane, Fatma Oudaï, and Khedija Lekhal. She revised her project, adding the fictional elements, Lila and her world, once she realized that she needed to bring together rural and urban women's voices in her exploration of Algerian history and memory (Delmas, "Assia Djebar," 18; Fanon, "Une femme, un film," 3). Then, by moving back and forth between fiction and documentary, she was able to create an interesting blend of the two, particularly when Lila, the fictitious interviewer, listens attentively to the conversations with former *moudjahidate* recorded by Djebar.[8]

As the fictional protagonist reenacts the role of historian, she interviews two types of informants, women who probe their personal past to recall their own war experiences and Zoulikha's family and friends, who, through memory, shed light on the life of the *chahida*, or martyr.[9] The testimonial narratives of the latter, however, remain incomplete, for only Zoulikha knows the full story of her life, including the last moments, and unfortunately, no record of her testimony exists. This "visible blank" will lead Djebar to choose novelistic liberty in recounting the martyred Zoulikha's life story, filling in the historical gaps through fiction.

As a hybrid work that privileges neither its documentary nor its fictional elements, the film also takes us into the realm of the symbolic. In one crucial sequence, Lila enters a cave to participate with a group of rural women of Chenoua in an evening of traditional dance and ritual. Adding her glowing candle to those placed in the cave by the other women and then joining in their dance, Lila takes her place in their world; her maternal lineage links her to them. Just as her symbolic gestures are crucial to reaffirming these ties to her maternal clan, so is the place where these rites take place: a dark, humid, mysterious cave. Here, traditional music, dance, and ritual draw her symbolically to the womb; through this ceremony of female bonding, she finds a new sense of self, and she is able to emerge with a new sense of direction.

After bonding with the women of Mount Chenoua, reconnecting to her maternal origins, Lila reemerges restored. Acknowledging these rural women as Lila's forebears, the critic Clarisse Zimra concludes that their healing trance in the ancestral cave brings Lila's quest to closure ("Sounding Off the Absent Body," 112). It remains unclear to the viewer whether this sequence is oneiric or "real," whether Lila is renewed through dream or through ritual. Hence, as the film often blurs the distinction between documentary and fiction, it also blurs the distinction between dream and reality.

Algerians of the Chenoua region—but certainly not all viewers—will connect this scene filmed in the Dahra caves with an earlier episode in Algerian history, one Djebar gleaned from colonial archives and regional oral tradition and describes in detail in *L'amour, la fantasia*. As described in chapter 2, in 1845, two separate incidents of *enfumade* occurred in the region when the French military set fire to caves used as refuge by the local tribes, asphyxiating the men, women, and children sheltered within. The chronicle of war and conquest became a chronicle of genocide in which the novelist's ancestors were victims. One officer, Pélissier, subsequently made his soldiers carry the bodies out of the cave for a macabre body count. His written testimony of the event unleashed a polemic against him, effectively ending his military career. The other officer, Saint-Arnaud, far more discrete and politically astute, sent a confidential report to the French military headquarters in Algiers, where it was promptly destroyed. Whereas the first incident was recorded and entered French colonial archives, the second was relegated to oral history, known only to the victims' descendants but never forgotten. Djebar, a historian by training, uses written archives and oral testimony to bring these episodes of colonial history to the attention of her readers.

We can view Lila's visit to the Dahra cave as a palimpsestic rewriting of Pélissier's brutal massacre. In other words, as Djebar films her protagonist participating in the ancestral dance ritual, she superimposes a new narrative, a symbolic rebirth occurring in the cave, upon the previous one, the death by asphyxiation of approximately fifteen hundred men, women, and children in their underground refuge. Thus, viewers find the film anticipating Djebar's later textual revisions of history. In this regard, the critic Winifred Woodhull notes that Djebar, in counterpoint to Pélissier's macabre act, brings to light elements of colonial history that have "a liberatory dimension for women" (*Transfigurations of the Maghreb*, 82). Because the incidents of *enfumade* are explicitly depicted in *L'amour, la fantasia*, critics tend to overlook the fact that indirect references to them appear first in the film.[10] Indeed, as we view the film today, we find early traces of several themes that Djebar develops more fully in later texts. For example, meditations on remembrance and mourning the dead are further explored in the collection of essays *Le blanc de l'Algérie* (*Algerian White*), of 1996, and in the collection of short stories *Oran, langue morte* (*The Tongue's Blood Does Not Run Dry: Algerian Stories*), of 1997, as well as in Djebar's reflections on making the film that appear in the novel, *Vaste est la prison* (*So Vast the Prison*), also published in 1997.

A final sequence in the film suggesting a "liberatory dimension" depicts Lila, wearing a burnous (traditional Berber garb), seated in a fishing boat heading for the open waters under a bright blue Mediterranean sky. Leaving two closed worlds behind, the home she had shared with her husband and the rural community of women she has come to know, Lila moves on alone. As she leaves behind the personal trauma of a failed marriage and a fruitless search for her dead brother, as well as the collective trauma of a long and violent anticolonial war that she now understands has touched everyone who experienced it, she sets out, literally and figuratively, in uncharted waters. Ironically, perhaps, *La nouba*, despite its fragmented, often interrupted, and tenuous story line—all elements of experimental cinema—provides viewers with a traditional happy ending, including the optimistic praise song to Zoulikha, as a closed universe opens and Lila embarks upon a future filled with promise.

Significantly, Djebar, like her protagonist, has also found a new beginning. Having felt uneasy as a Francophone writer, she discovers that the experience of making a film has led to new perspectives:

> Après *La Nouba*, je me suis remise à écrire. Ce film m'a fait accepter mon bilinguisme culturel avec sérénité. Mon rapport avec la langue française est

aujourd'hui plus clair. Si j'écris en français, c'est parce que j'ai choisi cette langue et non parce que je suis une colonisée. (Djebar, "Comment travaillent les écrivains," 69)

(After *La Nouba* I began to write again. This film made me accept my cultural bilingualism with serenity. My relationship to the French language is much clearer today. If I write in French, it is because I chose this language and not because I am a colonized person.)

Thus, just as Lila has become "the outsider who has come back to claim her place inside the house (and collective narrative) of women" (Martin, *Screens and Veils*, 54), so, in a sense, has Djebar. Alternately outsider and insider with respect to two cultural spaces, Algeria and France, Djebar now reconnects willingly and comfortably to the French language as she continues to pursue her dual quest: to find her "vanished" sisters and reconnect with her "vanished self." As we now follow Djebar retracing Zoulikha's life in text, we have acquired certain fragments—aural and visual—that will help us fit together fragments yet to come.[11]

The Woman without a Tomb

In her introduction to *La femme sans sépulture*, the novel that, in contrast to the film, focuses exclusively on Zoulikha's life story, Djebar states that she will intertwine fiction with historical truth, using *liberté romanesque*, novelistic liberty, to illuminate her life. She writes: "J'ai usé à volonté de ma liberté romanesque, justement pour que la vérité de Zoulikha soit éclairée davantage, au centre même d'une large fresque féminine—selon le modèle des mosaïques si anciennes de Césarée de Maurétanie (Cherchell)" (9; I liberally used my novelistic liberty so that the truth about Zoulikha might be more fully disclosed, in the very center of a large feminine fresco—according to the model of the ancient mosaics of Cesarea of Mauretania [Cherchell]). By blurring the distinction between history and fiction, Djebar's text fits the description of historiographic metafiction as defined by the critic Linda Hutcheon (*Poetics of Postmodernism*, 113).

Although the text appears at first to be a tightly woven quest narrative composed of twelve chapters framed by a prologue and an epilogue, with a key episode—the narrator's interpretation of an ancient mosaic—occurring midway through the novel, the seemingly tight structure is soon subverted as sequences become blurred and multiple voices introduce fragments of Zoulikha's life story into the text. This breakdown of the narrative structure introduces uncertainty, suggesting that as both the form (a classic linear narrative) and the content (a canonical historical biography) move in new, unexpected directions, they open the way for new possibilities, perspectives, and transformation.

This movement occurs, for example, when the narrator arrives at Zoulikha's house to interview her daughters, Hania and Mina, and discovers not only that their home is next to her father's house (although her parents no longer live there) but also that the mosaic tiles that decorate their patio resemble those in her father's house. She finds herself drawn to the antique mosaics in the courtyard of the Musée archeologique de Cherchell (the Cherchell Archaeological Museum), where her careful examination and interpretation of a mosaic tableau of Ulysses and the sirens contributes to a new understanding of her relationship to the city, its present and past. This transformation occurs as she also listens attentively to the voices of the women relating segments of Zoulikha's life story. Thus, by delving into both the distant past and the more recent past, she gains greater understanding.

Memories can be painful, however, as Zoulikha's elder daughter, Hania, reveals: "Elle n'avoue pas que ses genoux fléchissent, que les rappels si brusquent de ce passé la violentent" (47; She doesn't admit that her knees are weak, that the sudden memories of the past upset her). Hania's reaction to returning to the traumatic past is not surprising. As the postcolonial critic Homi Bhabha writes, "Remembering is never a quiet act of introspection or retrospection. It is a painful re-membering, a putting together of the dismembered past to make sense of the trauma of the present" (*Location of Culture*, 63).

In the text, multiple voices—of family, friends, the narrator, and Zoulikha—reconstitute the *moudjahida*'s life story. Zoulikha's daughters, Hania and Mina, bear witness to the irreparable loss of their mother. FLN militants who worked closely with Zoulikha in the women's resistance network, Dame Lionne in Cherchell and Aunt Oudia in the maquis of Mount Cherchell, attest to Zoulikha's political engagement. Along with Zoulikha and the narrator, they are the principal female voices in the text. Individual voices presenting fragments of the heroine's life story, they produce narratives that form a mosaic; in this way, they articulate a collective voice.

When the narrator interviews Zoulikha's friends and family, readers are led to believe she is listening to the very voices Djebar heard—and recorded—when she visited the region in the mid-1970s in preparation for her film. Similarly, readers may assume that Djebar, in her role as historian, has faithfully followed the sequence of events of Zoulikha's life—her childhood, her marriages, and, most important, her decision to take to the maquis, the rural underground, after her husband's death, a decision that involved leaving her young children behind with family members. Nevertheless, by choosing novelistic liberty, Djebar freely invents parts of the text pertaining to the family and friends who tell Zoulikha's story and, according to her family, aspects of the militant's life as well.[12]

When Zoulikha speaks, addressing her younger daughter and the narrator—monologues that occur in chapters 3, 7, 10, and 12—she draws us into the realm of fiction, if not the fantastic. She is speaking from beyond the tomb. In the first monologue, she describes her capture; in the second, the daily police interrogation she undergoes following her husband's death. In the third, she charts her life from her father's farm to the maquis; and in the fourth and last monologue she relates the final hours of her life, from the time of her capture to her death and burial.

In the fourth monologue, Zoulikha explains that her corpse was exposed to the sun and the jackals before being stolen by a young member of the resistance and secretly buried by him. This account of her burial contradicts the title of the text, *La femme sans sépulture* but is in part historically grounded. Although Zoulikha's remains had not been uncovered when Djebar made her film, they were found before she completed her novel in 2001. In 1982 an Algerian peasant disclosed having buried the body of a woman found on a country road during the late 1950s and indicated the spot. The unearthed remnants of bone and clothing were indeed those of Zoulikha; her remains were subsequently buried in the cemetery of Menaceur, a village near Cherchell.[13] In the text, Zoulikha acknowledges her burial but tells her daughter Mina that she will never find the burial site. Thus, she grants partial closure to her family's quest—the martyr to the anticolonial war was buried, but the family will never know where—choosing, in effect, to remain a haunting presence as well as a symbolic reference for other women combatants, many of whom remain lost to history.

Narrative, as we know, lends itself to theatrical staging. Beginning with the first monologue, Djebar appropriates theatrical elements for her text to transform Zoulikha from historical figure to legendary presence. "Staging" the arrival of the prisoner, she uses movement, gesture, and lighting to heighten the sense of drama as she depicts Zoulikha, captured by French soldiers, emerging from the forest. Bathed in bright light, the captive is brought into the clearing surrounded by soldiers, who guard her, and Algerian peasants, who look on. The assembled crowd is exclusively male except for one veiled female figure, whose rebellious gesture, a fist raised in rebellion and solidarity, gives Zoulikha the courage to address the weeping crowd, shouting: "Regardez, ô mes frères, tout ceci, seulement pour une femme!" (67; Look, my brothers, all this to capture one woman).

Although oral history has recorded Zoulikha's last public statement and the place of her capture has been identified, the subsequent ten days before her death in military custody remain obscure. Djebar uses novelistic liberty freely to invent a narrative in which facts have been lost, drawing readers into the realm of the fantastic as Zoulikha speaks from beyond the tomb. Moreover, because the prisoner dies in custody, she is, of course, dispossessed of the ability to tell her own story. Therefore, her narrative is the author's invention, a verbal staging that complements the visual staging of her capture. This invention allows Djebar to move her protagonist, originally anchored in Algerian historical reality, into mythic space.

Zoulikha's transformation from historic to mythic figure is quite evident in the fourth and final monologue, when her voice, emanating from her tortured body, associates the pain of physical torture with the pain of childbirth. Here, Djebar suggests that the martyred Zoulikha, in the throes of pain, is transformed symbolically into a "founding mother of the new Algeria" as she gives birth to the new nation:

> Mon corps, peut-être parce que corps de femme et ayant enfanté tant de fois—se met à ouvrir ses plaies, ses issues, à déverser son flux, en somme il s'exhale, s'émiette, se vide sans pour autant s'épuiser! [. . .] Peut-être qu'il cherche dans le noir, et hors du temps, quelque métamorphose? (198)

(My body, perhaps because a woman's body and having given birth many times, begins to open its wounds, its orifices, to give off its flux; in short, it exhales, crumbles, empties itself in order to exhaust itself! [...] Perhaps it searches in the night, and outside of time, for some metamorphosis?)

It is fitting that Zoulikha identifies herself in this way with the birth of the new nation. The mother of several children, she had become a mother figure for the younger freedom fighters of Mount Chenoua. In this same vein, as her body fluids seep out into the earth, nourishing the land for which she fought, her words convey her metamorphosis; physical death results in spiritual rebirth.

It is important to note that as Zoulikha becomes an increasingly symbolic figure, the narrator participates in the process. Alternately calling herself a visitor, a guest, an interviewer, a stranger, and "l'étrangère pas tellement étrangère" (213; the stranger who is not such a stranger), she reveals herself to be a gifted interpreter of sign and symbol. Speaking with Zoulikha's daughter Mina, she interprets a unique visual image for her, the two-thousand-year-old mosaic *Ulysses and the Sirens*. Inspired by Homer's *Odyssey*, it depicts Ulysses tied to the mast of his boat so that he may continue his voyage despite the sirens' attempts to lure him from his goal of returning home. In this mosaic, the sirens are depicted as three winged women holding musical instruments who are about to take flight; the body of one of the three is partially effaced.[14] Linking the winged women of the mosaic to Zoulikha, the narrator tells Mina: "Une seule femme s'est vraiment s'envolée: et c'est ta mère, ô Mina, c'est Zoulikha" (109; Only one woman really flew away: it was your mother, oh Mina, it was Zoulikha).

The evocation of the mosaic, the critic Mireille Calle-Gruber explains, has a pivotal function in transforming Zoulikha into legend. "Elle est ici et nulle part, ni femme réelle ni créature mythique, et l'une et l'autre cependant, car l'écriture lui confère l'incomparable dimension de l'art" ("L'écrire nomade," 78; She [Zoulikha] is here and nowhere, neither real woman nor mythical figure, and yet one and the other, for writing confers upon her the incomparable dimension of art). Calle-Gruber proposes three interpretations of the mosaic. First, it links the past to the present, Ulysses and the sirens to contemporary Algeria; the three "femmes-oiseaux," or bird women, represent today's Algerian women. Second, the sirens are portents of Zoulikha's death. They are winged figures, and Zoulikha is taken away in a helicopter and disappears. Third, and the most interesting interpretation, Zoulikha, the woman without a tomb, receives the funeral rites missing at her death from this written text. In other words, the book is her sepulcher; the narrator assumes the role of witness and *pleureuse,* or weeping mourner, and shares in Zoulikha's suffering. The martyr, Zoulikha, disappears, but her voice remains. Calle-Gruber notes that

> l'écrivain accueillant le chant de Zoulikha, c'est Ulysse à l'écoute des femmes-oiseaux. Mais elle qui écoute pour partager, elle ne se fait pas attacher, prend tous les risques du voyage au pays de mort et des revenants. A toute extrémité, elle accomplit le deuil. (79–80)
>
> (the writer listening to Zoulikha's song is Ulysses listening to the bird women. She, however, listens so as to share the story; she is not bound and immobile as Ulysses is. She takes all the risks of traveling to the land of the dead and back and completes the ritual of mourning the dead.)

Unlike Ulysses, the writer, according to Calle-Gruber, is both listener and scribe. Are the writer and the narrator one and the same?

The narrator first appears as the privileged ear to the reminiscences of Zoulikha's daughters. As they speak with her, they are able to free themselves of the trauma of Zoulikha's death. Hence, she facilitates the process of anamnesis, which allows healing to occur. Yet glimpses of the narrator's own life reveal her inability to find the peace of mind she seeks. This is particularly evident at the end of the novel, when she faults herself for taking twenty years to complete this text and wonders when, perhaps if, she will ever return to Caesarea, the site of her own father's tomb: "Là, où sous mille couches de ténèbres, dort désormais mon père, les yeux ouverts" (220; There where under a thousand layers of dark shadows lies my father, his eyes open).

Expressing a sense of culpability with respect to Zoulikha's children for not having brought their mother's life to light sooner, as well as guilt for not having visited her father's grave, the narrator is clearly a troubled soul. In this regard, the critic Nicole Aas-Rouparis suggests that "the woman without a tomb" is not Zoulikha but Djebar, the writer condemned to exile. Aas-Rouparis sees Djebar condemned to exile because of the physical danger that threatened artists in Algeria during the period in which she was completing the text ("La femme-oiseau de la mosaïque," 103). Although I concur with Aas-Rouparis that the title should be reassigned, I think that "the woman without a tomb" is the narrator rather than the author; despite the various parallels in their lives, we cannot assume that the anonymous narrator and the author are one and the same.

As she assigns the role of siren, one of the winged women musicians, to Zoulikha, the narrator situates herself within the mosaic as well. However, the narrator identifies herself with Ulysses, "le voyageur qui ne s'est pas bouché les oreilles de cire sans toutefois risquer de traverser la frontière de la mort pour cela, mais entendre, ne plus jamais oublier le chant des sirènes" (214; the traveler who did not plug his ears with wax without the risk of crossing the frontier of death for not doing so but was able to hear and never forget the sirens' song). With this reference to Ulysses, the narrator places herself in opposition to her countrymen, whom she accuses of living small, quiet lives and having chosen amnesia. Hence, Djebar, the writer, and her anonymous narrator may be distinct, but they share a common vision, the need to remember Algeria's women martyrs to the anticolonial war at a time when women's sacrifices are at risk of being forgotten.

As Djebar's protagonist, Zoulikha, becomes increasingly symbolic, she enters the realm of the imaginary through image as well as voice: the image of the winged woman in the mosaic, the voice of the ghost speaking from beyond the tomb. And if the novelist's immediate intent is to chart the militant's life, her larger goal seems to be more ambitious, extending beyond the sacrifice of a brave combatant to the Algerian liberation struggle. As the critic Michael O'Reilly explains, *La femme sans sépulture*, published in 2002, calls attention to contemporary Algerian figures tortured and killed in the postindependence period, the victims of two warring factions, Algeria's repressive military regime and Islamic radicals (70). Most significant are the Algerian government's refusal to accept the *FIS*'s victory in the 1991 elections and the ensuing violence brought about by radical Islamic activists. The new wave of brutality recalls, as a haunting memory, the violence that first occurred between colonized and colonizer during the colonial era. Just as Zoulikha was never appropriately laid to rest, violence continued to haunt Algeria during the 1990s, the period during which Djebar wrote this text.

Why does Djebar choose to tell Zoulikha's story? First, as the novelist explains, Zoulikha is a heroic figure of Mount Chenoua who happened to be a neighbor of Djebar's family in Cherchell. Djebar's tribute helps keep her memory alive, extending it beyond the Cherchell region. Second, her life story is unique in terms of her bravery and political commitment, thereby lending itself to a feminist reading. Few Algerian women of her age and generation were in the maquis. Although, as Amrane-Minne's research has shown, married women with children were active members of the resistance, they were largely *moussebilate,* women in supporting roles. Zoulikha, in contrast, held a key post in the FLN organization in Cherchell. Third, we learn of her exploits via oral transmission, women speaking to women. If, in *L'amour, la fantasia,* Baron Barchou's description of Algerian women dying on the battlefield in the 1830s is highly visual (and, with its emphasis upon violent details, conveys the Orientalist stereotype of the savage "other"), Djebar's text, in contrast, emphasizes oral transmission, foregrounding the role of the individual who, as a privileged listener, serves as its conduit.

We note, however, that the novelist grants the position of listener to Lila in the film and then to the narrator in the text. As young women who return to a place they once knew but no longer call home, each is in some sense "the stranger who is not such a stranger." Thus, as parallels emerge between Lila and the narrator, we see more clearly that the film indeed lays the groundwork for the text. Moreover, as both Lila and the narrator return to the place they once knew as home, the filmmaker follows a similar path. The film project brings the filmmaker back not only to Cherchell and neighboring Mount Chenoua but also to Arabic, her mother tongue. Thus, the writer and her two protagonists share the experience of becoming "the stranger who is not such a stranger." When Djebar returns to writing, she does so in French, the language she now embraces with no misgivings. Thus, by working in two media, film and text, Djebar manipulates the languages of the colonized and the colonizer to her advantage. And by using both Arabic and French, Djebar perhaps finds yet another way to pay tribute to Zoulikha, who, unlike many Algerian women of her generation, is reported to have had an excellent command of French as well as Arabic.

Finally, and perhaps most importantly, Zoulikha's life story, with few written records and therefore significant lacunae for the historian, opens the field of inquiry to embrace the imaginary, encouraging the writer to fill in the blank spaces of history. As Zoulikha speak from beyond the tomb, Djebar fills in the blanks much in the same way that the Senegalese novelist Boubacar Boris Diop introduces literary testimonies of massacred Rwandans in *Murambi, le livre des ossements* (*Murambi, the Book of Bones*). When the dead cannot speak, the writer can assume novelistic liberty.

As I have already noted, Djebar evokes Zoulikha's martyrdom in film and text at two difficult periods for Algerian women: first in the late 1970s, when, during Houari Boumediene's presidency, conservative forces threatened to impose laws relegating Algerian women to secondary status; then in the 1990s, when Islamic fundamentalists began threatening women they judged too modern. Zoulikha's life story becomes a cautionary tale against violence, injustice, and amnesia. In addition, by situating her film and her text in the region of Cherchell, Djebar draws attention to the city of her birth—in the text she calls it by its Roman name, Caesarea—which has specific historic significance. Examining memory sites in Djebar's writings, the critic Wolfgang Asholt explains that Cherchell has historically been a place of exchange, cross-cultural encounters, and hybridity ("Les villes frontalières," 151–52). Through the ages it has been a voice for multiculturalism. A city with Roman as well as Moorish vestiges, it welcomed the Muslims expelled from Spain in the late fifteenth century. It is not surprising, therefore, that the narrator, returning to her birthplace, challenges the reductive vision she now encounters in postcolonial Algeria. She does so by setting her memory of a multiplicity of cultures against a commonly heard refrain:

> Nous avons une seule langue, l'arabe
> Nous avons une seule foi, l'islam
> Nous avons une seule terre, l'Algérie! (71)

> (We have one language, Arabic
> We have one faith, Islam
> We have one land, Algeria!)

Speaking with Zoulikha's daughter Mina, she acknowledges three languages—Berber, Arabic, and French—as well as a history of three religions—Christianity, Islam, and Judaism—and reminds her of three heroic figures of Algerian history—Jugurtha, Kahena, and Emir Abdelkader. Yet Djebar adds a comment that reveals her protagonist's surprising timidity in the face of the reductive spirit that has taken hold in the country. Her belief in the importance of diversity is an opinion she keeps to herself (72).

Nevertheless, by recognizing the multilayered history of Caesarea, with its Phoenician, Berber, Roman, Arabic, Turkish, and French colonial periods, Djebar's narrator weaves a complex web of cultural elements that transform her into a figure of resistance. Hence, she, in her way, reflects Zoulikha's resistance to French colonialism during an earlier era. Just as the Holocaust survivor Elie Wiesel reminds us that memory is the tool for ensuring that genocide will not be forgotten,[15] Djebar uses memory as a weapon against her nation's amnesia at two critical moments of her nation's history, the postindependence period of the 1970s and the undeclared civil war of the 1990s. By using film and text as tools for gathering memories, Djebar reiterates the need to bear witness to heroism and never forget those who gave their lives to the liberation struggle, women as well as men.

Memory restored often leads to commemoration. On October 25, 2007, the fiftieth anniversary of Zoulikha's death, a commemoration of her life was held in Cherchell. It was understandably an extremely important event for Zoulikha's family, friends, and the community at large. The following year, on the fifty-first anniversary of Zoulikha's death, an article remembering her appeared in the Algerian newspaper *El Watan*. In the article, the journalist Abderrahmane Zakad having visited Zoulikha's tomb, encourages his fellow Algerians to read *La femme sans sépulture*. Moreover, he concludes his article with the passage from Djebar's text in which Zoulikha kneels before the cadaver of her husband, killed by the French; she dips her hands in his blood and vows to continue his struggle. First, the narrator speaks:

> Je vois peu à peu Zoulikha, appelée par les gens des collines et des vergers au-dessus de Césarée (la tribu des Oudaï), qui arrive chez eux à la nouvelle de la mort d'El Hadj, son mari, dont le corps vient d'être rendu aux siens par l'armée. Zoulikha s'isole dans ce vestibule devant le cadavre étendu, yeux fermés; elle s'incline, elle palpe de sa main les blessures à la poitrine, à la tempe et aux bras. Elle trempe ses deux mains dans le sang pas encore séché d'El Hadj. Elle ne pleure pas; ses lèvres murmurent, quoi, une prière islamique, un serment, "que dorénavant c'est à elle ... ," peut-être lui dit-elle des mots d'amour, la promesse qu'elle continuera son action. ("Pour vous dire Zoulikha," quoting *La femme sans sépulture*, 109–10)

(I slowly make out Zoulikha, called by the people of the hills and orchards above Caesarea, the tribe of the Oudaï, coming to meet them following the news of the death of her husband, El Hadj. His body was just returned to his family by the army. Zoulikha withdraws to the vestibule before the cadaver; the body is stretched out, the eyes are closed. She bends forward, her hands touching the wounds on his chest, temple, arms. She dips both hands in El Hadj's blood that has not yet dried. She doesn't cry. Her lips murmur, perhaps an Islamic prayer, a vow: "From now on, it is up to her." Perhaps she murmurs words of love, the promise that she will continue his struggle.)

Zoulikha, speaking in the first person, repeats this scene in her third monologue:

Quand, beaucoup plus tard, à l'instant fatal, El Hadj mort, son cadavre fut à mes pieds, je me baissai sans pleurer, soucieuse de toucher sa poitrine nue, son visage, partout où mon sang n'avait pas encore séché! Je suis rentrée à la maison, avec mes deux paumes serrées, parce qu'ensanglantées. J'ai voulu que son sang sèche sur moi, sur ma peau. (*La femme sans sépulture*, 174)

(When, much later, at the fatal moment, El Hadj was dead, his cadaver was at my feet, I bent down without crying, carefully touching his bare chest, his face, everywhere that his blood had not dried. I went back home, my two palms clenched because they were covered in blood. I wanted his blood to dry on my skin.)

Certainly in oral tradition repetition is a way of emphasizing an important passage. Djebar, by presenting this scene first from the narrator's perspective and then from Zoulikha's, clearly positions Zoulikha as her husband's successor in the struggle. The journalist's selection is significant not only for its dramatic quality, as a passage that forcefully depicts Zoulikha as a grieving widow, but also for showing Zoulikha faithfully assuming her husband's mission, one that until his death the couple had shared.

Zoulikha's son Mohammed offers a different interpretation of events in an email written to me on 25 May 2010: "Zoulikha n'a pas pris le maquis au décès de mon père, mais dénoncé aux forces coloniales en tant que Chef détenant les secrets, elle décida à 46 ans de prendre le maquis pour que la cellule FLN de Cherchell ne soit pas totalement démantelée" (Zoulikha did not take to the maquis at my father's death, but after she had been denounced to the colonial military forces as an FLN leader with secret information she decided, at the age of forty-six, to join the maquis so that the FLN cell would not be totally destroyed). Mohammed emphasizes the importance of his mother's role: she was the political and military leader in Cherchell, a post with decision-making powers generally assigned only to men. He states: "Jusque-là on présente la femme comme agent de liaison, poseuse de bombes, infirmière, couturière, mais jamais comme chef ayant un pouvoir de décision, un commandement qu'elle exerce sur des hommes et des femmes" (Until then, a woman was always seen as a liaison agent, bomb carrier, nurse, seamstress, but not as a leader with decision-making authority, a position of authority over men and women).

It is clear that Zoulikha's children, who are very proud of their mother, want not only to have her sacrifices and courage recognized; they also want her life to be depicted as accurately as possible. Hence, they openly refute several inaccuracies in the text. Khadidja, named Mina in the text, was a married woman with two children when she met with Djebar in 1976. Her unhappy love story recounted in the text is completely fictitious. Mohammed Oudaï, who became a general in the Algerian army, is mistakenly identified as a junior military officer. Abdelhamid, the youngest child, is written out of the text. And as with the novelist's portrayal of Khadidja, fiction appears to distort reality. Zoulikha's children affirm that their mother was a pious woman and far more conservative, they say, than the woman depicted as Zoulikha in the novel. However, since Mohammed and Abdelhamid were children at the time their mother was assassinated, they are not necessarily reliable witnesses. Khadidja, however, was thirteen years old when she lost her mother, so her memories are far more vivid.[16]

A thorny issue they raise, however, is the possibility that Djebar's "novelistic liberty" resulted in a more serious transgression. When questioned by the French military officer Coste, Zoulikha is shown to be erotically attracted to him. Thus, the novelist evokes the possibility of forbidden reciprocal desire between enemies. Although it is impossible to know the truth concerning the relationship of two individuals who were killed during the Algerian War, one by the French, the other by Algerian nationalists, we can ask whether Djebar has taken "novelistic liberty" too far and not paid enough respect to

Zoulikha's memory. Did the novelist betray the trust that Zoulikha's family members placed in her when they spoke to her of their relative?

The critic Anne Donadey suggests that Djebar's rewriting of Zoulikha's life in this way may reflect a desire to avoid turning Zoulikha into a museum piece; she suggests that Djebar wishes to shatter the myth around the *moudjahida* who died for her country ("African-American and Francophone Postcolonial Memory," 74). By allowing the unspeakable to be spoken, Djebar refuses any easy escape from the discomfort she creates for the reader. In the final analysis, readers are left with questions of authenticity. As we try to learn the historical truth, we often reach an impasse. However, by engaging in this quest for hidden histories and the individuals involved, be they victims or perpetrators, writers and readers ensure that historical figures such as Zoulikha and their important sacrifices are not forgotten. The biography that Djebar proposes of Zoulikha Echaïb Oudaï may not fit the image that family and friends in Cherchell wish to embrace, but it has served an important purpose.[17] As Zoulikha's son Abdelhamid has clearly stated, expressing his gratitude to the novelist following her burial in the cemetery of Cherchell on February 13, 2015: "Je n'oublierai jamais Assia Djebar qui a sorti ma mère de l'anonymat" (qtd. in Houaoura, "Inhumation hier," 2; I will never forget Assia Djebar, who brought my mother out of anonymity). Through Djebar's efforts, Zoulikha's courage and heroism have come to light; her story is there to be passed on to future generations. By commemorating a resistance figure in film and text, combining documentary and fictional elements in both, Djebar creates a tribute to an extraordinary individual that, in its fluidity, its openness to new and changing interpretations, offers an alternative to the classic monument to the dead, with its immutable stone inscription. One hopes that Zoulikha Echaïb Oudaï would have considered it a fitting tribute to her life and deeds.

CONCLUSION

The Silence Has Been Broken . . .

Revisiting a war that ended more than fifty years ago is a revelatory experience. A fifty-year time span grants historical perspective as former combatants and witnesses—some who were adults and others who were children during the war—have had the time to reflect upon historical events that marked their lives. Moreover, a period of five decades allows historical information and material, whether occulted, forgotten, or simply unknown, to emerge. For example, French archives pertaining to the Algerian War, closed until 1999, are now accessible to researchers. During these decades historians and writers have continued to revisit key moments of Algerian history in an attempt to better understand the past as the postcolonial nation has had to grapple with contemporary social, economic, political, and cultural issues. Finally, a significant number of former combatants, silent for decades, have chosen to speak, with several publishing memoirs in the last few years. All have contributed to unearthing history, filling in historical blanks, and repairing fallacies.

In this volume, I bring together works of written fiction, film, memoirs, and historical studies, convinced that fiction and nonfiction are necessary to our understanding of the complexity of the Algerian War. On the one hand, we need hard data, facts and figures, to support the truth about a given historical moment. On the other hand, it is necessary to put a human face on the events. There is indeed a special place for the artistic representation of the experience of war.

In the quest to define women's roles in the liberation struggle and to grasp the extent to which the war was a transformative and empowering experience, I began with Djamila Amrane-Minne's historical writings. Highly critical of the fact that women's commitment and sacrifices to the Algerian War were increasingly overlooked, Amrane-Minne repaired this omission with two publications: *La guerre d'Algérie (1954–1962): Femmes au combat* (1993) and *Des femmes dans la guerre d'Algérie* (1994), a collection of thirty interviews chosen from the eighty-eight she used for her doctoral research. As both texts brought in multiple women's voices, they affirmed women's commitment to the struggle, the transformative power of the war upon women participants, and the collective nature of the experience. Moreover, they broke a weighty silence. Notably, the interviews in the 1980s were following several decades later by a series of published memoirs, as former combatants brought their individual narratives into public space.

Turning to fiction, I found Assia Djebar's early war novels, *Les enfants du nouveau monde* (1962), *Les alouettes naïves* (1967), and *L'amour, la fantasia* (1985), supporting her conviction that Algerian women's empowerment remains an ongoing process and therefore is not limited to one moment in her nation's history. Yet, her three texts also depict the ravages of war, the violence and the trauma, elements that reemerge in Yamina Mechakra's novel *La grotte éclatée* (1979) and Maïssa Bey's *Entendez-vous dans les montagnes . . .* (2002), as well as in the other texts that appear in this study. Clearly, writers such as Mechakra, Bey, Sebbar, and the more than forty contributors to the latter's collective work of testimonials reveal the need of those who lived through the war as children to comprehend its effects upon them as adults.

A study of literary texts that cover a fifty-five-year period—from Djebar's *Les enfants du nouveau monde* (1962) to Leïla Sebbar's *Une enfance dans la guerre: Algérie, 1954–1962* (2016)—allows us to discern transformations in both style and content, to recognize stylistic innovations not present in earlier texts as well as changes in historical perspective.

First among these transformations, the significant lapse in time between the publication of fictional works and memoirs suggests that it is easier for the writer to articulate the experience of war indirectly, via fiction, than directly, through autobiographical narrative. For example, Bey uses fiction, writing about her father's death in one of her earliest novels, *Entendez-vous dans les montagnes . . .* , to come to terms with the tragic loss that, she explains, had taken the form of a haunting scene lived over and over in her imagination. In contrast, Ighilahriz and Lavalette publish memoirs recalling traumatic prison experiences of rape, torture, and electroshock treatments decades after the events took place.

Second, we find several examples of multidirectional memory, of works that engage with other historical eras. Bey and Sebbar reference World War II and Algeria's undeclared civil war of the 1990s in their novels.

Third, the *témoignage*, a key element of Amrane-Minne's historical inquiry, assumes increasing importance in fiction, memoir, and film, beginning with Djebar's fictional protagonist, Lila, interviewing the former combatants of Cherchell in her film *La nouba des femmes du Mont Chenoua*.

Finally, these works all reveal a world that, while conveyed in the language of Molière, is rooted in a non-Western culture. Arabic and Berber languages and Islam and pre-Islamic traditions remain integral to the cultural fabric of the nation. However, even though religious terminology is used to identify participants in the struggle—*moudjahid* and *moudjahida*, for example—the war is defined as an anticolonial struggle, not a *jihad*, or holy war for Islam. Interestingly, in Djebar's film *La nouba . . .* , the women of Mount Chenoua engage in a ritual of dancing and chanting in a mountain cave, which, as it suggests a maternal womb, recalls the distant past of a pre-Islamic matriarchal heritage.

Revisiting History

In the decades since the end of the Algerian War new analyses have emerged, shedding further light on the effects of the war. Hence, I conclude by turning to recent works of history, literature, and film that increase our understanding of the war as they point to new directions. I begin with the historian Natalya Vince, who, in her historical analysis *Our Fighting Sisters: Nation, Memory and Gender in Algeria, 1954–2012*, published in 2015, takes Amrane-Minne's research further by widening the temporal scope of the original study and applying a critical lens informed by additional data, including French archival material that had not been available to Amrane-Minne when she was conducting her research. Like her predecessor, Vince makes extensive use of oral interviews, selecting both high-profile women, such as Djamila Boupacha and Zohra Drif, and individuals whose commitment and sacrifices to the cause were not well known. Moreover, Vince, like Amrane-Minne, states that each woman interviewed considered her participation in the struggle a transformational experience. Since the war experience gave them a new sense of self-worth and offered the possibility of a larger world-view and wider horizons than they had previously imagined, returning to one's previous life was not possible.

Vince's findings challenge the prevailing view that Algeria's women were depoliticized following independence. Previously historians, including Amrane-Minne, had concluded that Algerian women militants returned to traditional roles following the war. Vince reveals their continued presence in public space, citing numerous professions—in medicine, civil service, media, law, education, business, women's organizations, and youth organizations—in which these women were professionally engaged (123). In addition, as Vince examines the shifting importance women give to gender as a frame for understanding both their own lives and the society in which they live, she discovers that those who first dismissed gender as a factor in Algerian society became keenly aware of its importance as a result of the nation's implementation of the Family Code of 1984.

During the 1960s and 1970s the Algerian government debated the composition of a new family code that would overhaul the family code inherited from the colonial period, which combined sharia law and French colonial legislation. The new code that emerged, however, confirmed Algerian women's inferior status before the law. Experiencing outrage, disillusionment, and betrayal, many women begin to mobilize politically against the restrictive code. Moreover, as several *moudjahidate* used their legacy as former combatants in the struggle for independence to put forth a feminist-nationalist position, they were increasingly portrayed in the Algerian media not only as representatives of the historical conscience of the nation but also as engaged citizens reacting against illegitimate and arbitrary power.

Citing the reemergence of *moudjahidate* in debates concerning gender, nation building, and memory, Vince argues that the liberation struggle remains a powerful metaphor for Algerian identity, one that continues to represent a sense of solidarity, sacrifice, and unity for the Algerian people. In her view, it provides a space within which criticism may be voiced and acknowledged. Urging her readers to view Algerian women as more than "wombs of the nation, guardians of national essence, courageous teenage fighters" (212), she cautions us to see them all—the few high-profile women whose names became known beyond Algeria and the many anonymous militants—as important contributors to an epic narrative of resistance that did not end in 1962.

The sociologist Feriel Lalami makes the Family Code of 1984 the focal point of her study *Les Algériennes contre le code de la famille: La lutte pour l'égalité* (Algerian women against the family code: The fight for equality), published in 2012.[1] She explains in detail how the code grants Algerian men domination over women, thereby violating article 29 of Algeria's constitution, which secures equality for all of its citizens.[2] The code permits polygamy (art. 8), requires women to have a *wali* (guardian) at the time of their marriage (art. 11), forbids women to marry non-Muslim men, although their male counterparts can marry non-Muslim women (art. 30), and allows men to divorce at will (art. 48). It clearly grants men rights pertaining to marriage, divorce, and family that discriminate against women. Thus, it is not surprising that the retrograde code became a rallying point for women's organizations intent upon fighting effectively against it.

Lalami constructs her text around the thesis that Algerian women's organizations are the leading voices in the fight against the discriminatory code. Dividing the work into two parts—the first dealing with the history of the code, its beginnings and its legally discriminatory consequences; the second charting the development of the women's movement and the associations fighting legal injustice—she shows how women's organizations, beginning with the Union Nationale des Femmes Algériennes (UNFA, National Association of Algerian Women), founded before the Algerian War began, have adapted to changing times. She also discusses their weaknesses, pointing out, for example, that Algerian women and the organizations that represent them do not present a united front. Indeed, associations of Islamic women support the code, some even calling for more stringent regulations on women, in marked contrast to the associations that form the Algerian women's movement fighting for equality (17).

Noting that during the violent period of the 1990s, various protests organized by progressive women's groups—public meetings, demonstrations, sit-ins—could not continue as before, Lalami recognizes that the generation of women formed by a nationalist movement against colonialism was not prepared to deal with radical Islamic elements in the country and the ensuing violence, which put individual lives as well as progressive women's associations in danger. With peace restored to Algeria in the early years of the twenty-first century as a result of the government's general amnesty, the struggle against the Family Code of 1984, somewhat modified in 2005, continued, with the goal of implicating Algerian society in a project of citizenship for all. Within this context, as Lalami explains, the struggle for women's rights, a feminist agenda, becomes part of a broad coalition with other progressive social movements. Expressing optimism in Algerian society, she considers the massive education of women and a drop in the birth rate in Algeria in recent years to be concrete signs of progress for Algerian women.[3]

Resistance Literature

Just as social scientists and filmmakers interrogate the past and evaluate Algerian women's participation in the construction of the postcolonial nation, so, of course, do writers. When Djebar, in search of a way to articulate Algerian women's war story in *Les enfants du nouveau monde*, chose the fragmented narrative as a strategy that would convey the sense of a revolution in the making and depict women moving into a world of new possibilities, neither she nor her contemporaries could anticipate the undeclared civil war of the 1990s. During that period, most women writers, confronted with, on the one hand, a military-backed government that had been in power for thirty years and, on the other hand, militant Islamic fundamentalists attempting to establish an Islamic state, joined with forces seeking a secular and democratic society. In addition to Djebar, these writers include Malika Mokeddem, Leïla Marouane, Nina Hayat, Malika Boussouf, Fatiah, Fériel Assima, Naïla Imaksen, Latifa Ben Mansour, Maïssa Bey, Rachida Titah, and Hafsa Zinaï Koudil.[4] Using the pen as a weapon, writing as a form of resistance, they documented the violence of the civil war in various genres: novels, short stories, poetry, and essays. Sadly, the trauma that marks the literature of Algeria's war of independence reappears in these new works as the postcolonial nation struggles in the 1990s with internal strife and violence. Picking up on Maria Tumarkin's phrase characterizing geographical spaces of violence, we find that Algeria once again became a "traumascape."

Although Algeria's undeclared civil war is not the focus of this work, it is important to acknowledge its implications.[5] As I noted in the introduction, a significant number of women writers drew parallels between their role in the turbulent 1990s and the role played by militants in the liberation struggle. For example, Amrane-Minne compares the women of the two periods in her introduction to *Des femmes dans la guerre d'Algérie;* she reminds her readers that the same courage and determination motivated Algerian women at two different times in Algeria's history. In both historical moments, women resisted with actions and words.

With resistance as an importance legacy of Algerian women's writing, all of which was in French, what are its implications for the future? I believe that we can expect Algerian women, whether writing in French or in Arabic, to continue to focus on gender issues. When Algerian writers turn to fiction, it is with the understanding that by drawing their protagonists into the realm of the imaginary, fiction offers Algerian women a path to empowerment (admittedly fleeting and/or illusory), which the harsh reality of life often renders impossible. With this thought in mind, I turn to Nassira Bellouma's novel *Terre des femmes* (Land of women), published in Algeria in 2014. Set among the novelist's native Chaouia population and grounded in the history of the Aurès region, this historical novel presents a sweeping epic of the French colonial period, from the 1840s to the Algerian War. Depicting the lives of several generations of women in one family, it shows how each protagonist draws upon the courage and resiliency of her foremothers to meets life's challenges, then transmits the same determination to the next generation of women.

If, by situating the text among the Chaouia of the Aurès, Bellouma's novel recalls Mechakra's *La grotte éclatée*, it also reflects elements of Djebar's *L'amour, la fantasia*, as it probes colonial historical archives to bring incidents of neglected history to light. Bellouma, like Djebar, uses historical documentation that reveals the nature and extent of colonial oppression. For example, she cites excerpts from the French Code de l'Indigénat, the decree of 1881 that relegated Algerians to second-class citizenship (*Terre des femmes*, 76). Thus, with its historical focus, multiple narratives, and emphasis upon women forging bonds with one another as they struggle against the oppressive forces of French colonialism and indigenous patriarchy, the novelist pays tribute to the Algerian women writers who preceded her as she cautions her Algerian sisters to look back as they move forward, keeping ancestral women's voices with them as they journey through life.

Women Filming Women

Although the title of this book appears to single out writing as the medium for retrospection, I have emphasized the importance of orality in confirming women's place in the war story and acknowledged the power of the visual arts, bringing Djebar's film *La nouba des femmes du Mont Chenoua* into the study. When Djebar made the film in 1977, she not only gave voice to Algerian women, she paved the way for future documentary filmmakers. In a film that combines fictional characters and episodes with oral interviews of former militants, Djebar shows the women of Chenoua breaking their silence as they recall their war experiences and remember a fellow militant, Zoulikha Oudaï, who sacrificed her life to the struggle. Reticent at first, they tell their stories upon encountering a sympathetic listener. Lila, the fictional protagonist, listens attentively and silently to the women before sharing her own war story with them. As the critic Florence Martin remarks, by giving her interviewees an intimate space in the film comparable to their homes, Djebar, through her intermediary, Lila, succeeds in transforming private stories into public ones (*Screens and Veils*, 55–56).

Almost four decades after Djebar made her film, a new generation of documentary filmmakers continues in her footsteps; they too create intimate space by filming the women in their homes.[6] For example, Fatima Sissani's film *Tes cheveux démêlés cachent une guerre de sept ans* (Your disheveled hair hides a seven-year war), of 2017, depicts Eveline Lavalette, comfortably seated in her living room, recalling events of her past. Similarly, in Nassima Guessoum's film *10949 femmes* (10,949 women), of 2014, viewers first encounter Nassima Hablal in her kitchen preparing coffee for the filmmaker. And like Djebar's protagonist, Lila, the two filmmakers listen attentively to their subjects, thereby recovering fragments of buried histories and forgotten memories. As the critic Sheila Petty writes, "For women documentary filmmakers in the Maghreb, recovering fragments of submerged histories and memories goes beyond reclaiming the gaze. It is also about listening as a revolutionary gesture, and 'giving voice' to those silenced by official histories and telling their own stories in their own voices" ("We All Invented Our Own Algeria," 126). If, as the critics Camille Deprez and Judith Pernin note, documentary film is one of the most vibrant, challenging, and creative areas in the visual arts today (introduction, 1), Sissani and Guessoum contribute to it by implementing new technology in the service of a traditional practice, listening attentively to their female elders.

The title of Guessoum's film refers to the number of women who, according to the archives of the Ministère des Anciens Combattants (Ministry of Former Combattants), actively participated in the Algerian War; Amrane-Minne uses the statistic in *La guerre d'Algérie* to illustrate women's participation in the war. The title of Sissani's film, *Tes cheveux démêlés cachent une guerre de sept ans,* is a line taken from a poem Lavalette wrote as the war came to an end, "Cessez-le-feu" (*Juste Algérienne,* 118–19). As both titles pay homage to Algeria's *moudjahidate,* so do both films, capturing via visual images and sound, the compelling oral testimonies of Algerian women in their twilight years reflecting upon experiences that had occurred more than five decades earlier.

Using the documentary to give Algerian history a human dimension, the filmmakers introduce historical figures who did not engage in spectacular feats such as organizing a general strike, blowing up a bridge, or planting bombs in strategic locations but assumed important strategic and essential tasks: creating and distributing false identity cards, typing tracts for the FLN and articles for its journal, *El Moudjahid,* moving people to and from the maquis, securing safe houses for militants in the cities. Thus, the filmed narratives confirm the extent to which the FLN and the ALN depended upon women militants' assuming these critical tasks. Having participated in the large resistance movement, they often paid a heavy price—imprisonment, torture, rape, even death—yet were never adequately recognized for their courage and profound nationalism. The documentaries contribute to bringing them their due recognition, although admittedly quite late in life.

The two films are structured differently, with Guessoum focusing on one former militant, Nassima Hablal, whereas Sissini interviews three, Eveline Safir Lavalette, Alice Cherki, and Zoulikha Bekaddour. As Guessoum interviews Hablal over a period of several years, from 2007 to 2014, she retraces her life as a militant through conversations that take place intermittently, primarily in Hablal's home in Algiers but sometimes at other sites in the city. During this period, Hablal's health fails; the filmmaker finishes her documentary shortly after the former militant's death in 2014.

Sissani begins filming Lavalette shortly after she published her memoir, *Juste Algérienne,* in 2013. With her subject's health failing as well, she, like

Guessoum, concludes her documentary posthumously. Two former militants and close friends of Lavalette, Alice Cherki and Zoulikha Bekaddour, add their voices and narratives to the film, describing their lives during the war and expressing tributes to their departed friend.[7] As Sissani's film widens the spectrum to include interviews with Cherki and Bekaddour, Cherki evokes the anti-Semitism that she, as an Algerian Jew, was subjected to during the Vichy era in Algeria. Bekaddour recalls the social pattern of separation between Algerians and the European population. Lavalette, in turn, expresses her outrage at the way the Muslim community is rendered invisible, explains her decision to join the FLN once the war is declared, and describes her activity as a courier between Algiers and Oran, followed by her arrest and prison experience. Those who have read her memoir will find few new details. Most importantly, Sissani creates intimate space for her subject to reveal her indomitable spirit. In a moment of self-reflection that borders on self-deprecation, Lavalette admits that she may indeed be "puérile," childishly silly and immature, then concludes, "Je vis avec foi dans ce people" (I live with faith in the people), a faith that served her well throughout the eighty-six years of her life.

Although both documentaries end with scenes of close friends and family visiting their protagonists' graves in Algiers, they remain tributes to politically committed women who lived extraordinarily courageous lives, not objects of mourning. Guessoum's film captures Hablal's personality, spirit, and particularly her love of song. Sissani's, in turn, transmits the beauty of Lavalette's poetry as the latter reads aloud one of her poems. Finally, even though their subjects pass away before the films' conclusions, both filmmakers complete the important act of oral transmission, passing on each woman's story to the next generation. If, in the process, as Petty suggests, the documentary filmmaker creates a symbiotic relationship between memory and cultural identity, I would add that the filmmaker, as attentive listener, also establishes very strong bonds with the speaking subject. Thus, a documentary film, as a historical document, may become a vibrant memorial to the departed, offering the promise never to forget.

In this vein, I note with sorrow that the ranks of former combatants, journalists, historians, writers, critics, and filmmakers have thinned significantly in recent years. Since 2012, the year that marked the fiftieth anniversary of the end of the Algerian War, a number of individuals have passed away.

They include the *moudjahidate* Samia Lakhdari, Jacqueline Guerroudj, Eveline Lavalette, and Nassima Hablal; the novelists Yamina Mechakra and Assia Djebar; the historians Jean-Luc Einaudi and Djamila Amrane-Minne; and the literary critic Clarisse Zimra. As we pay tribute to them, we can only hope that future generations will continue to transmit the Algerian war story—in historical narrative or fiction, prose, poetry, or film—so that this extraordinary struggle, in all its complexity, will not be forgotten.

In conclusion, I believe this study shows that Algeria's war of independence was an empowering experience for many, if not most, of the women who participated in it as *moudjahidate, fidayate,* or *moussebilate.* Unfortunately, however, women's participation in a nationalist cause, a powerful motivating force that might mean women's liberation, rarely ends in social transformation. When the nationalist cause has been won, women are expected to resume their traditional gender roles. As the political scientists Joyce P. Kaufman and Kristen P. Williams note in their study of war's impact on women, rarely are gender norms overturned once the conflict has ended: "Very rarely are women brought into the formal political structure: what happens is that gender roles and norms remain entrenched even if they were suspended for the duration of the fight. Gender norms, while they may be challenged, particularly in times of conflict and war, are rarely overturned" (*Women at War,* 51). This paradigm surely applies to postcolonial Algeria, where political events of the postindependence era—including a disappointing family code approved by the National Assembly in 1984 and the *décennie noire,* Algeria's dark decade of the 1990s—confirm the strength of residual patriarchy.[8]

Unfortunately, the experience of militant women losing their political momentum at the end of a nationalist struggle in which they fought long and hard has been repeated in other areas of the African continent since the end of Algeria's anticolonial war. For example, in 1980 Zimbabwe won independence from the Rhodesian white settler regime following a guerrilla war in which women had been trained to engage in combat. Yet, women's active involvement brought them neither the equality nor the access to political power they had envisioned.[9] Sadly, women in many African nations—Algeria, Zimbabwe, Mozambique, and elsewhere—have learned that it is easier to fight against a foreign enemy than to dismantle a patriarchal system at home. Thus, it is not surprising that neither the historians nor the creative writers whose work I explore in this study chart a gender revolution. They do, however, indicate the possibilities of collective transformation. They confirm that when challenged by extraordinary historical events, individuals test their mettle in ways that definitively alter their sense of self. In other words, individual change occurs even when social transformation lags behind. Hence, I conclude this text on a note of guarded optimism for the future of Algeria's women. I hope that this study confirms that Algerian women have secured their rightful place in their nation's history and that the "fight to write," the struggle to become the legitimate chronicler of one's story, has been won by women committed to replacing amnesia with remembering, and silence with reflective and articulate testimony and creative works.

NOTES

Introduction

1. See Horne, *Savage War of Peace*. Horne devotes just four of the more than six hundred pages of his volume on the Algerian War to "the family and Muslim women at war."
2. Unless otherwise noted, translations are mine.
3. The era concluded with the Concorde civile, the government policy of reconciliation implemented in 1999 to bring the civil war to an end by granting amnesty to Islamist jihadists who were willing to give up the struggle and return to civilian life. The Algerian novelist Maïssa Bey is highly critical of the amnesty policy. Her 2010 novel *Puisque mon coeur est mort* (Since my heart is dead) tests the limit of the government policy of reconciliation in her portrayal of an individual traumatized by jihadist violence. Following the publication of her text, she engaged in a series of public discussions, affirming her position: no pardon is possible without bringing the assassins to justice.
4. Unfortunately, Alcott contracted typhoid fever during the period she spent at the hospital in Georgetown and never fully regained her health.
5. Less well known is Helen Zenna Smith's account of World War I, *Not so quiet . . .*, published in 1930.
6. Today, however, women compose about 15 percent of America's armed forces. For a study of three women who served in Iraq and Afghanistan, see Thorpe, *Soldier Girls*.
7. See, e.g., Monique Gadant's study of the journal *El Moudjahid* from 1956 to 1962, *Islam et nationalisme en Algérie,* published in 1988, which reflects the ambiguities involved with negotiating between "tradition" and "modernity" with respect to women's place in postcolonial society.
8. Cooke's harshest criticism is directed at Fadéla M'Rbat's studies *La femme algérienne* (1964) and *Les algériennes* (1967).
9. See Ireland, "Voices of Resistance."
10. See Mosteghanemi, *Dhakirat al-jasad;* and Ellen McLarney's critical study of the novel, "Unlocking the Female in Ahlam Mosteghanemi."

1. Writing Women into History

1. The historical text was published in France and Algeria. I am using the Algerian edition. The French edition, published in 1991, is titled *Les femmes algériennes dans la guerre*.
2. Guerroudj's memoir, *Des douars et des prisons* (1993), describes her experiences as a militant and then a prisoner during the Algerian War. The former combatant died in Algeria at the age of ninety-five on 15 January 2015.
3. The Battle of Algiers took place from January to September 1957, when the city of Algiers was under the control of the French military. During this period it was extremely difficult for the Algerian population to move around the city.
4. During this period, Danièle's four younger siblings lived with the Guerroudj family in Algeria.
5. Nassima Guessoum used the figure 10,949 in the title of her documentary film *10949 femmes* (2014), discussed in the conclusion.
6. Yasmina Belkacem's interview appears in Amrane-Minne, *Des femmes dans la guerre d'Algérie*, 124–27.
7. Tried and convicted, the three women spent the rest of the war years in prison. Interviewing the former militants years later, Amrane-Minne obtained their perspectives on their actions in their own words. Her interview with Malika Ighilahriz, one of Louisette Ighilahriz's sisters, appears in Amrane-Minne, *Des femmes dans la guerre d'Algérie*, 147–51.
8. The differing backgrounds gave rise to a division of labor within the units. Rural women, largely illiterate, were frequently assigned kitchen chores. Urban women, generally educated, formed the nursing staff; many had trained as nurses before joining the maquisards.
9. It is not clear from the entry whether Ghanoudja is her relative or a sister in arms.
10. Amina's photo with a group of maquisards appears in the text's annex.
11. Yamina Mechakra's novel *La grotte éclatée*, examined in chapter 3, depicts in detail the life of a nurse in the maquis.
12. The three are Djamila Bouhired, Samia Lakhdari, and Zohra Drif, who describes her mission in her memoir, *Mémoires d'une combattante de l'ALN*. See chapter 6.
13. Steiner's poems appear in Amrane-Minne, *La guerre d'Algérie*, 175–76. The chapter "Militantes d'origine européenne" in Amrane-Minne, *Des femmes dans la guerre d'Algérie*, includes interviews with Jaqueline Guerroudj, Annie Steiner, Elyette Loup, and Rose Serrano.
14. For more recent interviews with former women combatants, see Vince, *Our Fighting Sisters*.
15. This same disappointment is expressed in Lazreg, *Eloquence of Silence*; Gadant,

Le nationalisme algérien et les femmes; and Taleb Ibrahimi, "Les Algériennes et la guerre de libération nationale."

16. Other prisoners whose poems she cites include Annie Steiner, Zehor Zehari, and Baya Hocine.
17. Written in July 1962, the poem was awarded a first prize by the magazine *Jeune Afrique* that year. It appears in its entirety in Barrat, *Espoir et parole,* 147–51.
18. Here, Amrane-Minne is also respectful of an experience that she did not share with them; she was never tortured, nor was her mother, Jacqueline Guerroudj.
19. In June 1999 the French National Assembly and Senate ordered access to military archives related to the Algerian War officially opened, leading to new scholarly publications that deal with torture. See Branche, *La torture et l'armée,* on torture by the French military; and Thénault, *Une drôle de justice,* on the complicity of the French juridical system with military practices of torture.
20. In her article "Transgressing Boundaries" (2010), which draws on interviews with former women combatants and uses French military and FLN internal documents from army and colonial archives to complement the study, Natalya Vince considers the sexual abuse and rape that women often experienced when captured or raided by the French army.
21. A chart on p. 107 of *La guerre d'Algérie* lists the bombs placed during the Battle of Algiers, from January 7 to August 15, 1987. including the three on January 26, 1957, set at the Coq Hardi, the Cafétéria, and the Otomatic. Amrane-Minne designates each FLN operative only as a *fidaïa.* Djamila Bouzza placed the first; Hassiba Ben Bouali, the second; and Danièle Minne, the third. Thus, she includes herself in the record but remains anonymous.
22. For a discussion of the film that looks at various ways in which it diverges from documentary realism, particularly in aesthetic terms, see Harrison, "Pontecorvo's 'Documentary' Aesthetics."
23. For Drif's account of the event, see chapter 6.
24. Generally called Saadi Yacef by Anglophone historians, in the film he plays himself, under the pseudonym Jaffar. His text *Souvenirs de la Bataille d'Alger décembre 1956–septembre 1957* (1962) was the original basis for the film.
25. Amrane-Minne notes that Horne acknowledges difficulty in finding guides and informants and that he attributes it to the collective nature of the Algerian War of Independence, a political struggle in which individuals refrained from drawing attention to themselves out of a sense of solidarity (*La guerre d'Algérie,* 277). I would add that Horne's remark confirms Amrane-Minne's unique position as an insider who had access to former combatants that many historians probably would not have had.
26. As noted in the introduction, n. 1, Horne devotes few pages to Algerian women's role in the war.

27. See Amrane-Minne, "Women and Politics in Algeria," 68–73; and Lalami, *Les Algériennes*.

2. Herstory Is the War Story

1. In her discussion, Cooke distinguishes between the Algerian Revolution, which she terms a modern war, in contrast to postmodern wars, "the products as well as the consumers of the technological revolution" ("Wo-man, Retelling the War Myth," 179).
2. Cooke translates the passage from Arabic.
3. See Zimra, afterword; Bigelow, "Revolution and Modernity"; Schyns, *La mémoire littéraire de la guerre*; and Quinan, "Veiling Unveiled."
4. For a pedagogical approach to the text, see Mortimer, "Seeds of Change."
5. The critic Diane Labontu-Astier's 118-page monograph *Assia Djebar* (2014) may signal a renewed interest in the text.
6. The couple later divorced, and she married the Algerian poet Malek Alloula. While they were married, she and Garn collaborated on a play, *Rouge l'aube* (Red is the dawn).
7. For further biographical details, see Schyns, *La mémoire littéraire de la guerre*, 72–73; and Zimra, afterword.
8. The educational reform at the university that required history courses to be taught in Arabic influenced Djebar to leave for Paris in 1965. She returned to the University of Algiers in 1974 to teach French literature in the French Department. Calle-Gruber, *Assia Djebar*, chronology, unpaginated.
9. For further discussion of Touma and her betrayal of her society, see Quinan, "Veiling Unveiled," 742–45.
10. Djebar stated in an interview with Wadi Bouzar that "la position de Lila, à côté et en même temps dedans et témoin, c'est un peu moi" (Bouzar, "Interview," 160; Lila's position, on the periphery and at the same time within and a witness, that's somewhat me).
11. Djebar, "Entretien."
12. Said writes: "In the counterpoint of Western classical music, various themes play off one another, with only a provisional privilege being given to any particular one; yet in the resulting polyphony there is concert and order, an organized interplay that derives from the themes, not from a rigorous melodic or formal principle outside the work." *Culture and Imperialism*, 51.
13. In her article "Writing Woman: The Novels of Assia Djebar" Zimra concludes that the novel ends with the failure of both politic commitment and erotic fulfillment (73).

14. Three of the four projected volumes of her "Algerian Quartet" appeared: *L'amour, la fantasia* (1985), *Ombre sultane* (1987), and *Vaste est la prison* (1995).
15. Donadey explains in "Rekindling the Vividness of the Past," 885, that she is drawing on the critic Nancy K. Miller's essay "Arachnologies" a study that proposes the strategy of "overreading" or "reading women back in" (292).
16. The episodes recounted by Zohra and Chérifa appear in Djebar's film *La nouba des femmes du Mont Chenoua* and in the novel.
17. Although they share the same name, this Chérifa and the protagonist of *Les enfants du nouveau monde* are not the same individual.
18. A historian of fascist Italy, Portelli acknowledges the influence of William Faulkner's novel *Absalom, Absalom!* in determining his work on oral history. Portelli, *The Order Has Been Carried Out*, 18.
19. Djebar wrote about Malek Sahraoui El Berkani in the poem "Le pays sans mémoire," published in *Poèmes pour l'Algérie heureuse*, 39–40.

3. Mapping the Traumascape

1. Caruth writes: "It is always the story of a wound that cries out, that addresses us in the attempt to tell us of a reality or truth that is not otherwise available." *Unclaimed Experience*, 4.
2. In his preface to *La grotte éclatée*, Kateb Yacine informs the reader that Mechakra witnessed the torture and death of her father, to whom she dedicates the work (7–8). Mokhtari refutes this account, stating that the father died after the war, on 12 January 1974. Mechakra's sister confirms Mokhtari's account. Dalila Mechakra Martini, conversation with author, 14 April 2017.
3. The first and only full-length study of Mechakra's work, Rachid Mokhtari's *Yamina Mechakra: Entretiens et lectures*, appeared in 2015, two years after her death.
4. The French anthropologist Germaine Tillion, who worked among the Chaouia before World War II, first brought the Chaouia to the attention of the French public through her studies exploring their cultural traditions and revealing their extreme poverty. She arrived in Arris in 1934, moving from the town to a more remote rural area to do her ethnographic work.
5. For Rothberg's analysis of traumatic realism in holocaust literature, see *Traumatic Realism*, 99–106.
6. Arris is not only the name of the town but also the name of the narrator's husband and child. She distinguishes between them by using all capital letters when referring to the town.
7. La Kahina, however, has been claimed by several other groups, who also dispute her origins and her religious background. Lazreg, *Eloquence of Silence*, 21.

8. See MacMaster, *Burning the Veil,* 316; and Amrane-Minne, *La guerre d'Algérie,* 247; both refute Fanon.
9. For further discussion of the testimonies that have appeared in *El Moudjahid,* see Chaulet-Achour, *Noûn,* 73–79.
10. Mechakra would not have read it when it first appeared; she was a ten-year-old child at the time. However, as Chaulet-Achour suggests, the novelist may have consulted this series, or others *Noûn,* 87.
11. Taleb Ibrahimi references *Présence de femmes,* of the Atelier de recherches sur les femmes algériennes (ARFA), published sometime in the 1980s, as her source for this text, whose author, Drifa, does not give her last name. See Taleb Ibrahimi, "Les Algériennes," 208.
12. Remaining in the maquis throughout the war, Cherrad narrowly escapes death again when her second infirmary is obliterated two years later by French bombers. Having left for the village that day, she escapes the fate of her coworkers and the wounded soldiers in their care; all are killed in the attack (Amrane-Minne, *Des femmes,* 57).
13. For further discussion, see Chaulet-Achour, *Noûn,* 90–92.
14. According to Mechakra's sister Dalila, the novelist began asking her father about his participation in the war when she was fourteen or fifteen years old, recording his statements in a notebook that remains in the family's possession. Dalila Mechakra Martini, conversation with author, 14 April 2017.
15. For an extensive study of the cave as symbol, see Chevalier and Gheerbrant, *Dictionnaire des symboles,* 180–84.
16. We should note that Pélissier's brutal military campaign is also mentioned in Mechakra's novel as an example of French colonial violence against the colonized. See *La grotte éclatée,* 61.
17. For further discussion of maternity in the novel, see Jones, "La caverne algérienne."
18. I borrow this expression from Marie-Denise Shelton, who (herself taking the expression from the Chicana poet Gloria Anzaldua) uses it in her study of Haitian women's ability to create and preserve a sense of home in diasporic space. For a further discussion of the concept, see Shelton, "Haitian Women's Fiction."
19. It is in this same spirit that Eveline Safir Lavelette entitles her memoir *Juste Algérienne: Comme une tissure.* With a reference to the intersection of the warp and woof of woven fabric, which she uses figuratively, she conceptualizes her role as that of a weaver; her memoir, a woven carpet or tapestry. See chapter 6.
20. See Vivier, "La symbolique dans l'art populaire algérien." The catalog was prepared to accompany the exhibition "Djazair, une année de l'Algérie en France"

(Djazair, Algeria's year in France), 22 October 2003–1 February 2004, held at the Pavillon des arts, Les Halles, in Paris.
21. Pears follows her ethnographically centered reading with an interesting interpretation based on the poststructuralist reading of codes and voices by Roland Barthes in *S/Z*.
22. "Roman d'itinéraire, le récit libère sa parole et celles des autres" (Chaulet-Achour, *Noûn*, 90; Novel of an itinerary, the narrative frees her words and those of others).
23. *Les Aveugles*, oil on canvas, 1982, Musée public national des beaux-arts, Algiers. Orlando adds: "Blindness is, indeed, one of the driving themes in *La grotte éclatée*. Lack of (in)sight defines the heroine as she navigates the present trauma of war while pondering what the Algerian postcolonial nation will become. Issiakhem's painting, chosen for its haunting qualities, depicts two androgynous figures who appear as wanderers in an opaque desert, searching as they move forward in a timeless space. The work is a fitting visual image that carries through to the end of the novel." Orlando, *Algerian New Novel*, 258.
24. In an interview, Mechakra explains that after completing the manuscript in 1973, she found it difficult to get it published because it didn't fit in with the politics of the time. Mokhtari, *Yamina Mechakra*, 64.

4. Wounded Memories

1. For a discussion of the different positions of historians and creative writers, see Semujanga, "*Murambi*," 153–55.
2. For a book-length study of the theme of traumatic memory, see Heimberg, *Mémoires blessées*.
3. Achille extends the comparison between the two texts, comparing the "improbable encounter" on the train in Bey's novel to Meursault's trial in Camus's work. "Des Arabes, j'en suis sûre!," 258–59.
4. Originally published in German in 1995 as *Der Vorleser*, Schlink's novel was widely translated, and it was made into a film in 2008. Directed by Stephen Daldry, the German and American film starred Kate Winslet as Hanna, Ralph Fiennes as the adult Michael, and David Kross as the young Michael. The English translation of the novel by Carol Brown Janeway appeared in 1997.
5. Delbo's trilogy comprising *Aucun de nous ne reviendra* (1970), *Une connaissance inutile* (1970), and *Mesure de nos jours* (1971) was published in English as *Auschwitz and After* in 1995.
6. See Daeninckx, *Meurtres pour mémoire*; Huston, *L'empreinte de l'ange*; Sebbar, *La Seine était rouge*; and Lallaoui, *Une nuit d'octobre*.

7. Analyzing postmemory, Hirsch writes: "Postmemory characterizes the experience of those who grew up dominated by narratives that preceded their birth, whose own belated stories of the previous generation are shaped by traumatic events that they can neither understand nor re-create." "Projected Memory," 8.
8. For an informative article on PTSD, see Brody, "War Wounds that Time Can't Heal."
9. In an appearance on CBS's *60 Minutes* on 23 January 2002, Aussaresses was asked by host Mike Wallace whether he would use torture on Al Queda suspects. Aussaresses responded in English, "It seems to me that it's obvious." Publisher's introduction to the English translation of the general's memoirs, *The Battle of the Casbah*, iii.
10. See Dakia, *Dakia, fille d'Alger*, 38. In this text, Djaout's words, known throughout Algeria as the writer's motto, appear on a banner carried through the streets of Algiers.
11. The association won an important victory with the establishment of a new library early in this century. Having lost its library in 1990, when Islamic fundamentalists won the municipal elections in Sidi-bel-Abbès and subsequently shut down the public library, Paroles et Écriture obtained a grant from the European Union a decade later to build a new one. For Bey, a writer who has brought other writers into her own literary texts and often commented on the multiple ways in which her reading has enriched her world, this victory was substantial.
12. See McIlvanney, "Fictionalising the Father," 209. In this vein, the critic notes: "This book is about the partial healing of both autobiographical and national wounds through the narrativization of the past" (218).

5. Collective Trauma, Collective Memory

1. See Barrière, "La bibliothèque de Radio Orient."
2. See Haroun, *La 7e wilaya*; Cole, "Remembering the Battle of Paris"; and Rice, "Remembering 17 October 1961."
3. See Lionnet, *Postcolonial Representations*; Donadey, "Retour sur mémoire"; and Mortimer, "On the Road."
4. For a further exploration of Sebbar's sense of a fractured identity, see Vassallo, *Body Besieged*.
5. See Stora, *La gangrène et l'oubli*; and Branche, *La guerre d'Algérie*.
6. Haroun claims that the Conseil national de la révolution algérienne (CNRA) had designated the Fédération the seventh district in the summer of 1959 but that following independence this high-level decision generally went unrecognized by politicians within Algeria, whom he derides as opportunistic. Haroun, *La 7e wilaya*, 6.

7. Cole puts the figure between twenty thousand and forty thousand. Cole, "Remembering the Battle of Paris," 23.
8. For details of the planning of the strike, see Haroun, *La 7e wilaya*, 361–65; Levine, *Les ratonnades d'octobre*, 82–83; and Einaudi, *La Bataille de Paris*, 92–96.
9. Because the police reported that they found her body in the Canal Saint-Denis on October 31, Einaudi cannot confirm conclusively that she was murdered on October 17. He interviewed her family in 1987 and 1988. Einaudi, *La Bataille de Paris*, 171.
10. For a study of three novels published during the 1980s—Nacer Kettane's *Le sourire de Brahim* (1985), Mehdi Lallaoui's *Les beurs de Seine* (1986), and Tassadit Imache's *Une fille sans histoire* (1989)—see Jones, "Les fantômes d'une mémoire meurtrie."
11. "J'ai écrit ce texte pour me permettre de comprendre cette journée particulière, violente, que j'avais moi-même ignoré" (I wrote this text in order to understand that particular violent day, which I myself had ignored). Sebbar to author, 27 May 2007.
12. Sebbar to author, 27 May 2007.
13. Of these early works, Didier Daeninckx's *Meurtres pour mémoire* (1984), a very popular detective novel that brings events of World War II and the October 17 massacre together, overshadowed the others.
14. For brief sketches of these earlier works, see Donadey, "Retour sur mémoire," 24–28.
15. In *Mes Algéries en France* Sebbar speaks of her parents' friendship with the militants Jacqueline and Djilali Guerroudj, sentenced to death as terrorists and pardoned at the end of the war. They were Djamila Amrane's mother and stepfather.
16. By 1999, when Sebbar's text was published, French movie theaters had begun showing other films related to 17 October 1961: Denis Lévy's *Mémoires en blanc* (1981), Agnès Denis and Mehdi Lallaoui's *Le silence du fleuve* (1992), Philip Brooks and Alan Hayling's *Une journée portée disparue* (1992), Bourlem Guerdjou's *Vivre au paradis* (1999).
17. Sebbar, discussion with author, 1 July 2009.
18. During a visit to the United States in the spring of 2002, Sebbar visited Professor Michel Laronde's literature classes at the University of Iowa. Discussing the novel with his students, she evoked the women's silence. I thank Michel Laronde for sharing the video of the classroom session with me.
19. For further details concerning the women's protest, see Einaudi, *La Bataille de Paris*, 209–10; and Haroun, *La 7e wilaya*, 369.
20. Sebbar, discussion with author, 1 July 2009.
21. An exception would be Waciny Laredj, whose childhood is divided between his life before and his life after the death of his father.

22. See, e.g., *L'Algérie des contes et légendes* (2003), *Contes du Djebel Amour* (2006), and most recently, *La femme de Djiha* (2013).
23. Suleiman references Agemben, *Remnants of Auschwitz*, 17. She also qualifies her statement by stating that we have the survivor in mind when we speak of testimony "in a nonjuridical sense." Suleiman, *Crises of Memory*, 133.

6. Testimonial Literature

1. Drif discusses this incident in the preface to *Mémoires d'une combattante de l'ALN*, which is not included in the English translation.
2. Pontecorvo reproduces this scene in his film *The Battle of Algiers*. For a fifty-year retrospective of the film, see Daulatzai, *Fifty Years of "The Battle of Algiers."*
3. As noted in chapter 1, her point of view is not shared by Djamila B., who admits to a crisis of conscience when faced with the task of placing a bomb. Amrane-Minne, *La guerre d'Algérie*, 98.
4. This position is shared by Germaine Tillion, who, as she attempted to negotiate between the French and the Algerians, condemned both populations for engaging in deadly atrocities that killed the innocent. *Les ennemis complémentaires*, 47; *Fragments de vie*, 311.
5. For further discussion of the roles and representations of Algerian women as agents and victims of violence, see Flood, "Women Resisting Terror."
6. On the architecture of the Casbah, see Ravéreau, *La Casbah d'Alger*.
7. For a study of *Pépé le Moko*, see Rolot and Ramirez, "La Casbah des insoumis."
8. Tuan, *Space and Place*, 54. See Tuan's book for an extended analysis of the ways in which space becomes place.
9. Walter writes: "A place is a matrix of energies, generating representations and causing changes in awareness." Walter, *Placeways*, 131.
10. During this period, Drif becomes acquainted with the future historian Djamila Amrane, then only a teenager; they live in the same house briefly and meet again in prison. *Mémoires d'une combattante de l'ALN*, 273–74; *Inside the Battle of Algiers*, 171–72.
11. In Algiers for a meeting of the Commission internationale contre le régime concentrationnaire (CIRCC, International commission against concentration camp regimes), Tillion, as her notes on the meetings with Saadi reveal, is unable to get the French government to agree to the FLN proposal; she is, however, impressed with the FLN leader's sincerity in their negotiations.
12. Translation modified.
13. Both Tillion and Drif note the importance of Tillion's intervention in their memoirs. See Tillion, *Fragments de vie*, 323–30; and Drif, *Mémoires d'une combattante de l'ALN*, 563–75 (this passage is omitted in the English translation).

14. Two important works appeared later: Vidal-Naquet's *La torture dans la république* (1972) and, more recently, Branche's *La torture et l'armée* (2001).
15. As Amrane-Minne explains in her study of Algerian women combatants, these women encountered astonishment, suspicion, admiration, and hostility on the part of Algerian men, but never indifference. *La guerre d'Algérie*, 238.
16. For a detailed discussion of the Day of the Dead celebration in Mexico, see Haley and Fukada, *Day of the Dead*.
17. Khaoula Taleb Ibrahimi states in her study of Algerian women's participation in the war that the majority chose to remain silent. Taleb Ibrahimi, "Les Algériennes," 225.
18. For an interview with Lavalette, see Sissani's documentary *Tes cheveux démêlés cachent une guerre de 7 ans*.
19. On the participation of Frenchwomen of pied-noir descent engaged in the struggle for Algerian independence, see Doré-Audibert, *Des Françaises d'Algérie*.
20. For a further examination of the role of the liberal Catholics in the war, see Fontaine, *Decolonizing Christianity*.
21. Formed in 1919 as a Catholic workers' union, the CFTC evolved from a union on the political right to a clandestine organization that opposed Vichy and participated in the resistance in World War II. In 1960 it sought a negotiated solution for Algeria, and in 1964 it dropped all religious reference and become the CFDT, the Confédération française démocratique du travail (French Democratic Workers' Union).
22. After only two years of publication, *Consciences maghrébines* ceased publication, shut down by the government for its support of the FLN.
23. An elected member of the first National Assembly, Lavalette remained a public servant, holding various positions in the Ministère du Travail (Ministry of Labor) until her retirement in the early 1990s.
24. See Vivier, "La symbolique dans l'art populaire algérien," 15.

7. Remembering Zoulikha in Assia Djebar's Film and Fiction

1. Amrane-Minne, interview by author, Algiers, April 2009.
2. Clarisse Zimra explains in "Sounding Off the Absent Body," 121n1, that this quotation is taken from notes she took at a session she chaired of the symposium "Women in Films," in which Djebar participated, on 19 March 1998.
3. In this region, the urban population speaks Arabic; the rural inhabitants, although now schooled in Arabic, have retained Tamazight (Berber). Djebar is not a Tamazight speaker. For a study of Djebar's relationship to her Berber ancestry, see Aïtel, *We Are Imazighen*, chap. 5. Aïtel states that Djebar views Tamazight as

the language of resistance, the language in which she says no even though she does not speak it (207).
4. The film is in Arabic but subtitled in French.
5. Djebar, "La nouba des femmes du Mont Chenoua," 46.
6. In her last published work, *Nulle part dans la maison de mon père* (Nowhere in my father's house), Djebar writes of her mother's mastery of Andalusian music and the influence of this traditional form of North African music upon her in her youth.
7. For a recent historical study of the royal couple, see Roller, *World of Juba II and Kleopatra Selene*.
8. It is interesting that Djebar and Amrane-Minne, one in Cherchell, the other in Algiers, were interviewing former women militants at approximately the same time, in the late 1970s.
9. I use the term *martyr* in a secular sense, to mean an individual who sacrificed all for the greater good of his or her country's liberation.
10. Clarisse Zimra notes in "Sounding Off the Absent Body" that the scene that takes place in the cave "triggers the occulted memory of another colonial war against the French, that of 1845" (112), but she does not draw the specific parallel between their healing ritual and the *enfumade* that killed their ancestors.
11. For a further analysis of the film in terms of the Arabic language, see Bentahar, "Voice with an Elusive Sound."
12. Zoulikha's children contend that Djebar invented too much. Mohammed and Abdelhamid Oudaï, interview by author, Cherchell, 21 April 2009; Khadidja Oudaï Chemmi, interview by author, Algiers, 15 November 2013.
13. The account of the discovery of Zoulikha's remains appears in Zakad, "Pour vous dire Zoulikha."
14. Unfortunately, the museum has no reproductions of this mosaic and forbids visitors to photograph it.
15. Wiesel, *Silences et mémoires d'homme*.
16. Khadidja Oudaï Chemmi, conversation with author, Algiers, 16 November 2013.
17. In 2016 a biography of Zoulikha was published: Kamel Bouchama's *Lalla Zoulikha Oudaï, la mère des résistants*.

Conclusion

1. For further analysis of Algerian women's political movements and the Family Code of 1984, see Gadant, *Le nationalisme algérien et les femmes*, 117–71.
2. Article 29 reads: "All citizens are equal before the law. No discrimination shall prevail because of birth, race, sex, opinion or any other personal or social condition or circumstance."

3. Feriel Lalami, conversation with author, 25 May 2017.
4. I borrow this list from Susan Ireland's informative study of women's resistance literature of the undeclared civil war, "Voices of Resistance," 171.
5. For studies of the literature of this period, see Ireland, "Voices of Resistance"; Landers, "Representing the Algerian Civil War"; and Geesey, "Violent Days."
6. Faouzia Fekiri (*Les porteuses de feu,* 2007), Alexandra Dols (*Moudjahidate,* 2007), and Habiba Djahnine (*Lettre à ma soeur,* 2006) belong to this new generation of documentary filmmakers, but I exclude them because their films predate 2012. In addition, Dols, unlike Sissani and Guessoum, is not retracing her female lineage of transmission, and Djahnine's documentary, a poignant homage to her martyred sister, gunned down by Islamic terrorists in 1995, is not concerned with the Algerian War of Independence.
7. For an interview with Bekaddour by Feriel Lalami-Fatès, see Lalami-Fatès, "Une femme dans la guerre."
8. See Amrane-Minne, "Women and Politics," 68–73.
9. See Lyons, "Guerrilla Girls and Women."

BIBLIOGRAPHY

Aas-Rouparis, Nicole. "La femme-oiseau de la mosaïque: Image et chant dans *La femme sans sépulture* d'Assia Djebar." *Nouvelles études francophones* 19, no. 2 (Autumn 2004): 97–108.
Accad, Evelyne. "Assia Djebar's Contribution to Arab Women's Literature: Rebellion, Maturity, Vision." *World Literature Today* 70, no. 4 (1996): 801–12.
Aceval, Nora. *L'Algérie des contes et légendes*. Paris: Maisonneuve et Larose, 2003.
———. *Contes du Djebel Amour*. Paris: Seuil, 2006.
———. *La femme de Djiha*. Paris: El Manar, 2013.
Achille, Étienne. "'Des Arabes, j'en suis sûre!': Rompre le silence dans *Entendez-vous dans les montagnes . . .* de Maïssa Bey." *French Forum* 38, no. 1 (2013): 251–65.
Achour, Christiane. *Abécédaires en devenir: Idéologie et langue française en Algérie*. Algiers: Entreprise Algérienne de Presse, 1985.
———, ed. *Diwan d'inquiétude et d'espoir: La littérature féminine algérienne de langue française*. Algiers: ENAG/Editions, 1991.
Agemben, Giorgio. *Remnants of Auschwitz: The Witness and the Archive*. New York: Zone Books, 1999.
Ahmed, Sara. *Strange Encounters: Embodied Others in Post-Coloniality*. London: Routledge, 2000.
Aïtel, Fazia. *We Are Imazighen: The Development of Algerian Berber Identity in Twentieth-Century Literature and Culture*. Gainesville: University Press of Florida, 2014.
Alcott, Louisa May. *Hospital Sketches and Camp and Fireside Stories*. Boston: Roberts Brothers, 1869.
———. *Little Women: or Meg, Jo, Beth and Amy*. 1926. Reprint, New York: Aladdin Classics, 2000.
Ali-Benali, Zineb. "Yamina Mechakra: Pour une autre histoire." In Achour, *Diwan d'inquiétude et d'espoir*, 100–115.
Alleg, Henri. *La question*. Paris: Minuit, 1958.
Alloula, Malek. *Le harem colonial: Images d'un sous-érotisme*. Paris: Seguier, 2001.

Translated by Myrna Godzich and Wlad Godzich as *The Colonial Harem* (Minneapolis: University of Minnesota Press, 1986).

Amrane-Minne, Danièle Djamila. *Des femmes dans la guerre d'Algérie.* Paris: Karthala, 1994.

———. *La guerre d'Algérie (1954–1962): Femmes au combat.* Algiers: Editions RAHMA, 1993. Originally published as *Les femmes algériennes dans la guerre* (Paris: Plon, 1991).

———. "Women and Politics in Algeria from the War of Independence to Our Day." *Research in African Literatures* 30, no. 3 (1999): 62–77.

———. "Women at War: The Representation of Women in *The Battle of Algiers*." Trans. Alistair Clarke. *Interventions* 9, no. 3 (2007): 340–49.

Armes, Roy. *African Filmmaking: North and South of the Sahara.* Indianapolis: Indiana University Press, 2006.

———. *Postcolonial Images: Studies in North African Film.* Indianapolis: Indiana University Press, 2005.

Arnaud, Georges, and Jacques Vergès. *Pour Djamila Bouhired.* Paris: Minuit, 1957.

Asholt, Wolfgang. "Les villes frontalières d'Assia Djebar." In Calle-Gruber, *Assia Djebar: Nomade entre les murs*, 147–60.

Aussaresses, Général Paul. *Services spéciaux en Algérie, 1955–1957.* Paris: Perrin, 2001. Translated by Robert L. Miller as *The Battle of the Casbah: Terrorism and Counter-Terrorism in Algeria: 1955–1957* (New York: Enigma Books, 2002).

Barrat, Denise, ed. *Espoir et parole, poèmes algériens.* Paris: Seghers, 1962.

Barrière, Loïc. "La bibliothèque de Radio Orient." *Radio Orient*, 18 April 2017.

Barthes, Roland. *S/Z.* Paris: Seuil, 1970.

Beaugé, Florence, "Le Général Massu exprime ses regrets pour la torture en Algérie." *Le Monde*, 22 June 2000.

Beauvoir, Simone de, and Gisèle Halimi. *Djamila Boupacha.* Paris: Gallimard, 1962.

Bekkadour, Zoulikha. "Une femme dans la guerre: Entretien avec Zoulikha Bekkadour." Interview by Feriel Lalami-Fatès. In *De l'Indochine à l'Algérie: La jeunesse en mouvements des deux côtés du miroir colonial, 1940–1962*, ed. Nicole Bancel, Daniel Denis, and Youcef Fatès, 94–111. Paris: La Découverte, 2003.

Bellouma, Nassira. *Terre des femmes.* Algiers: Chihab, 2014.

Bensmaïa, Reda. "*La nouba des femmes du Mont Chenoua:* Introduction to the Cinematic Fragment." *World Literature Today* 70, no. 4 (1996): 877–84.

Bentahar, Ziad. "A Voice with an Elusive Sound: Aphasia, Diglossia, and Arabophone Algeria in Assia Djebar's 'The Nouba of the Women of Mount Chenoua.'" *Journal of North African Studies* 21, no. 3 (2016): 411–32.

Bey, Maïssa. *À contre-silence: Entretien avec Martine Marzloff.* Grigny: Paroles d'Aube, 1999.

———. *Au commencement était la mer.* Paris: Marsa, 1996.

———. *Bleu, blanc, vert*. La Tour d'Aigues: L'Aube, 2006.
———. *Cette fille-là*. La Tour d'Aigues: L'Aube, 2001.
———. *Entendez-vous dans les montagnes . . .* La Tour d'Aigues: L'Aube; Algiers: Barzakh, 2002.
———. "Faut-il aller chercher des rêves ailleurs que dans la nuit." In *Journal intime et politique: Algérie, 40 ans après*, 9–51. With Mohamed Kacimi, Boualem Sansal, Nourredine Saadi, and Leïla Sebbar. La Tour d'Aigues: L'Aube, 2003.
———. "Fragments." In *Mon père*, ed. Leïla Sebbar, 65–74. Montpellier: Chèvre-feuille étoilée, 2007.
———. *Hizya*. La Tour d'Aigues: L'Aube, 2015.
———. "Interview: Algerian Novelist Maïssa Bey: The Rebel's Daughter." By Suzanne Ruta. *Women's Review of Books* 23, no. 4 (July–August 2006): 16–17.
———. "Mon père, ce rebelle." In Bey, *À contre-silence*, 80–90. Translated by Suzanne Ruta as "My Father, the Rebel," in *World Literature Today* 81, no. 6 (2007): 27–30.
———. *Nouvelles d'Algérie*. Paris: Grasset, 1998.
———. *Pierre sang papier ou cendre*. La Tour d'Aigues: L'Aube, 2008.
———. *Puisque mon coeur est mort*. La Tour d'Aigues: L'Aube, 2010.
———. *Sous le jasmin la nuit*. La Tour d'Aigues: L'Aube, 2004.
———. *Surtout ne te retourne pas*. La Tour d'Aigues: L'Aube, 2005.
———. *L'une et l'autre*. La Tour d'Aigues: L'Aube, 2009.
Bhabha, Homi. *The Location of Culture*. London: Routledge, 1994.
Bigelow, Gordon. "Revolution and Modernity: Assia Djebar's *Les enfants du nouveau monde*." *Research in African Literatures* 34, no. 2 (Summer 2003): 13–27.
Bouchama, Kamel. *Lalla Zoulikha Oudaï, la mère des résistants*. Algiers: Juba, 2016.
Bourdieu, Pierre. *Sociologie de l'Algérie*. Paris: Presses Universitaires de France, 1958. Translated by Alan C. M. Ross as *The Algerians* (Boston: Beacon, 1962).
Bouslimani, C. "La nouba des femmes du Mont Chenoua." *El Moudjahid*, 8 March 1978, 7.
Branche, Raphaëlle. *La guerre d'Algérie: Une histoire apaisée?* Paris: Seuil, 2005.
———. *La torture et l'armée pendant la guerre d'Algérie*. Paris: Gallimard, 2001.
Brody, Jane. "War Wounds That Time Can't Heal." *New York Times*, 7 June 2016, D5.
Brooks, Philip, and Alan Hayling, dirs. *Une journée portée disparue*. 1992.
Calle-Gruber, Mireille, ed. *Assia Djebar*. Paris: ADPF, Ministère des affaires étrangères, 2006.
———. "L'écrire nomade—Ici ailleurs à une passante." In *Assia Djebar: Nomade entre les murs . . . ; pour une poétique frontalière*, ed, Calle-Gruber, 67–80. Paris: Maisonneuve & Larose, 2005.
Caruth, Cathy. "Introduction: Recapturing the Past." In Caruth, *Trauma*, 151–57.
———, ed. *Trauma: Explorations in Memory*. Baltimore: Johns Hopkins University Press, 1995.

———. *Unclaimed Experience: Trauma, Narrative, and History*. Baltimore: Johns Hopkins University Press, 1996.
Chaulet-Achour, Christiane. *Noûn: Algériennes dans l'écriture*. Biarritz: Séguier, 1999.
Cheever, Susan. *Louisa May Alcott: A Personal Biography*. New York: Simon & Schuster, 2010.
Cherki, Alice. *Mémoire anachronique: Lettre à moi-même et à quelques autres*. La Tour d'Aigues: L'Aube, 2016.
Chevalier, Jean, and Alain Gheerbrant. *Dictionnaire des symboles: Mythes, rêves, coutumes, gestes, forms, figures, couleurs, nombres*. 1966. Reprint, Paris: Robert Laffont, 1986.
Clark, Jan. "*Moudjahidate:* Women's Participation in the Algerian War of Independence as Represented in the Works of Algerian Women Writers." *Bulletin of Francophone Africa* 4, no. 7 (Spring 1995): 77–92.
Cole, Joshua. "Remembering the Battle of Paris: 17 October 1961 in French and Algerian Memory." *French Politics, Culture & Society* 21, no. 3 (2003): 21–50.
Cooke, Miriam. "Wo-man, Retelling the War Myth." In *Gendering War Talk*, ed. Miriam Cooke and Angela Woollacott, 177–204. Princeton, NJ: Princeton University Press, 1993.
———. *Women and the War Story*. Berkeley: University of California Press, 1996.
Courrière, Yves. *La guerre d'Algérie*. 4 vols. Paris: Fayard, 1968–71.
Crane, Stephen. *The Red Badge of Courage*. New York: Norton, 1969.
Daeninckx, Didier. *Meurtres pour mémoire*. Paris: Gallimard, 1984.
Dakia. *Dakia, fille d'Alger*. Paris: Castor Poche Flammarion, 1996.
d'Almeida, Irène Assiba. *Francophone African Women Writers: Destroying the Emptiness of Silence*. Gainesville: University Press of Florida, 1994.
Daulatzai, Sohail. *Fifty Years of "The Battle of Algiers": Past as Prologue*. Minneapolis: University of Minnesota Press, 2016.
Delbo, Charlotte. *Aucun de nous ne reviendra: Auschwitz et après I*. Paris: Minuit, 1970. Translated by Rosette Lamont as *Auschwitz and After: I* (New Haven, CT: Yale University Press, 1995).
———. *Les belles lettres*. Paris: Minuit, 1961.
———. *Une connaissance inutile: Auschwitz et après II*. Paris: Minuit, 1970. Translated by Rosette Lamont as *Auschwitz and After: II* (New Haven, CT: Yale University Press, 1995).
———. *Le convoi du 24 janvier*. Paris: Minuit, 1965.
———. *Mesure de nos jours: Auschwitz et après III*. Paris: Minuit, 1971. Translated by Rosette Lamont as *Auschwitz and After: III* (New Haven, CT: Yale University Press, 1995).
Delmas, Jean. "Assia Djebar: Regarder et écouter les femmes." *Jeune cinéma*, February 1979, 16–21.

Denis, Agnes, and Mehdi Lallaoui, dirs. *Le silence du fleuve*. 1992.
Deprez, Camille, and Judith Pernin. Introduction to Deprez and Pernin, *Post-1990 Documentary*, 1–17.
———, eds. *Post-1990 Documentary: Reconfiguring Independence*. Edinburgh: Edinburgh University Press, 2015.
Derrida, Jacques. *Acts of Literature*. Ed. Derek Attridge. New York: Routledge, 1992.
Dib, Mohammed. *Qui se souvient de la mer*. Paris: Seuil, 1962.
Diop, Boubacar Boris. *Murambi, le livre des ossements*. Paris: Stock, 2000. Translated by Fiona McLaughlin as *Murambi, the Book of Bones* (Indianapolis: Indiana University Press, 2006).
Djahnine, Habiba, dir. *Lettre à ma sœur*. 2006.
Djebar, Assia. *Les alouettes naïves*. Paris: Julliard, 1967.
———. *L'amour, la fantasia*. 1985. Reprint, Paris: Albin Michel, 1995. Translated by Dorothy S. Blair as *Fantasia, An Algerian Cavalcade* (London: Quartet Books, 1985).
———. *Le Blanc de l'Algérie*. Paris: Albin Michel, 1996. Translated by Marjolijn de Jager and David Kelley as *Algerian White* (New York: Seven Stories, 1999).
———. *Ces voix qui m'assiègent*. Paris: Albin Michel, 1994.
———. "Comment travaillent les écrivains: Assia Djebar. Interview by Samia Barrada-Smaoui. *Jeune Afrique*, 27 June 1984, 66–68.
———. *Les enfants du nouveau monde*. Paris: Julliard, 1962. Translated by Marjolijn de Jager as *Children of the New World: A Novel of the Algerian War* (New York: Feminist Press, 2005).
———. "Entretien avec Assia Djebar, écrivain algérien." By Mildred Mortimer. *Research in African Literatures* 19, no. 2 (Summer 1988): 197–205.
———. *La femme sans sépulture*. Paris: Albin Michel, 2002.
———. *Les impatients*. Paris: Julliard, 1958.
———. "Interview avec Assia Djebar (30 May 1975)." By Wadi Bouzar. In *Lectures maghrébines*, 155–61. Algiers: OPU; Paris: Publisud, 1984.
———, dir. *La nouba des femmes du Mont Chenoua*. 1977. New York: Women Make Movies, 2007. DVD.
———. "La nouba des femmes du Mont Chenoua." *Les deux écrans*, July 1978, 46.
———. *Nulle part dans la maison de mon père*. Arles: Actes Sud, 2007.
———. *Ombre sultane*. Paris: Albin Michel, 1987. Translated by Dorothy S. Blair as *A Sister to Scheherazade* (London: Quartet Books, 1987).
———. *Oran, langue morte*. Arles: Actes Sud, 1997. Translated by Tegan Raleigh as *The Tongue's Blood Does Not Run Dry: Algerian Stories* (New York: Seven Stories, 2010).
———. *Poèmes pour l'Algérie heureuse*. Algiers: SNED, 1969.
———. "Un regard de femme." *Courrier de l'UNESCO*, no. 91 (October 1989).

———. "Le romancier dans la cité arabe." *Algérie-Actualité*, no. 159 (November 3, 1968): 118–19.

———. *La soif.* Paris: Julliard, 1957. Translated by Francis Frenaye as *The Mischief* (New York: Simon & Schuster, 1958).

———. *Vaste est la prison.* Paris: Albin Michel, 1995. Translated by Betsy Wing as *So Vast the Prison* (New York: Seven Stories, 1999).

Djebar, Assia, and Walid Garn. *Rouge l'aube.* Algiers: SNED, 1969.

Dols, Alexandra, dir. *Moudjahidate.* 2007.

Donadey, Anne. "African-American and Francophone Postcolonial Memory: Octavia Butler's *Kindred* and Assia Djebar's *La femme sans sépulture.*" *Research in African Literatures* 39, no. 3 (Fall 2008): 65–81.

———. "Anamnesis and National Reconciliation: Re-membering October 17, 1961." In *Immigrant Narratives in Contemporary France*, ed. Susan Ireland and Patrice J. Proulx, 47–56. Westport, CT: Greenwood, 2001.

———. "Between Amnesia and Anamnesis: Remembering the Fractures of Colonial History." *Studies in Twentieth Century Literature* 23, no. 1 (Winter 1999): 111–16.

———. "'Une certaine idée de la France': The Algeria Syndrome and Struggles of 'French Identity.'" In *Identity Papers: Contested Nationhood in Twentieth Century France*, ed. Steven Ungar and Tom Conley, 215–32. Minneapolis: University of Minnesota Press, 1996.

———. *Recasting Colonialism: Women Writing between Worlds.* Portsmouth, NH: Heinemann, 2001.

———. "Rekindling the Vividness of the Past: Assia Djebar's Films and Fiction." *World Literature Today* 70, no. 4 (1996): 885–92.

———. "Retour sur mémoire: *La Seine était rouge* de Leïla Sebbar." In *Leïla Sebbar*, ed. Michel Laronde, 187–98. Paris: L'Harmattan, 2003.

Doré-Audibert, Andrée. *Des Françaises d'Algérie dans la guerre de libération.* Paris: Karthala, 1995.

Drif, Zohra. *Mémoires d'une combattante de l'ALN: Zone autonome d'Alger.* Algiers: Chihab, 2013. Translated by Andrew Farrand as *Inside the Battle of Algiers: Memoir of a Freedom Fighter* (Charlottesville, VA: Just World Books, 2017).

———. *La mort de mes frères.* Paris: Maspéro, 1960.

Durmelat, Sylvie. "Revisiting Ghosts: Louisette Ighilahriz and the Remembering of Torture." In Hargreaves, *Memory, Empire, and Postcolonialism*, 14–159.

Einaudi, Jean-Luc. *La Bataille de Paris: 17 octobre 1961.* Paris: Seuil, 1991.

El Nossery, Névine. "The Fictionalisation of History in Maïssa Bey's *Entendez-vous dans les montagnes....*" *Journal of North African Studies* 21, no. 2 (2016): 273–82.

Elshtain, Jean Bethke. *Women and War.* 1987. Reprint, Chicago: University of Chicago Press, 1995.

Erikson, Kai. "Notes on Trauma and Community." In Caruth, *Trauma*, 183–99.

Fanon, Frantz. "L'Algérie se dévoile." In *Sociologie d'une révolution: L'An V de la révolution algérienne*, 16–50. Paris: Maspéro, 1968. Translated by Haakon Chevalier as "Algeria Unveiled" in *A Dying Colonialism* (New York: Grove Press, 1967), 35–67.

———. *Les damnés de la terre*. Paris: Maspéro, 1961. Translated by Constance Farrington as *The Wretched of the Earth* (1968; reprint, New York: Grove Press, 1978).

Fanon, Josie. "Une femme, un film, un autre regard: *La nouba des femmes du Mont Chenoua*." *Demain l'Afrique*, September 1977, 3–5.

Fekiri, Faouzia, dir. *Les porteuses de feu*. 2007.

Flood, Maria. "Women Resisting Terror: Imaginaries of Violence in Algeria (1966–2002)." *Journal of North African Studies* 22, no. 1 (2017): 109–31.

Fontaine, Darcie. *Decolonizing Christianity: Religion and the End of Empire in France and Algeria*. New York: Cambridge University Press, 2016.

Friedman, Susan Stanford. "Bodies on the Move: A Poetics of Home and Diaspora." *Tulsa Studies in Women's Literature* 23, no. 2 (Fall 2004): 189–212.

Gadant, Monique. *Islam et nationalisme en Algérie: D'après "El Moudjahid," organe central du FLN*. Paris: L'Harmattan, 1988.

———. *Le nationalisme algérien et les femmes*. Preface by Mohammed Harbi. Paris: L'Harmattan, 1995.

Geesey, Patricia. "Violent Days: Algerian Women Writers and the Civil Crisis." *International Fiction Review* 27, nos. 1–2 (2000): 48–59.

Genette, Gérard. *Palimpsestes: La littérature au second degré*. Paris: Seuil, 1982.

Gilmore, Leigh. *The Limits of Autobiography: Trauma and Testimony*. Ithaca, NY: Cornell University Press, 2001.

Guerdjou, Bourlem, dir. *Vivre au paradis*. 1999.

Guerroudj, Jacqueline. *Des douars et des prisons*, Algiers: Barzakh, 1993.

Guessoum, Nassima, dir. *10949 femmes*. 2014.

Haley, Shawn D., and Curt Fukada. *The Day of the Dead: When Two Worlds Meet in Oaxaca*. New York: Berghahn Books, 2004.

Haneke, Michael, dir. *Caché*. 2005.

Harbi, Mohammed. Preface to Gadant, *Le nationalisme algérien et les femmes*, 5–7.

Harbi, Mohammed, and Benjamin Stora, eds. *La guerre d'Algérie, 1954–2004: La fin de l'amnésie*. Paris: Robert Laffont, 2004.

Hargreaves, Alec. Introduction to Hargreaves, *Memory, Empire, and Postcolonialism*, 1–8.

———, ed. *Memory, Empire, and Postcolonialism: Legacies of French Colonialism*. Lanham, MD: Lexington Books, 2005.

Harlow, Barbara. *Resistance Literature*. New York: Methuen, 1987.

Haroun, Ali. *La 7e wilaya: La guerre du FLN en France, 1954–1962*. Paris: Seuil, 1986.

Harrison, Nicholas. "Pontecorvo's 'Documentary' Aesthetics." *Interventions* 9, no. 3 (2007): 389–404.

Heimberg, Charles. *Mémoires blessées*. Geneva: Métis, 2012.
Henke, Suzette. *Shattered Subjects: Trauma and Testimony in Women's Life Writing*. London: Macmillan, 2000.
Herrero, Dolores, and Sonia Baelo-Allué, eds. *The Splintered Glass: Facets of Trauma in the Post-Colony and Beyond*. New York: Rodopi, 2011.
Hiddleston, Jane. *Assia Djebar: Out of Algeria*. Liverpool: Liverpool University Press, 2006.
Hirsch, Marianne. "Projected Memory: Holocaust Photographs in Personal and Public Fantasy." In *Acts of Memory: Cultural Recall in the Present*, ed. Mieke Bal, Jonathan Crew, and Leo Spitzer, 3–23. Hanover, NH: University Press of New England, 1999.
Horne, Alistair. *A Savage War of Peace: Algeria, 1954–1962*. New York: Penguin, 1977. Translated by Philippe Bourdrel as *Histoire de la guerre d'Algérie* (Paris: Albin Michel, 1980).
Houaoura, M'Hamed. "Inhumation hier de la romancière algérienne: Cherchell fière d'accueillir sa fille Assia Djebar." *El Watan*, 14 February 2015.
House, Jim, and Neil MacMaster. "Une journée portée disparue: The Paris Massacre of 1961 and Memory." In *Crisis and Renewal in France, 1918–1962*, ed. Kenneth Mouré and Martin S. Alexander, 267–90. New York: Berghahn Books, 2002.
Huston, Nancy. *L'empreinte de l'ange*. Arles: Actes Sud, 1998.
Huston, Nancy, and Leïla Sebbar. *Lettres parisiennes: Autopsie de l'exil*. Paris: Bernard Barrault, 1986.
Hutcheon, Linda. *A Poetics of Postmodernism: History, Theory, Fiction*. New York: Routledge, 1998.
Ighilahriz, Louisette. *Algérienne, récit recueilli par Anne Nivat*. Paris: Fayard/Calmann-Lévy, 2001.
Imache, Tassadit. *Une fille sans histoire*. Paris: Calmann Lévy, 1989.
Ireland, Susan. "The Algerian War Revisited." In Hargreaves, *Memory, Empire, and Postcolonialism*, 201–15.
———. "Voices of Resistance in Contemporary Algerian Women's Writing." In *Maghrebian Mosaic: A Literature in Transition*, ed. Mildred Mortimer, 171–93. Boulder: Lynne Rienner, 2001.
Ireland, Susan, and Patrice J. Proulx. "Cultural Trauma and Narrative Recovery in Marie-Célie Agnant's *Un alligator nommé Rosa* (Haïti) and Maïssa Bey's *Entendez-vous dans les montagnes...* (Algeria)." *New Zealand Journal of French Studies* 36, nos. 1–2 (2015): 101–20.
Jaccomard, Hélène. "L'autobiographie de Louisette Ighilahriz ou la biographie d'une nation torturée." *Expressions maghrébines* 10, no. 1 (2011): 131–44.
Jones, Christa. *Cave Culture in Maghrebi Literature*. Lanham, MD: Lexington Books, 2012.

———. "La caverne algérienne chez Yamina Mechakra et Georges Buis: Lieu de résistance, de maternité ou de combat." *Nouvelles études francophones* 21, no. 1 (Spring 2011): 135–49.
Jones, Kathryn N. "'Les fantômes d'une mémoire meurtrie': Representing and Remembering *La Bataille de Paris*." *Romance Studies* 24, no. 2 (2006): 91–104.
Kateb Yacine. *Nedjma*. Paris: Seuil, 1956. Translated into English by Richard Howard with an introduction by Bernard Aresu. Charlottesville: University Press of Virginia, 1991.
———. *Le polygone étoilé*. Paris: Seuil, 1966.
———. Preface to Mechakra, *La grotte éclatée*, 7–8.
Kaufman, Joyce P., and Kristen P. Williams. *Women at War, Women Building Peace: Challenging Gender Norms*. Boulder, CO: Kumarian, 2013.
Kettane, Nacer. *Le sourire de Brahim*. Paris: Denoël, 1985.
Khannous, Touria. "The Subaltern Speaks: Remaking/Her/Story in Assia Djebar's *La Nouba des femmes du Mont Chenoua*." In *African Images: Recent Studies and Text in Cinema*, ed. Maureen Eke, Kenneth W. Harrow, and Emmanuel Yewah, 51–71. Trenton, NJ: Africa World Press, 2000.
Khatibi, Abdelkébir. *La mémoire tatouée*. 1971. Reprint, Paris: Denoël, 2002.
Labontu-Astier, Diane. *Assia Djebar: Les alouettes naïves*. Paris: Honoré Champion, 2014.
Lachman, Kathryn. "The Allure of Counterpoint: History and Reconciliation in the Writing of Edward Said and Assia Djebar." *Research in African Literatures* 41, no. 4 (Winter 2010): 162–86.
Lalami, Feriel. *Les Algériennes contre le code de la famille: La lutte pour l'égalité*. Paris: Presses de Sciences Po, 2012.
Lallouli, Mehdi. *Les beurs de Seine*. Paris: L'Arcantère, 1986.
———. *Une nuit d'octobre*. Paris: Alternatives, 2001.
Landers, Neil Grant. "Representing the Algerian Civil War: Literature, History and the State." PhD diss., University of California, Berkeley, 2013.
Laronde, Michel. *Autour du roman beur: Immigration et identité*. Paris: L'Harmattan, 1993.
———. "'Effets d'histoire': Représenter l'histoire coloniale forclose." *International Journal of Francophone Studies* 10, nos. 1–2 (2007): 139–55.
Laub, Dori. "Truth and Testimony: The Process and the Struggle." In Caruth, *Trauma*, 61–75.
Lavalette, Eveline Safir. *Juste Algérienne: Comme une tissure*. Algiers: Barzakh, 2013.
Lazreg, Marnia. *The Eloquence of Silence*. London: Routledge, 1994.
———. *Torture and the Twilight of Empire: From Algiers to Baghdad*. Princeton, NJ: Princeton University Press, 2008.
Lejeune, Philippe. *Le pacte autobiographique*. Paris: Seuil, 1975.

Levine, Michel. *Les ratonnades d'octobre: Un meurtre collectif à Paris en 1961*. Paris: Ramsay, 1985.
Lévy, Denis, dir. *Mémoires en blanc*. 1981.
Lionnet, Françoise. *Postcolonial Representations: Women, Literature, Identity*. Ithaca, NY: Cornell University Press, 1995.
Lyons, Tanya. "Guerrilla Girls and Women in the Zimbabwean National Liberation Struggle." In *Women in African Colonial Histories*, ed. Jean Allman, Susan Geiger, and Nakanyike Musisi, 305–26. Bloomington: Indiana University Press, 2002.
MacMaster, Neil. *Burning the Veil: The Algerian War and the "Emancipation" of Muslim Women*. Manchester: Manchester University Press, 2009.
Malkmus, Lizbeth, and Roy Armes. *Arab and African Film Making*. London: Zed Books, 1991.
Mammeri, Mouloud. *L'opium et le bâton*. Paris: Plon, 1965.
Martin, Florence. *Screens and Veils: Maghrebi Women's Cinema*. Bloomington: Indiana University Press, 2011.
Marx-Scouras, Danielle. "Yacef Girls." *Maghreb Review* 21, nos. 3–4 (1996): 256–66.
Mattei, Georges. *La guerre des gusses*. Paris: Balland, 1982.
McIlvanney, Siobhán. "Fictionalising the Father in Maïssa Bey's *Entendez-vous dans les montagnes*. . . ." *Hawwa: Journal of Women of the Middle East and the Islamic World* 12 (2014): 195–220.
McLarney, Ellen. "Unlocking the Female in Ahlam Mosteghanemi." *Journal of Arabic Literature* 33, no. 1 (2002): 24–44.
Mechakra, Yamina. *Arris*. *Algérie Littérature/Action*, nos. 33–34 (September–October 1999): 5–91.
——. "L'éveil du mont." In Achour, *Diwan d'inquiétude et d'espoir*, 525–28.
——. *La grotte éclatée*. Algiers: SNED, 1979.
Medeiros, Ana. "Fantastic Elements in Assia Djebar's *La femme sans sépulture*." *Portal: Journal of Multidisciplinary International Studies* 4, no. 2 (July 2007):1–13.
Michel-Chich, Danielle. *Lettre à Zohra Drif*. Paris: Flammarion, 2012.
Miller, Nancy K. "Arachnologies: The Woman, the Text, and the Critic." In *The Poetics of Gender*, 270–95. New York: Columbia University Press, 1986.
Milò, Giuliva. *Lecture et pratique de l'histoire dans l'oeuvre d'Assia Djebar*. Brussels: Peter Lang, 2007.
Mohammedi-Tabti, Bouba. "Assia Djebar: *Les Enfants du nouveau monde* ou la clôture du lieu." In *Assia Djebar*, ed. Najib Redouane and Yvette Bénayoun-Szmidt, 115–28. Paris: L'Harmattan, 2008.
Mokhtari, Rachid. *Yamina Mechakra: Entretiens et lectures*. Algiers: Chihab, 2015.
Mortimer, Mildred. "Language and Space in the Fiction of Assia Djebar and Leïla Sebbar." In "Special Issue on Women's Writing," *Research in African Literatures* 19, no. 3 (Fall 1988): 301–11.

———. "Nouveau regard, nouvelle parole: Le cinéma d'Assia Djebar." In "With Open Eyes: Women and African Cinema," ed. Kenneth W. Harrow, 93–109. Special issue, *Matatu* 19, no. 1 (1997): 93–109.

———. "On the Road: Leïla Sebbar's Fugitive Heroines." In "North African Literature," special issue, *Research in African Literatures* 23, no. 2 (Summer 1992): 308–13.

———. "Probing the Past: Leïla Sebbar, *La Seine était rouge/The Seine was Red*." *French Review* 83, no. 6 (May 2010): 1246–56.

———. "Seeds of Change: Assia Djebar's *Les enfants du nouveau monde/Children of the New World*; A Novel of the Algerian War." In *Approaches to Teaching the Works of Assia Djebar*, ed. Anne Donadey, 37–43. New York: Modern Language Association, 2017.

———. "Tortured Bodies, Resilient Souls: Algeria's Women Combatants Depicted by Danièle Djamila Amrane-Minne, Louisette Ighilahriz, and Assia Djebar." *Research in African Literatures* 43, no. 1 (Spring 2012): 101–17.

———. "Women and War: *La Grotte Éclatée*, by Yamina Mechakra." *CELFAN Review* 7, nos. 1–2 (November 1987–February 1988): 14–17.

———. "Zoulikha, the Martyr of Cherchell in Film and Fiction." *PMLA* 131, no. 1 (2016): 134–39.

Mosteghanemi, Ahlam. *Dhakirat al-jasad*. Beirut: Dar al-Adab, 1998. Translated by Peter Clark as *Memory in the Flesh* (Cairo: American University in Cairo Press, 2004).

M'Rabet, Fadéla. *Les algériennes*. Paris: Maspéro, 1967.

———. *La femme algérienne*. Paris: Maspéro, 1965.

Nora, Pierre. "Entre mémoire et histoire: La problématique des lieux." In *Les lieux de mémoire*, xvii–xlii. Paris: Gallimard, 1984. Translated by Marc Roudebush as "Between Memory and History: Les lieux de mémoire," *Representations*, no. 26 (Spring 1989): 7–24.

O'Reilly, Michael. "Place, Position, and Postcolonial Haunting in *La femme sans sépulture*." *Research in African Literatures* 35, no. 1 (Spring 2004): 66–86.

Orlando, Valérie. *The Algerian New Novel: The Poetics of a Modern Nation, 1950–1979*. Charlottesville: University of Virginia Press, 2017.

———. *Of Suffocated Hearts and Tortured Souls: Seeking Subjecthood through Madness in Francophone Women's Writing of Africa and the Caribbean*. Lanham, MD: Lexington Books, 2003.

Pears, Pamela A. *Remnants of Empire in Algeria and Vietnam: Women, Words, and War*. Lanham, MD: Lexington Books, 2004.

Penijel, Jacques, dir. *Octobre à Paris*, 1962.

Petty, Sheila. "'We All Invented Our Own Algeria': Letter to My Sister as Memory-Narrative." In Deprez and Pernin, *Post-1990 Documentary*, 125–37.

Platt, Katherine. "Places of Experience and the Experience of Place." In *The Longing* for Home, ed. Leroy S. Rounder, 112–27. Notre Dame, IN: University of Notre Dame Press, 1996.

Pontecorvo, Gillo, dir. *The Battle of Algiers*. 1966.

Portelli, Alessandro. *The Order Has Been Carried Out: History, Memory, and Meaning of a Nazi Massacre in Rome*. New York: Palgrave, 2003.

Quandt, William B. *Revolution and Political Leadership: Algeria, 1954–1968*. Cambridge, MA: MIT Press, 1969.

Quinan, Christine. "Veiling Unveiled: Female Embodiment and Action in Assia Djebar's *Les Enfants Du Nouveau Monde* and *Les Alouettes Naïves*." *Women's Studies* 40, no. 6 (September 2011): 723–47.

Ravéreau, André. *La Casbah d'Alger, et le site créa la ville*. Paris: Sinbad, 1989.

Rezzoug, Simone. "Écritures féminines algériennes: Histoire et société." *Maghreb Review* 9, nos. 3–4 (1984): 86–89.

Rice, Alison. *Polygraphies*. Charlottesville: University of Virginia Press, 2012.

———. "Remembering 17 October 1961: The Role of Fiction in Remembering the Battle of Paris." *L'Esprit créateur* 54, no. 4 (2014): 90–102.

Ricoeur, Paul. *La mémoire, l'histoire, l'oubli*. Paris: Seuil, 2000. Translated by Kathleen Blarney and David Pellauer as *Memory, History, Forgetting* (Chicago: University of Chicago Press, 2004).

Rocca, Anna. *Assia Djebar, Le Corps Invisible: Voir sans être vue*. Paris: L'Harmattan, 2004.

Roller, Duane R. *The World of Juba II and Kleopatra Selene: Royal Scholarship on Rome's African Frontier*. New York: Routledge, 2003.

Rolot, Christian, and Francis Ramirez. "La Casbah des insoumis: Alger dans *Pépé le Moko* de Julien Duvivier." In *Alger: Une ville et ses discours*, ed. Naget Khadda and Paul Siblot, 379–90. Montpellier: Praxiling, 1996.

Rothberg, Michael. *Multidirectional Memory: Remembering the Holocaust in the Age of Decolonization*. Stanford, CA: Stanford University Press, 2009.

———. *Traumatic Realism: The Demands of Holocaust Representation*. Minneapolis: University of Minnesota Press, 2000.

Rotman, Patrick, and Bernard Tavernier. *La guerre sans nom: Les appelés d'Algérie, 1954–1962*. Paris: Seuil, 1992.

Rousso, Henry. *Le syndrome de Vichy (1944–198 . . .)*. Paris: Seuil, 1987.

Ruedy, John Douglas. *Modern Algeria: The Origins and Development of a Nation*. 1992. Reprint, Bloomington: Indiana University Press, 2005.

Saadi, Yacef. *La Bataille d'Alger*. 3 vols. Paris: Publisud, 2002.

———. *Souvenirs de la Bataille d'Alger, décembre 1956–septembre 1957*. Paris: Julliard, 1962.

Said, Edward. *Culture and Imperialism*. New York: Knopf, 1993.

———. "The Mind of Winter." *Harper's Magazine*, September 1984, 49–55. Reprinted in a modified version as "Reflections on Exile" in *Reflections on Exile, and Other Essays* (Cambridge, MA: Harvard University Press, 2000), 173–86.

Schlink, Bernhard. *Der Vorleser*. Zurich: Verlag AG, 1995. Translated by Carol Brown Janeway as *The Reader* (New York: Random House, 1997).

Schyns, Désirée. *La mémoire littéraire de la guerre d'Algérie dans la fiction algérienne francophone*. Paris: L'Harmattan, 2012.

Sebbar, Leïla. *Les carnets de Shérazade*. Paris: Stock, 1985.

———. *Une enfance dans la guerre: Algérie, 1954–1962*. Saint-Pourçain-sur-Sioule: Bleu Autour, 2016.

———. *Le fou de Shérazade*. Paris: Stock, 1991.

———. *Je ne parle pas la langue de mon père*. Paris: Julliard, 2002.

———. *Mes Algéries en France*. Saint-Pourçain-sur-Sioule: Bleu Autour, 2004.

———. *La Seine était rouge*. Paris: Thierry Magnier, 1999. Translated by Mildred Mortimer as *The Seine Was Red* (Bloomington: Indiana University Press, 2008).

———. "La Seine était rouge." *Actualité de l'émigration hébdo*, no. 207 (1990). Reprinted as "La force de la mémoire" in *Le Maghreb littéraire* 2, no. 3 (1998): 95–98.

———. *Shérazade, 17 ans, brune, frisée, les yeux verts*. Paris: Stock, 1982.

Seferdjeli, Ryme. "Rethinking the History of the Mudjahidat during the Algerian War." *Interventions: International Journal of Postcolonial Studies* 14, no. 2 (2012): 238–55.

Semujanga, Josias. "*Murambi*: La métaphore de l'horreur ou le témoignage impossible." In *Configurations mémorielles et identités francophones*, ed. Kanaté Dahouda and Sélom K. Gbanou, 85–101. Paris: L'Harmattan, 2007.

Shelton, Marie-Denise. "Haitian Women's Fiction." *Callaloo* 15, no. 3 (1992): 770–77.

Shepard, Todd. *The Invention of Decolonization: The Algerian War*. Ithaca, NY: Cornell University Press, 2006.

Sissani, Fatima, dir. *Tes cheveux démêlés cachent une guerre de 7 ans*. Le Mans: 24 Images-Djinn Production-Thelma Film, 2017.

Smith, Helen Zenna. *Not So Quiet . . . 1930*. Reprint, New York: Feminist Press, 1989.

Stora, Benjamin. *L'Algérie: Formation d'une nation*. Biarritz: Atlantica, 1998.

———. *La gangrène et l'oubli: La mémoire de la guerre d'Algérie*. Paris: La Découverte, 1991.

———. "La guerre des mémoires." *Maghreb-Machrek*, no. 197 (Autumn 2008): 13–19.

———. *La guerre invisible: Algérie, années 90*. Paris: Presses de Sciences Po, 2001.

———. "Women Writing between Two Algerian Wars." *Research in African Literatures* 30, no. 3 (1999): 78–94.

Suleiman, Susan Rubin. *Crises of Memory and the Second World War*. Cambridge, MA: Harvard University Press, 2006.

Taleb Ibrahimi, Khaoula. "Les Algériennes et la guerre de libération nationale: L'émergence des femmes dans l'espace public et politique au cours de la guerre et l'après-guerre." In Harbi and Stora, *La guerre d'Algérie*, 197–226.
Teguia, Mohamed. *L'Algérie en guerre*. Algiers: OPU, n.d.
Thénault, Sylvie. *Une drôle de justice: Les magistrats dans la guerre d'Algérie*. Paris: La Découverte, 2001.
Thorpe, Helen. *Soldier Girls: The Battles of Three Women at Home and at War*. New York: Scribner, 2014.
Tillion, Germaine. *Les ennemis complémentaires*. Paris: Minuit, 1960.
———. *Fragments de vie*. Paris: Seuil, 2009.
Tuan, Yi-Fu. *Space and Place: The Perspective of Experience*. Minneapolis: University of Minnesota Press, 1997.
Tumarkin, Maria. *Traumascapes: The Power and Fate of Places Transformed by Tragedy*. Carleton, Victoria, Australia: Melbourne University Publishing, 2005.
Vassallo, Helen. *The Body Besieged: The Embodiment of Historical Memory in Nina Bouraoui and Leïla Sebbar*. Lanham, MD: Lexington Books, 2012.
Vidal-Naquet, Pierre. *La torture dans la république: Essai d'histoire et de politique contemporain*. Paris: Minuit, 1972.
Vince, Natalya. *Our Fighting Sisters: Nation, Memory and Gender in Algeria, 1954–2012*. Manchester: Manchester University Press, 2015.
———. "Saintly Grandmothers: Youth Reception and Reinterpretation of the National Past in Contemporary Algeria." *Journal of North African Studies* 18, no. 1 (2013): 32–52.
———. "Transgressing Boundaries: Gender, Race, Religion, and 'Françaises musulmanes' during the Algerian War of Independence." *French Historical Studies* 33, no. 3 (2010): 445–74.
Vivier, Marie-France. "La symbolique dans l'art populaire algérien." In *Algérie: Mémoire de femmes, au fil des doigts*, ed. Beatrice Riollet El-Habib and Marie-France Vivier, 15–25. Paris: Somogy Editions d'Art, 2003.
Walter, Eugene Victor. *Placeways: A Theory of the Human Environment*. Chapel Hill: University of North Carolina Press, 1988.
Weltman-Aron, Brigitte. "Lectures de Zohra Drif." *L'Esprit créateur* 54, no. 4 (Winter 2014): 51–63.
Wiesel, Elie. *Silences et mémoires d'homme*. Paris: Seuil, 1989.
Woodhull, Winifred. *Transfigurations of the Maghreb: Feminism, Decolonization, and Literatures*. Minneapolis: University of Minnesota Press, 1993.
Zakad, Abderrahmane. "Pour vous dire Zoulikha." *El Watan*, 2 November 2008. http://www.elwatan.com/Pour-vous-dire-Zoulikha.
Zimra, Clarisse. Afterword to *Children of the New World: A Novel of the Algerian War*, by Assia Djebar, trans. Marjolijn de Jager, 201–33. New York: Feminist Press, 2005.

———. "In Her Own Write: The Circular Structures of Linguistic Alienation in Assia Djebar's Early Novels." *Research in African Literatures* 11, no. 2 (Summer 1980): 206–23.

———. "Sounding Off the Absent Body: Intertextual Resonances in 'La femme qui pleure' and 'La femme en morceaux.'" *Research in African Literatures* 30, no. 3 (Fall 1999): 108–24.

———. "Writing Woman: The Novels of Assia Djebar." In "Translations of the Orient: Writing the Maghreb." Special issue, *SubStance* 21, no. 3 (1992): 68–84.

INDEX

Aas-Rouparis, Nicole, 205–6
Accad, Evelyne, 57
Aceval, Nora, 156–57
Achille, Etienne, 109, 231n3
Achour, Christiane. *See* Chaulet-Achour, Christiane
agency of women: in patriarchal system, 23, 52, 56–57; in speaking out about trauma and torture, 177. *See also* voice
Ahmed, Sara, 111–12
AJAAS (Association de la jeunesse algérienne pour l'action sociale; Association of Algerian Youth for Social Action), 178
Alcott, Louisa May, 4, 225n4
Algerian syndrome (France's inability to deal with Algerian past), 134, 136, 146–47
Algerian War: fatalities and displaced persons from, 1–2, 165; French amnesia about, 104, 134, 136, 146–47, 191, 209; Holocaust linked to, 115–16; influence and legacy of, 1, 3; militants' bombings in Algiers, 22, 26–27, 43, 45, 160, 163–65, 227n21; military archives on, public access to, 227n19; new analyses of, 215–18. *See also* Battle of Algiers; torture; women's role in war; *specific women writers*
Algiers (Hollywood film), 166

Ali-Benali, Zineb, 82
Alleg, Henri, *La question,* 12, 170
Alloula, Malek (second husband of Djebar), 45, 228n6
ALN (Armée de libération nationale), 1, 84, 87, 221
alouettes naïves, Les (Djebar; The naïve larks), 17, 60–68, 214; "alouettes naïves," use of term in, 67; autobiographical nature of, 63, 65; complex narrative structure of, 61; counterpoint realms in, 62–63, 65; *Les enfants du nouveau monde* and, 58, 61–62; on transformation of women due to war, 50–52, 65; on Tunisian life of Algerian exiles, 53, 61, 63; uncertain future of war and postwar world in, 62, 65; withdrawal of heroine from public to private realm in, 65–66
Amato, Alain, 155
Amina (young *moudjahida* and diarist), 28–32, 226n10
amour, la fantasia, L' (Djebar; *Fantasia: An Algerian Cavalcade*), 17, 68–74, 214; alternating between first- and third-person pronouns in, 111; autobiographical nature of, 58, 68, 72; Barchou de Penhoën's story and, 69–70, 74, 189, 207; collaboration between informant and her scribe

amour, la fantasia, L' (continued)
in, 73–74; compared to Bellouma's *Terre des femmes*, 219; compared to *Les alouettes naïves* and *Les enfants du nouveau monde*, 68; *Les enfants du nouveau monde* prefiguring, 58; *enfumade* (asphyxiation by fire) killing Algerians hiding in caves, 92–93, 198–99; multiple women's war testimonies in, 29, 72–75; part of "Algerian Quartet," 229n14; time periods (conquest of 1830 and war for independence) covered in, 51–52, 69

Amrane, Rabah (husband of Amrane-Minne), 23

Amrane-Minne, Danièle Djamila, 17, 21–48; anonymity of interviewees of, 35–36, 43–44; as Battle of Algiers bomber for FLN, 22, 37, 45, 227n21; biographical background of, 22–23; "Boqala" (poem), 41–42; compared to Djebar, 190; compared to Ighilahriz, 175; compared to Lavalette, 180; compared to other historians of Algerian War, 35, 36, 71; compared to Vince, 216; Drif and, 234n10; Fanon refuted by, 25–26; *Des femmes dans la guerre d'Algérie*, 21, 35, 38, 87, 214, 219, 226nn6–7; as hidden informant in her writing, 43, 74; on history vs. memory, 16; Horne and, 46, 227n25; on incarceration's psychological effects, 37–42, 226n7; on interviews as conversations, 44; on literature dealing with women's role in Algerian War, 2, 19, 21, 48; male gaze challenged by, 44–47, 235n15; oral testimony and its interpretation of history used by, 35–37, 74, 214; other writers relying on interviews collected by, 85–88; poetry written during her incarceration and subsequent release, 39–42, 227n17; on Pontecorvo's film *The Battle of Algiers*, 44–45; sources used by, 23, 25–28, 46; subjectivity in interview process, 36–37, 148; on "terrorist" as term applied to *fidayine*, 34; on transformation of women due to war, 49–50, 84, 214; "Women at War: The Representation of Women in *The Battle of Algiers*," 44; on women's organizations, 24; on women's status and treatment, 11, 24, 99, 207; Zoulikha unknown to, 188. See also *guerre d'Algérie (1954–1962), La: Femmes au combat*

anamnesis (recovery of historical memory), 18, 20, 132, 138, 140, 144, 146, 175

Anzaldua, Gloria, 230n18

Arabic language, 19, 192, 207, 215, 228n8, 235n3

Arnaud, Georges, *Pour Djamila Bouhired* (with Vergès), 12, 170

Arris (mountain village), 82, 229n6

Asholt, Wolfgang, 208

Assima, Fériel, 218

Association des femmes musulmanes algériennes (AFMA; Association of Algerian Muslim Women), 24–25

Atelier de recherches sur les femmes algériennes (ARFA), 230n11

Aussaresses, Paul, 122, 147, 170, 232n9

Ayoun, Monique, 153–54

Barchou de Penhoën, Baron, 69–70, 74, 189, 207

Barthes, Roland, 231n21

Bartok, Bela, 192–93

Battle of Algiers (January–September 1957), 226n3; bombings conducted by women in, 22, 37, 45, 160, 227n21; Drif's memoir on her role in, 159, 160, 170, 186; started by French bombing Casbah (August 10, 1956), 45, 163; young girls as FLN operatives in, 32–34

Battle of Paris (October 17, 1961), 18, 131, 132, 135–38, 146, 233n7, 233n16

bearing witness and testimonial literature, 158–87, 213; in Amrane-Minne's *La guerre d'Algérie,* 29–32; compared with narratives and fictions typically inspired by war, 187; difficulty of women to speak out, 12, 175–77; Drif, Ighilahriz, and Lavalette as writers of, 159, 186–87; as part of healing process, 13, 129–30, 143, 170, 173; search for meaning and involvement in independence struggle, 159, 187; in Sebbar's *La Seine était rouge,* 141–44. *See also* Drif, Zohra; Ighilahriz, Louisette; Lavalette, Eveline Safir; *témoignages*

Beauvoir, Simone de (with Halimi), *Pour Djamila Boupacha,* 12, 170

Bédar, Fatima, 136, 233n9

Bekaddour, Zoulikha, 221, 222

Belaskri, Yahia, 154

Belguembour, Khadidja, 88

Belkacem, Yasmina, 27, 226n6

Bellouma, Nassira, *Terre des femmes* (Land of women), 219

Benameur, Samia. *See* Bey, Maïssa

Benameur, Yagoub (father of Maïssa Bey), 106–9, 110

Ben Bella, Ahmed, 150

Ben Bouali, Hassiba, 161, 167–69, 227n21

Beni Manacer (Algerian tribe), 72

Ben Mansour, Latifa, 218

Ben M'Hidi, Larbi, 167

Ben Mohamed, Mimi, 31

Benosmane, Fatima, 38

Bensmaïa, Réda, 195

Berber language, 19, 215, 235n3

Berque, Jacques, 67

Bey, Maïssa: on amnesty granted to Islamist jihadists, 225n3; *Au commencement était la mer,* 10–11, 106; autobiographical writing of, 109–10, 113, 214; Samia Benameur taking Maïssa Bey as pen name, 106; biographical background of, 104–5, 106–9; on childhood knowledge of helicopters called *alouettes,* 155; compared to Djebar, 110–11, 113; compared to Ighilahriz, 175; compared to Lavalette, 185; compared to Mechakra, 104–5; compared to Sebbar, 132–33, 139; during *décennie noire* of 1990s, 10, 127–28; Delbo and, 117; encouraging other women writers, 10–11, 128; "Faut-il aller chercher des rêves" (diary), 128–29; "Fragments," 107–8; *Hizya,* 106; intertextuality in work of, 113; on literature as significant form of resistance to injustice and tyranny, 105–6, 116, 126–29; on literature widening her horizons, 113; "Mon père, ce rebelle," 106–7; multidirectional memory and, 215; *Pierre sang papier ou cendre,* 106; *Puisque mon coeur est mort,* 106, 225n3; relationship between fact and fiction in work of, 111, 127; return to meaningful place transformed by death of her father, 108–9; Sebbar's work as reference source for, 132; *L'une et l'autre,* 113; writing fiction of traumatic experiences, 159. *See also Entendez-vous dans les montagnes...*

Bhabha, Homi, 201
Bigeard, Colonel, 27
Bigelow, Gordon, 55, 59
Borzeix, Jean-Marie, preface to *Une enfance dans la guerre*, 154
Bouhired, Djamila, 45, 46, 160, 161, 167, 170, 226n12
Bouhired-Hattari, Fatiha (Oukhiti), 161, 167
Boumedienne, Houari, 150, 189, 208
Boupacha, Djamila, 12, 215
Bourdieu, Pierre, 59
Bousafi, Kheira, 87
Boussouf, Malika, 218
Bouzza, Djamila, 227n21
Branche, Raphaëlle, 134, 227n19
Brenot, Jacqueline, 153, 155

Calle-Gruber, Mireille, 204–5
Camus, Albert, *L'Étranger (The Stranger)*, 109, 231n3
Caruth, Cathy, 13–14, 78–79, 94, 104, 171, 229n1
Casbah of Algiers, 165–69; as authentically Algerian space, 167–69; in Battle of Algiers, 44, 45; destruction of, in Algerian War, 3; Western imagery of, 165–66; young girls used as FLN operatives to come and go between European parts of Algiers and, 32–34; ZAA in, 160. *See also* Battle of Algiers
cave's real and metaphoric role, 85, 92–94, 197–99, 230n15, 236n10. *See also enfumade*
CFTC (Confédération française de travailleurs chrétiens; French Confederation of Christian Workers), 178, 235n21
Chaouia (Berber ethnic group), 79, 219, 229n4
Charef, Mehdi, 154

Chaulet-Achour, Christiane, 41, 85, 90, 99, 156, 230n10
Cherki, Alice, 184, 221, 222
Cherrad, Yamina, 86, 89–90, 230n12
Chouaki, Salah, 128
civil war in Algeria: amnesty granted to Islamicists to end (1999), 225n3; Bey on, 11, 105, 125–26, 215; Djebar on, 206; Islamicist targeting intellectuals and defenders of cultural pluralism, 10, 183, 206; Lavalette and, 183–84; resistance literature of women writers during, 218–19; Sebbar on, 139, 215; silencing of women and, 9–10, 189. *See also* dark decade of 1990s (*décennie noire*)
Cole, Joshua, 16, 135, 148, 149–50, 233n7
colonialism. *See* French conquest and colonialism
conscience, issues of, 33–34, 66, 122, 124, 163–65, 226n7, 234n3
Consciences maghrébines (journal), 178, 235n22
Conseil national de la révolution algérienne (CNRA), 232n6
Cooke, Miriam, 9, 49, 50, 56, 75, 225n8, 228n1; "Silence Is the Real Crime," 8; *Women and the War Story*, 7–8
Courrière, Yves, 35, 46
Crane, Stephen, *Red Badge of Courage*, 5

Daeninckx, Didier, 117, 138, 233n13
d'Almeida, Irène Assiba, 19
dark decade of 1990s (*décennie noire*), 2–3, 9–12, 23, 47, 106, 125–26, 132, 183–84, 223
Day of the Dead (Mexico), 174, 235n16
décennie noire. *See* dark decade of 1990s
decolonization. *See* Algerian War; postcolonial era

Delacroix, Eugène, 165; *Femmes d'Alger dans leur appartement* (painting), 10
Delanoë, Bertrand, 146
Delbo, Charlotte, 116–17, 231n5
Deprez, Camille, 220
Derrida, Jacques, 110
Dib, Mohammed, *Qui se souvient de la mer*, 92
Diop, Boubacar Boris, 208
Djahnine, Habiba, 237n6
Djaout, Tahar, 127, 232n10
Djebar, Assia, 49–76, 189–212; "Algerian Quartet," projected volumes of, 229n14; autobiographical elements in writing and film of, 58, 63, 65, 68, 72, 190, 192, 194; *Le blanc de l'Algérie*, 199; biographical background of, 52–53, 228n8, 228n10; *Ces voix qui m'assiègent*, 62; compared to Amrane-Minne, 190; compared to Bey, 110–11, 113; compared to Fanon, 59; compared to Mechakra, 97; during *décennie noire* of 1990s, 10, 189, 218; family history relayed by women of her family, 71, 75; as filmmaker in Arabic dialect, 192; fragmented story telling by, 58–59, 191, 195, 197–98, 199–200; *Les impatients*, 50; *Nulle part dans la maison de mon père*, 236n6; *Ombre sultane*, 58, 229n14; *Oran, langue morte*, 10, 199; recognition as great French novelist, 50; *La soif*, 50; trilogy of early novels of 1950s and 1960s, 51–52; *Vaste est la prison*, 199, 229n14; on women's empowerment, 50–52, 54–57, 65, 76, 214; writing fiction of traumatic experiences, 159; on younger women writers ("nouvelles femmes d'Alger"), 10; on Zoulikha's role in resistance, 16, 18, 188–212. See also *alouettes naïves, Les; amour, la fantasia, L'; enfants du nouveau monde, Les; femme sans sepulture, La; nouba des femmes du Mont Chenoua, La*
Djeghloul, Abdelkader, 137
Dols, Alexandra, 237n6
Donadey, Anne, 70–71, 74, 133, 143–44, 146, 189, 212, 229n15
Drif, Zohra: Amrane-Minne and, 234n10; arrest of Drif, 169; biographical background, 159–60; bombing in Algiers executed by Drif, 45, 160, 163–65; Casbah as spatial referent for, 166–69; compared to Ighilahriz, 175; compared to Lavalette, 177, 178; covert work for FLN, 160, 162–64; education in colonial schools, 162; friendship with Samia Lakhdari, 162–63; incarceration of, 169; *Mémoires d'une combattante de l'ALN*, 18, 34, 159–70, 226n12, 234n1; *La mort de mes frères*, 160; personal testimony in memoir by, 159, 186; silence and, 43; Tillion negotiations over treatment of Algerian political prisoners, 168, 234n13; torture, 18, 167–68; ZAA role of, 165, 167
Durmelat, Sylvie, 173
Duvivier, Julien, *Pépé le Moko* (film), 166

Einaudi, Jean-Luc, 233n9; *La Bataille de Paris: 17 octobre 1961*, 136, 141–42, 147, 148, 149
El Berkani, Malek Sahraoui, 75, 229n19
El Berkani, Mohammed Ben Aissa, 75
El Moudjahid, 26, 52, 63, 85, 178, 221
El Nossery, Névine, 110–11
Elshtain, Jean Bethke, *Women and War*, 4–6, 7, 17, 33, 83, 87, 164

empowerment of women: Amrane-Minne's focus on, 23, 214; Bey encouraging women writers and, 10–11, 128; Cooke on war's destabilization of identity and community creating possibilities for, 75–76; Djebar's focus on, 50–52, 54–57, 65, 76, 214; fiction as path to, 219; mobility and, 7; self-understanding of colonialist past and, 121; testimonials of women enabling, 158

enfance dans la guerre, Une (Sebbar; A childhood in war), 17, 18, 132, 150–57; Arab and Berber communities experiencing violence directly, 153; collection of essays on childhood memories of those who lived through Algerian War, 151–53; identity development of children in, 155–56; preface by Borzeix, 154; Sebbar's recollections of childhood, 155; traumatic memories in, 154–55, 157

enfants du nouveau monde, Les (Djebar; Children of the New World), 17, 53–60, 214; *Les alouettes naïves* and, 58, 61–62; autobiographical nature of, 58; on gender differences in war experiences, 54; multivoiced discourse or contrapuntal perspective, use of, 59–60, 62–63; narrative's fragmented structure mirroring unstable and changing world, 58–59, 218; sources for novel's story, 53; on tranformation of women due to war, 50–51, 55–57, 75; on women as witnesses to war, 53–54

enfumade tactic of French to kill Algerians hiding in caves, 16, 71–72, 92–93, 198–99

Entendez-vous dans les montagnes . . . (Bey; Do you hear in the mountains), 18, 103–30; allegory of Franco-Algerian relations, 105; childhood experiences of war, effect of, 117–18, 132; compared to Mechakra's *La grotte éclatée*, 119–20; compared to Sebbar's *La Seine était rouge*, 143; exile and loss of home in, 125–26; identity and encounters with others in, 111–13; metaphor of politically engaged literature as resistance to injustice and tyranny, 126–29; PTSD and moral injury syndrome and, 120, 124; repressed traumatic recollections in, 105, 120, 124, 171, 214–15; returning to Algeria through memory in, 118–21; Schlink's *The Reader* in, 112–16; shared memory and healing process in, 129–30, 143; unhealed wound metaphor in, 104, 118, 119, 129, 232n12

equality. *See* gender equality/inequality

Erikson, Kai, 13, 43, 96, 139

exile from Algeria, 51, 53, 61, 63, 64–65, 84, 125–26, 133

Family Code (Algeria 1984), 47, 216–18, 223

Fanon, Frantz, 33, 59; "L'Algérie se dévoile," 6–7, 25–26, 34; *Les damnés de la terre*, 164

Fanon, Josie, 192

Faraday, Michael, 181

Faulkner, William, 229n18

Fédération de France du FLN, 134, 135, 143, 150, 232n6

Fédération démocratique internationale des femmes (FDI; International Democratic Federation of Women), 25

Federman, Raymond, 150

Fekiri, Faouzia, 237n6

feminism: Cooke and, 49; Djebar and, 51, 52, 207; Fanon and, 25–26; Mechakra and, 97; struggle for women's rights and, 218. *See also* empowerment of women

femme sans sepulture, La (Djebar; Woman without a tomb), 16, 18, 110, 188–91, 200–212; ancient mosaic's role in, 200–201, 204–6; authenticity issues created in, 210–11; civil war's brutality linked to earlier war of independence, 206; compared to Bey, 110; compared to film *La nouba*, 194; exile of author at time of writing, 205–6; fragmented approach to plot and character in, 191, 201; as historiographic metafiction, 110, 200, 203, 211; individual voices forming a collective remembrance in, 190, 202; oral tradition's use of repetition in, 210; transforming Zoulikha from historical to mythic figure, 190–91, 200, 202, 203–4, 206–7; Zoulikha's children's critique of, 211–12, 236n12; Zoulikha's remains, disposition of, 202

FIS (Front islamique du salut; Islamic Salvation Front), 9–10, 125, 206

flashbacks, use of, 59, 61, 82, 95, 120, 133, 139

FLN (Front de libération nationale; National Liberation Front), 22, 37, 45, 227n21; armed women combatants, photos used for propaganda by, 87; Bey's father working in, 106–7; in conflict with Mouvement national algérien, 142; election challenge from FIS, 9–10; first attack in war for independence (November 1, 1954), 1; FIS in elections against, 125; French claiming to have dismantled (1957), 27; negotiating with French on treatment of Algerian political prisoners, 234n11; news reporting French success in dismantling, 27; Paris student strike organized by (1956), 52; power struggles within toward end of war, 135; retaliatory attacks by, 165; Sebbar's father working with, 139; strike of January 1957 ordered by, 168; women combatants as heroic symbols for, 84; women not considered as essential fighters, 84–85, 87; women's participation in, 25–26, 221; Zoulikha as member of, 207, 211. *See also* Battle of Algiers; La Fédération de France du FLN

folk music, 193

folk narratives, 81, 157

France: Djebar's recognition in, 50; racism against North Africans in, 133, 136; women from, joining anticolonial militants, 35. *See also* Algerian War; Battle of Algiers; Battle of Paris; French conquest and colonialism; Paris, protest march of Algerian women

French Code de l'Indigénat (1881), 219

French conquest and colonialism: Algerian women in colonial era, 24; Bey on, 106; duration and commitment of French to maintain, 1, 3; educational system and, 24, 68–69; treatment of indigenous Algerians, 67, 120–21. See also *enfumade* tactic; Staoueli, battle of

French language used by Algerian women, 10, 19, 74, 113, 161, 171, 207

Freudian concepts, 13, 78, 171

Friedman, Susan Stanford, 99–100

Gadant, Monique, 225n7
Garn, Walid (first husband of Djebar), 52, 228n6
gender equality/inequality: after Algerian War, lack of equality persists, 6, 52, 223; colonial cultural norms and, 59; colonial educational system and, 68–69; family code in post-colonial era and, 216–18; Islamic fundamentalists' denial of equal rights to women, 10; male gaze toward women combatants, 44–47, 235n15; in maquis and rural areas, 83–86; men's role vs. women's role in war, 4–5, 54, 84, 143, 164, 173, 193. *See also* patriarchy
Gilmore, Leigh, 95, 175–76
GPRA (Gouvernement provisoire de la République algérienne), 150
grotte éclatée, La (Mechakra; The shattered cave), 14, 18, 78–102, 214, 226n11; accuracy of war story in, 81–82; autobiographical nature of, 79, 230n14; cave's real and metaphoric role in, 85, 92–94; Cherrad's testimony paralleling protagonist's role in, 89–90, 230n10; compared to Bellouma's *Terre des femmes*, 219; constructing a new society at end and expressing hope for the future, 101–2; critical reception of, 82; displaced person's search for home in, 99–101; fragmented narrative in, reflecting disrupted time and dislocated memory, 82, 95; identity quest and transformative experiences as key plot elements in, 81–82; life in maquis depicted in, 79, 85–88; madness of protagonist in, 80, 95–96; nationalist fervor expressed in praise song in, 90–91; nurse as protagonist in, 79, 83; outsider background of orphan protagonist in, 80–82, 97; patriarchal constraints, ability of protagonist to escape from, 97; poetic images in, 91; recovery from war's trauma in, 94–99; reliability of narrator becoming questionable in, 95–96; return to site of trauma in, 101; rural setting of maquis in, 83, 86; shift from *I* to *we* by narrator in, 99; as story of traumatic realism, 81, 82, 89–90; trauma/traumascape in, 79, 96, 104; weaving as metaphor in, 98–99, 179; Yacine's preface to, 83, 229n2
Groupe Islamique Armée (GIA; Armed Islamic Group), 10
guerre d'Algérie, La (1954–1962): Femmes au combat (Amrane-Minne; The Algerian War [1954–1962]: Women in combat), 2, 214, 221; Amina's journal depicting life of women in maquis, 28–32, 88, 226n10; bombs placed during Battle of Algiers, list of, 227n21; civil militants in, 28, 32, 56; diversity of women covered in, 22; doctoral dissertation, focus of, 21; on exclusion of Algerian women from political life, 24; *fidayate* (female urban guerrillas) in, 32–34; oral testimony as basis of, 35–37; solidarity among women combatants in, 38; Stora's concern for overabundance of revelations and, 148; torture and trauma in, 42–44
Guerroudj, Djilali (stepfather of Amrane-Minne), 22, 233n15
Guerroudj, Jacqueline (mother of Amrane-Minne), 35, 223, 226n2, 226n13, 226n18, 233n15

Guessoum, Nassima, *10949 femmes* (film), 220–21, 222, 226n5

Hablal, Nassima, 220, 221, 222, 223
Hadj, Messali, 26
Halimi, Gisèle (with Beauvoir), *Pour Djamila Boupacha*, 12, 170
Hamoud, Nafissa, 84
Haneke, Michael, *Caché* (film), 149
Harbi, Mohammed, *La guerre d'Algérie, 1954–2004: La fin de l'amnésie* (preface with Stora), 15–16, 36, 47, 96, 104
Hargreaves, Alec, 147
harkis (Algerian collaborators with French), 2, 141, 148
Harlow, Barbara, 127
Haroun, Ali, 134, 232n6
Hayat, Nina, 218
Hegel, Georg Wilhelm Friedrich, *Phenomenology of the Spirit*, 5
Hiddleston, Jane, 58–59, 63, 65–66, 74
Hirsch, Marianne, 117, 232n7
history and memory. *See* memory
Hocine, Baya, 227n16
Holocaust, 13, 78, 114–17; Israel's recognition of those who saved Jews during, 185; need to remember to prevent future genocide, 209; Suleiman on Perec and Federman as child survivors of, 150–51; Vichy deportation of Jews, 146
"home," meaning of term, 99–101, 230n18
Homer's *Odyssey*, 204–6
Horne, Alistair, 22, 45–46, 225n1, 227nn25–26
House, Jim, 136
Hovnanian, Dr., 185
Huston, Nancy, 117, 133–34
Hutcheon, Linda, 200

identity development: of children in Sebbar's *Une enfance dans la guerre*, 155–56; cross-class and cross-ethnic boundaries, 9; destabilization of identity in war creating opportunity for empowerment, 75–76; imperial vs. national identity, 122; in Mechakra's *La grotte éclatée*, 81–82
Ighilahriz, Louisette: *Algérienne*, 12, 18, 170–77; alternating between singular and plural in telling her story (synecdoche), 176; choice of French publisher, 171; compared to Amrane-Minne, 175; compared to Bey, 175; compared to Lavalette, 171, 177, 178, 184–85, 186; compared to Mechakra, 175; exposing torture and rape, 12, 121–22, 159, 168, 170, 174–75, 186–87; female bonding with sister Ourdïa and journalist Nivat to support telling her story, 171–74, 175, 177, 184; FLN and, 171, 174; individual vs. collective testimony and, 175–77; personal testimony in memoir by, 159, 174–75, 186–87, 215; recognizing French doctor Richaud who saved her life, 172–74; silence and, 43, 171, 176, 184–85
Ighilahriz, Malika, 27, 32–33, 226n7
Imaksen, Naïla, 218
incarceration, psychological effects of, 37–42
Ireland, Susan, 129, 143, 237n4
Islamic fundamentalists. *See* civil war in Algeria; FIS
Issiakhem, M'hammed, *Les Aveugles* (The blind ones; painting), 102, 231n23
Iveton, Fernand, 22

Jaccomard, Hélène, "L'autobiographie de Louisette Ighilahriz," 171, 176
Jews in World War II. *See* Holocaust; Vichy government
Jones, Christa, 92
Jospin, Lionel, 137

Kateb Yacine: *Nedjma*, 92; *Le polygone étoilé*, 68–69; preface to *La grotte éclatée*, 83, 91, 229n2
Kaufman, Joyce, 47, 223
Kettane, Nacer, 138
Khalifa, Sahar, *Abbad al-shams* (Sunflower), 49
Khatibi, Abdelkébir, 69
Koriche, Malika, 27
Koudil, Hafsa Zinaï, 10, 218

Labontu-Astier, Diane, 228n5
Lachman, Kathryn, 60
Lacoste, Robert, 169
Lakhdari, Samia, 45, 160, 161, 162–63, 165, 223, 226n12
Lalami, Feriel, *Les Algériennes contre le code de la famille: La lutte pour l'égalité* (Algerian women against the family code: The fight for equality), 217–18
Lallaoui, Mehdi, 117, 138
Langlois, Anne-Marie, 153
La Pointe, Ali, 167–69
Laredj, Waciny, 155, 233n21
Laronde, Michel, 136, 233n18
Laub, Dori, 13, 95, 171, 175
Lavalette, Eveline Safir: biographical background, 177–78, 235n23; "Cessez-le-feu" (poem), 221; choice of title for memoir, 179; compared to Amrane-Minne, 180; compared to Bey and Sebbar, 185; compared to Drif, 177,

178; compared to Ighilahriz, 171, 177, 178, 184–85, 186; compared to Mechakra, 179; exile during civil war, 183–84; FLN role of, 178; incarceration and torture, 178, 180–83, 185; *Juste Algérienne: Comme une tissure*, 18, 111, 177–87, 230n19; "La prison centrale" (poem), 180–83; in Sissani's film, 220, 221; personal testimony in memoir by, 159, 177, 179–80, 187, 215; preserving privacy for fellow prisoners and her family, 186; prison poems of, 180; recognizing Dr. Hovnanian as one of the just, 185; silence and, 43, 184–85, 186; "Un tapis pour Amar," 179
Lazreg, Marnia: *The Eloquence of Silence*, 8–9, 19, 226n15; *Torture and the Twilight of Empire*, 121, 122, 125
Lejeune, Philippe, 158
Lenzina, José, 156
Loup, Elyette, 35, 226n13

MacMaster, Neil, 84–85, 87–88, 136
Mammeri, Mouloud, *L'opium et le bâton*, 92
maquis (guerrilla camp), 28–32, 60, 79, 84–88, 230n12. *See also* cave's real and metaphoric role
Marche pour l'égalité et contre le racism, La (Marche des Beurs), 136
Marouane, Leïla, 10, 218
"Marseillaise, La" (French national anthem), 103, 118–19
Martin, Florence, 196, 220
Marx-Scouras, Danielle, "Yacef Girls: The First Bombs," 45–46
Massu, Jacques, 147, 170
Mattei, Georges, 138
McIlvanney, Siobhán, 123, 127, 232n12

McLarney, Ellen, 225n10
Mechakra, Yamina: *Arris* (sequel to *La grotte éclatée*), 79; biographical background of, 79, 229n2; compared to Bey, 104–5; compared to Djebar, 97; compared to Ighilahriz, 175; compared to Lavalette, 179; difficulty in getting work published, 231n24; "L'éveil du mont," 79; psychiatric training of, reflected in writing, 82; Sebbar's work as reference source for, 132; writing fiction of traumatic experiences, 159. See also *grotte éclatée, La*
Medeiros, Ana, 190
memoirs. *See* bearing witness and testimonial literature; Drif, Zohra; Ighilahriz, Louisette; Lavalette, Eveline Safir
memory: collective amnesia toward Algerian War, 134, 136, 146–47, 191, 209; commemoration resulting from memory restored, 209; countermemory of massacre in Paris (October 17, 1961), 136; individual vs. collective testimony, 152, 157, 175–77, 190, 202, 214; *lieux de mémoire* (places of memory), 145–46, 196; Mechakra's *La grotte éclatée* and dislocated memory, 82, 95; multidirectional memory, 116–17, 133, 139, 185, 215; postmemory generation, 117, 232n7; relationship with history, 14–16, 20, 175; repressed traumatic recollections, 105, 120, 124, 129, 171, 175, 185; Sebbar on collective memory, 138–41; Sebbar's traumatic memories of childhood in *Une enfance dans la guerre,* 154–55; shared memory and healing process, 13, 96, 129–30, 143,
173, 194; Stora on repressed memories of war, 170, 175, 191; survivor's testimony, 234n23; Zoulikha's life as woman combatant and, 189. *See also* anamnesis
men. *See* gender equality/inequality; patriarchy
Michel-Chich, Danielle, 165
Miller, Nancy K., 229n15
"Min Djibalina" (Algerian revolutionary song), 103, 119
Minne, Danièle. *See* Amrane-Minne, Danièle Djamila
Minne, Jacqueline Netter (mother of Amrane-Minne), 22. *See also* Guerroudj, Jacqueline
Mohammedi-Tabti, Bouba, 54
Mokeddem, Malika, 10, 218
Mokhtari, Rachid, 82, 83, 229n3
Molina, Simone, 155
moral injury syndrome, 120, 124
Mosteghanemi, Ahlam, 19, 225n10
moudjahidate (female FLN militants), 32, 47, 190, 197, 212, 215, 216, 221, 223
Mouffok, Ghania, 186
moussebilate (civil urban militants), 28, 32, 56, 207, 223
Mouvement national algérien (rival party to FLN), 142
M'Rbat, Fadéla, 225n8
multiculturalism, 10, 208–9, 215
multidirectional memory, 116–17, 133, 139, 185, 215

napalm, 3, 81, 94
newspapers as research source on women's role in war, 26–28
Nivat, Anne, 171–72, 184
Nora, Pierre, 14–15, 36, 145, 196

nouba des femmes du Mont Chenoua, La (Djebar's film), 16, 18, 92, 188, 190–200, 229n16; choice of title, 192; collective and individual memory of Algerian War in, 190; Djebar's purpose in, 197; female bonding ceremony in, 197–98, 215; fragmented approach to plot and character in, 191, 195, 197–98, 199–200; hope for Algeria's future at end of, 192, 199; influence on future filmmakers, 220; interviews with former combatants in, 194, 197, 215; liberatory scene in, 199; meditations on remembrance and mourning in, 190, 199; musical references in, 192–93, 194–95, 236n6; protagonist revisiting childhood village to come to terms with her past in Algerian War, 194, 200; themes from, more fully elaborated in later writings by Djebar, 199; women sharing stories of anticolonial war as opening gateway to healing, 194; Zoulikha's introduction and story in, 189, 190–91, 197, 220

Noweir, Sawan, 194

nurses' role in war, 4, 30–31, 79, 83, 84–86, 230n12

OAS (Organisation de l'armée secrète), 153, 154

official archives, access to, 25–26, 137, 227n19

"1.5 generation," 117, 151, 157

oral history and tradition: Armane-Minne's use of, 23, 41, 148; Djebar's use of, 71, 73–75, 193, 198, 203, 207, 210; Drif's role in transmitting for Casbah, 167; Sebbar's reference to, 18, 141

O'Reilly, Michael, 206

Orientalism, 10, 69, 133, 165–66

Orlando, Valérie, 101–2, 231n23

Oudaï, Yamina Echaïb. *See* Zoulikha

Oudaï children (Zoulikha's children), 17, 210–12

Oukhiti (Fatiha Bouhired-Hattari), 161, 167

outsider or other status: in Bey's *Entendez-vous* . . . , 111–13; in Djebar's film *La nouba*, 200; in Mechakra's *La grotte éclatée*, 80–82, 97; Sebbar considering herself as, 134

palimpsest, creation of, 70–71

Papon, Maurice, 135, 141, 146–47, 149

Paris, protest march of Algerian women (October 20, 1961) in reaction to Battle of Paris, 143, 233n19. *See also* Battle of Paris

Paroles et Écriture (women's writing association), 11, 128, 232n11

Parti communiste algérien (PCA; Algerian Communist Party), 24

Parti du peuple algérien–Mouvement pour le triomphe des libertés démocratiques (PPA-MTLD; Algerian People's Party–Movement for the Triumph of Democratic Liberty), 24

patriarchy: agency of women and, 23, 52, 56–57; Bellouma's fiction on, 219; Djebar's fiction on, 50; emotional wounds of women stemming from, 97; in FLN thinking about women activists, 87; in postcolonial era, 47, 52, 193; power of, 7, 65–66, 97; silence of women in submission to, 8

Pears, Pamela, 83, 95, 98–99, 231n21
Pélissier, Aimable, 71, 72, 93, 198–99, 230n16
Penijel, Jacques, *October à Paris* (documentary), 141
Perec, Georges, 150
Pernin, Judith, 220
Petty, Sheila, 220, 222
pieds-noirs (French Algerians): excluding indigenous Algerians from equal legal status and land rights, 120–21; fleeing independent Algeria, 2; local press of, 26; OAS extremist group of, 153, 154; in Sebbar's *Une enfance dans la guerre*, 148, 150, 153; women joining anticolonial militants, 35, 177, 235n19
political parties' treatment of women, 24. *See also specific parties*
Pontecorvo, Gillo, *Battle of Algiers* (film), 5–6, 33, 44–45, 166, 227n22, 234n2
Portelli, Alessandro, 73–74, 172, 229n18
postcolonial era: Algerians unprepared for challenges of, 60; former women combatants' treatment in, 24, 39, 102; male depiction of women's role in war as continuation of colonial paradigm, 45; patriarchy continuing in, 47, 49, 52, 193. *See also* civil war in Algeria; silence
post-traumatic stress disorder (PTSD), 120
privacy: Amrane-Minne preserving for interviewees, 35–36, 42–43; Lavalette preserving for fellow prisoners and her family, 186
Proulx, Patrice J., 129, 143
Proust, Marcel, 154

Quandt, William B., 35
Quinan, Christine, 67

racism, 136, 156
rape and torture. *See* torture
retribution, killings and violence as, 33–34, 164–65
Rice, Alison, *Polygraphies*, 109–10, 113, 123
Richaud, Commandant, 172–75
Ricoeur, Paul, *La mémoire, l'histoire, l'oubli* (*Memory, History, Forgetting*), 14, 176–77
Rothberg, Michael, 81, 116, 133, 139, 229n5
Rousso, Henry, 146
rural vs. urban life, 83, 86, 153
Rwandan genocide, 13, 78, 208

Saadi, Nourredine, 155
Saadi, Yacef, 22, 45–46, 159, 163, 166, 167–69, 227n24
Safir, Abdelkader (husband of Lavalette), 183
Said, Edward, 59–60, 64–65, 228n12
Saint-Arnaud, Armand Jacques de, 71, 93, 198
Schlink, Bernhard, *The Reader*, 112–16, 117–18, 231n4
Schyns, Désirée, 95
Sebbar, Leïla, 17, 18, 117, 131–57, 214; Algerian war story as focus of writing by, 132; as daughter of Arab father and French mother, 156; biographical background of, 131, 137–39; compared to Bey, 132–33, 139; *Je ne parle pas la langue de mon père*, 139; *Lettres parisiennes: Autopsie de l'exil* (letters exchanged with Huston),

Sebbar, Leïla (*continued*)
133–34; *Mes Algéries en France*, 233n15; multidirectional memory and, 215; role in postcolonial literary studies, 131; at University of Iowa, Laronde's literature class (2002), 233n18; compared to Lavalette, 185; Shérazade trilogy, 133. See also *enfance dans la guerre, Une*; *Seine était rouge, La*

Sebbar, Mohammed (father of Leïla), 139

Seine était rouge, La (Sebbar; *The Seine was Red*), 14, 18, 132, 137–50, 233n11; anamnesis and choice of protagonists in, 140, 144; bearing witness in, 141–44; collective memory and trauma revealed in, 138–41, 150; *lieux de mémoire* in, 145–46; memory tags by editing commemorative plaques in, 144–50; modeled after Einaudi's *La Bataille de Paris*, 141–42; multiple historical conflicts referenced in, 139

self-worth: of fictional protagonist in Djebar's film *La Nouba*, 198; of orphan protagonist in Mechakra's *La grotte éclatée*, 80; of women combatants, 37–38, 57, 216. See also identity development

Shelton, Marie-Denise, 230n18

Shepard, Todd, 104

silence: in Algerian colonial period vs. in postcolonial era, 8; choice to remain silent, 19, 235n17; gender dynamics and, 3; Ighilahriz and, 43, 171, 176, 184–85; institutional silence on massacre of Algerians in Paris (October 17, 1961), 136; Islamic fundamentalists and, 9–10; Lavalette and, 43,

184–85; listening instead of speaking, 97; as path to spirituality, 19; in Pontecorvo's film *The Battle of Algiers*, 44; reasons for, 142–43; as resistance to injustice, 19; Sebbar's father's silence, 139; Sebbar's own silence, 156; of soldier who witnessed torture, 122; of survivors, negative effects of, 171; torture and trauma, silence as way of coping with, 43; victims' silence on massacre of Algerians in Paris (October 17, 1961), 138–39. See also bearing witness and testimonial literature; voice

Sissani, Fatima, *Tes cheveux démêlés cachent une guerre de sept ans* (Your disheveled hair hides a seven-year war), 220–22

Slimani, Fatima, 27

Smith, Helen Zenna, 225n5

solidarity, 38, 85, 227n25

sources of information on women's role in the war, 23, 25–28, 46, 53, 132, 198, 213, 215–16. See also official archives

Staoueli, battle of, 16, 69–72, 189–90

Steiner, Annie, 35, 226n13, 227n16

Stora, Benjamin, 15–16, 36, 38, 104, 121, 134; on Amrane-Minne's purpose in writing, 21, 46–47; on anamnesis as gateway to healing, 175; on overabundance of revelations as dangerous, 147–48; on repressed memories and national amnesia, 170, 191

Suleiman, Susan, *Crises of Memory and the Second World War*, 117, 150–52, 155, 157, 234n23

Taleb Ibrahimi, Khaoula, 85–86, 87, 227n15, 230n11, 235n17

Teguia, Mohamed, 35
témoignages (testimony of eye witnesses), 14, 36, 148, 215
"terrorist," use of term, 34
testimonial literature (memoirs). *See* bearing witness and testimonial literature
Thénault, Sylvie, 227n19
Tillion, Germaine, 168, 169, 229n4, 234n4, 234n11, 234n13
Titah, Rachida, 218
torture: Amrane-Minne and, 42–44, 227n18; definition of, 122; Djebar and, 73; Drif and, 18, 167–68; French engaging in, 12, 42–44, 121–25, 167–68, 170, 227n19; Ighilahriz and, 12, 121–22, 159, 168, 170, 174–75, 186–87; Lazreg and, 122, 125; sexual torture of Algerian women combatants, 170, 175
trauma: belatedness in recalling, 13–14, 175–77; Caruth on, 78–79; personal history of trauma placed within collective history as context, 175; repressed traumatic recollections in Bey's *Entendez-vous . . .* , 105; shared trauma, creating sense of community, 96; traumascape vs., 78; Tumarkin on, 78; as unclaimed experience, 78–79, 229n1; war's effect on both Algeria and France, 103; as a wound, 12–16, 78, 104, 118, 119, 129, 232n12. *See also* memory; *specific women writers*
traumascapes referring to places of violence, war, and terror, 13, 78, 79, 100–101, 119–20, 145, 165, 218
traumatic realism, 81, 82, 89–90, 229n5
truth and reliability of narrator, 14, 171
Tuan, Yi-Fu, 166, 234n8
Tucker, Judith, 6

Tumarkin, Maria, *Traumascapes: The Power and Fate of Places Transformed by Tragedy*, 13, 77–79, 94, 100–101, 218

Ulysses, 100, 201, 204–6
Union des femmes d'Algérie (UFA; Union of Algerian Women), 24–25
Union Nationale des Femmes Algériennes (UNFA; National Association of Algerian Women), 217
University of Algiers, 24, 228n8

veil, use of, 6–7
Vergès, Jacques, 167; *Pour Djamila Bouhired* (with Arnaud), 12, 170
Vichy government: anti-Semitism of, 222; CFTC opposition to, 235n21; crimes against humanity committed during, 147, 149; deportation of Jews by, 139; Vichy syndrome (France's inability to deal with Vichy past), 146
Vietnam war against French colonialism, 13, 78
Vince, Natalya, 16, 47, 49–50, 74, 76, 85, 88, 215–16, 227n20
Virgil, *Aeneid*, 77, 102
Vivier, Marie-France, 98–99
voice: in Amrane-Minne, collective voice emerging from sources, 23, 35–37, 214; appropriation of, 19, 52, 74; in Bey's *Entendez-vous . . .* , 123; counterdiscourse of Algerian women's narratives and, 131; in Djebar, multivoiced discourse (polyphony), 59–60, 62–63, 65; first-person vs. third-person narratives, 19, 111, 177, 184; handicraft of women as metaphor for weaving

INDEX | 269

voice (*continued*)
together multiple women's voices, 98–99, 179, 230nn19–20; individual as representative of the many, 152, 157, 190, 202; loss of authority over war story and, 5, 7–8, 224; male vs. female voice in describing women's role in war, 45–46; Rice on polyphony of Francophone Algerian women writers, 109–10; in Sebbar's *La Seine était rouge*, multiple voices on past events, 141–42; trauma survivors' need to articulate their experience, 95. *See also* bearing witness and testimonial literature

Walter, Eugene Victor, 109, 166, 234n9
war crimes and crimes against humanity, 114–16, 147. *See also* torture
weaving metaphor for collective voicing by women, 98–99, 179, 230nn19–20
Weltman-Aron, Brigitte, 164, 165
Wiesel, Elie, 209
Williams, Kristen, 223
women's organizations, 24–25, 217–18, 236n1
women's role in war: age of women combatants, 28; anonymity of, 35–36, 43–44, 82, 161, 186, 188, 190, 203, 217; as Beautiful Souls, 5; as bombers, 22, 37, 45, 160, 163–65, 227n21, 234n3; death statistics for women combatants, 28; as demonstrators, organizers, and fighters, 6, 70, 84, 87, 158; earning respect for their militant role, 9, 224; Fanon on Algerian women combatants, 6, 25–26; "ferocious few," term attributed to legendary women warriors, 5, 17, 33, 83, 87, 164; *fidayate* (female urban guerrillas), 28, 32–34, 44, 84, 223; in French campaign of 1830s to establish colonization, 69–70; life in maquis, 28–32, 85–88; men's role vs., 4–5, 45, 54, 84, 143, 164, 173, 193; moral code imposed on women, 86; motivation for women, 26; newspapers as source on, 26–28; non-combatant women's supportive role, 99; perspective to study, 3; political awareness of women and, 7–8, 159; rural vs. urban women, 83, 86; sense of self, effect on, 9, 49–52, 65, 214; social transformation not achieved through, 47, 75; supportive and active participant role, 23, 33, 44, 56, 83, 87, 99, 107, 140, 207; tradition vs. modernity and, 225n7; voting rights of, 24; as weepers, 5, 87; Zoulikha's importance in lead role, 211. *See also* gender equality/inequality; nurses; women's role in war; women writers and filmmakers

women writers and filmmakers: autobiographical writing of, 29, 58, 63, 65, 68, 72, 109–10, 113, 190, 192, 194, 214, 230n14; counterdiscourse of Algerian women's narratives, 131; during *décennie noire* of 1990s, 10, 218; filmmakers after Djebar, 220–24, 237n6; resistance literature, 218–19; selection of writers for study, 19. *See also* bearing witness and testimonial literature; voice; *specific writers by name*

Woodhull, Winifred, 7, 72, 199
World War II: in Bey's *Entendez-vous…*, 113, 215; French Resistance in, 34; memorials edited to proclaim heroism in Algerian War, 144; in Sebbar's *La*

Seine était rouge, 139, 215; women as active combatants in, 25. *See also* Holocaust; Vichy government

Yacine, Tassadit, 155

ZAA (Zone Autonome d'Alger, Algiers Autonomous Sector), 45, 159–60, 165, 167
Zakad, Abderrahmane, 209
Zehari, Zehor, 227n16
Zerrouki, Malika, 30–31, 87
Zimra, Clarisse, 54, 63, 191, 198, 223, 228n13, 235n2, 236n10

Zoulikha (Yamina Echaïb Oudaï), 16–17, 18, 188–212; anonymity to other resistance fighters, 188; biographical background of, 188, 236n17; Cherchell commemoration of life of (on fiftieth anniversary of her death), 209; Djebar's work about, 16, 18, 189, 220; FLN role of, 207, 211; as martyr of Cherchell, 188, 203–4; symbolism of fight against violence, injustice, and amnesia, 189. See also *femme sans sepulture, La; nouba des femmes du Mont Chenoua, La*

www.ingramcontent.com/pod-product-compliance
Lightning Source LLC
Chambersburg PA
CBHW030822230426
43667CB00008B/1329